A TIME REMEMBERED

A TIME REMEMBERED

American Women in the Vietnam War

Olga Gruhzit-Hoyt

PRESIDIO

To all the Americans who volunteered for Vietnam War service.

Published by Presidio Press
505 B San Marin Drive, Suite 300
Novato, CA 94945-1340

Library of Congress Cataloging-in-Publication Data

Gruhzit-Hoyt, Olga, 1922–
    A time remembered : American women in the Vietnam War /
Olga Gruhzit-Hoyt.
        p. cm.
    Includes bibliographical references and index.
    ISBN: 0-89141-669-2
    1. Vietnam Conflict, 1961–1975—Women—United States. 2.
Women—United States Bibliography. I. Title.
DS559.8.W6 G78 1999
959.704'082—dc21
[B]   99-28442
                                            CIP

Printed in the United States of America

Contents

Acknowledgments

I am grateful to so many people who helped me complete this project. Especially important were those who assisted me in locating women who served in Vietnam or Southeast Asia. I hope I have not forgotten thanks where they are due. It was difficult to locate women who were willing to share their experiences with me so that I could provide firsthand accounts in my chapters.

The following are but a few of the many I would like to thank. These people provided leads, ideas, and recommendations that enabled me to communicate with the women whose services are chronicled in the book: Constance Moore, Army Nurse Corps Historian, The Center for Military History, Department of the Army, who took over for Iris West; Jake Jones; Bernard F. Cavalcante, head of the Operational Archives Branch, Naval Historical Center; Mary Stremlow, Deputy Director, State of New York, Division of Veterans Affairs; Celin V. Shoen, executive director, Delaware County Chapter, American Red Cross; *The Register,* Karen Austin, Women in Military Service for America Memorial Foundation, Inc.; Diane Carlson Evans, founder and chair, Vietnam Women's Memorial Project, Inc.; Retired Army Nurse Corps Association; Constance E. Miller, *Carry On,* Women's Overseas Service League, the *Oversea'r,* American Red Cross Overseas Association; Faith Richards, *WMA News,*

Women Military Aviators; *New York Times Book Review;* Cannon Free Library, Delhi, New York; Ann Kelsey, Associate Director, Learning Resource Center, County College of Morris; Agnes Feak, Chair, Women Veterans, Mark Leepson, book editor, Vietnam Veterans of America (VVA); Cathleen Cordova; Linda Grant DePauw; Chuck Howard; John G. Eastman; David Elder, Paul E. Skoglund, American Friends Service Committee; Marsha Four; Frenchy McDaniel; Kelly Snodgrass; Penny King; Marion Richards; George Badgley; Jean London; Carol Beechy; Col. Mac Snodgrass; Betty Bowers; Walton S. Moody, Historian, Department of the Air Force; Margaret Salm; Women Veterans Working Group, Readjustment Counseling Service, U.S. Department of Veterans Affairs; James R. Peluso, Division of Veterans Affairs, State of New York; Sister Search; Minerva Center; Don Luce, International Voluntary Services, Inc., Vietnam; Jennifer L. Blanck, USO; *Military Affairs,* American Military Institute, Kansas State University; *The Officer,* Reserve Officers Association of the United States; Fleet Reserve Association; *The Retired Officer,* Retired Officers Association; *The American Legion Magazine; V.F.W. Magazine,* Veterans of Foreign Wars; *Naval Affairs Magazine,* Women's Army Corps Veterans Association, Fort McClellan, Alabama; Maggie M. White, Women Marines Association, Area 1; Air Force Women Officers Association; Navy Nurse Corps Association; United Women Veterans; WAC Veterans Association; Women Veterans of America; Army Special Services Association; The Circle of Sisters; Retired Army Medical Specialist Corps; Vietnam Veterans of America (more than one hundred U.S. chapters); Mary Beth Straight, "Notebook" editor, *U.S. Naval Institute Proceedings; Sea Power,* Navy League of the United States; Marine Corps Association; Noncommissioned Officers Association; Joy A. Lane, Society of Retired Air Force Nurses, Inc.; Gerald Baker, Veterans of the Vietnam War, Inc.; Elise Hines; John Wisby; Faith Richards; Robert Johnson, director, Delaware County Veterans Service Agency; *Mail Call,* Gioia Grasso Cattabriga, VA Medical & Regional Office Center, White River Junction, Vermont; Joan Furey, Department of Veterans Affairs, Washington, D.C.; *Stars and Stripes;* Chel Avery, American Friends Service Committee; Roger Herrick (Internet); *The Daily Star,* Oneonta, New York; *The Reporter,* Walton, New York; Kimberly

S. Smith, Communications Specialist, American Nurses Association; Bill and Liz Brossi, Delaware Business Systems; Diana Dell; Anne Wood, *Marine Corps Gazette;* Tess Johnston, Shanghai; Mary Stewart, Retired Nurses Association for Navy Nurse Corps; Scott Peters, education, Department of the Army; Sharon Dickerson; Helen Hegelheimer; Will Molineux, book editor, *The Daily Press,* Newport News, Virginia; Ron Bailey; *Soldiers,* U.S. Army; The Society of Retired Air Force Nurses; Virginia Allred, editor, '*Nouncements;* Linda DuMoulin, Women Military Aviators; and *Athena.*

I would like to thank, in particular, my agent, Henry Shaw, for his help and encouragement, and my editor, E. J. McCarthy, for his enthusiasm and, of course, knowledgeable guidance.

Special love and thanks are given to my family: my son-in-law Ben Berliner for his computer expertise, my son-in-law Dick Mroczynski for his e-mail cheer-ons, my daughter Diana for her unwavering support, my son Chris Hoyt for his Texas efforts, and my daughter Helga for her reading and copyediting of the manuscript and her wholehearted understanding of my project.

And lastly, to all the hundreds of women who wrote me with good intentions of telling about their Vietnam days, intentions which came to naught, but were well meant and most encouraging.

And of course, sincerest thanks to those women who were willing to share their emotion-filled Vietnam days with me.

Introduction

Almost everyone remembers the Vietnam War with a shudder of horror. It was America's longest and perhaps most brutal war. More than half a million American servicemen fought and more than 300,000 were wounded, many with multiple amputations. It was a savage war.

Estimates of the number of women who served in Vietnam vary, ranging from 7,500 to 11,000 military women, with the greatest number being nurses. Add to this arbitrary figure the hundreds and hundreds of women sponsored by civilian organizations, and the figure could be near thirty thousand.

Women played a vital role, whether succoring the wounded, mourning the dead, or desperately trying to raise the morale of the fighting men and keep it high. All the women who served in Vietnam and Southeast Asia volunteered, and they did so for almost as many reasons as there were women—to support the armed forces, for adventure, to see the world, to escape boredom, or to do what they could to help.

The enemy seemed to be everywhere, with the din of rockets and mortars and the danger of booby traps, land mines, grenades, and unsuspected snipers. The women endured the hot, humid, bug-ridden, disease-filled lowlands and were chilled in the mountains and highlands. They took care of men in hospitals, in litters of patients at sea, or in evacuation planes in the air. Their presence cheered the men who sought to forget the bloody, debilitating war for a few moments.

As women flocked to help in Vietnam, the antiwar feeling in the United States grew by leaps and bounds, until returning veterans were almost universally scorned. By the time the women finished their tours of duty, many felt ambivalent about returning to the United States; they anticipated the enjoyment of a happy, normal home life, but they knew they would sorely miss the tight community of friends they had made in Vietnam. The most difficult aspect came when they arrived home and were rebuffed for participating in what many Americans claimed was an unjust war. They hid their uniforms and their hearts.

Each woman reacted to her Vietnam experience in her own fashion. Many were proud to have served, but few loudly proclaimed that the cause was just. For some it was just a stop on a career path; for others the experience became a sinkhole of pain in post-traumatic stress disorder.

It took hundreds of letters and four years to solicit the accounts of the women who were willing to share their Vietnam experiences for use in this book.

Surprisingly, after more than thirty years, there are still women who cannot—dare not—vividly recall their Vietnam days. The memories of the dreadful death and destruction are still there. To those whose lives were irretrievably scarred by their exposure, I admire their fortitude in attempting to regain emotional sanity and stability. To those who gave of themselves without the resultant pain and devastation of themselves, I congratulate them for their innate strength.

The days of the Vietnam War were indeed a time to remember.

Army Nurse Corps

Anne N. Philiben

Anne Philiben was born and raised in Chicago, and lived there and in its suburbs. She took her nurse's training in the city, and after graduation she had various nursing jobs: railroad stewardess/nurse, health consultant for an insurance company, and duty in nearby hospitals. She joined the Army Nurse Corps in August 1966 to serve in Vietnam. After basic training, she worked at Walter Reed Army Medical Center in Washington, D.C., on an orthopedic ward where most of the patients were amputees or had fractured femurs, the majority the result of Vietnam wounds.

Anne Philiben arrived in Vung Tau in February 1967 to take up duty at the new 36th Evacuation Hospital. Vung Tau was the old French town of Cap Street.

St. Jacques, which, in its heyday, was a renowned resort. Now the white beaches were covered with military Quonset huts, aircraft, garbage, and debris from the construction buildup. The streets, lined with brilliant orange bougainvillea and palm trees, were littered with filth and jammed with bicycles, motorcycles, and three-wheeled vehicles.

Vietnamese children played in the streets and in the sewage-clogged ditches. Beautiful Vietnamese women strolled along in their graceful white gowns, each carrying a black umbrella for protection from the sun. Anne found Vietnam colorful, exotic, exciting, and at first contact, not frightening. She had come to Vietnam for many reasons: a broken romance, escape from boredom, and the lure of adventure and travel.

Surprisingly, living conditions were pleasant and hospital work was hard—sometimes rewarding, sometimes devastatingly sad, but always demanding. A series of Quonset huts that served as the hospital were located near the beach next to the airfield and could hold four hundred patients. The only running water was in the operating room, the laboratory, and two shower/toilet facilities. The corpsmen lived in tents across the street from the hospital, and the physicians, medical specialists, nurses, and Red Cross workers all lived several miles away.

The officers, including the nurses, were billeted in a three-story building, the Villa Dubois, which was comfortable by war standards. Each room was a double with a shower and a toilet. The octagonal building in front, known as the gazebo, was the party center, open twenty-four hours a day and in almost constant use. Everything was celebrated there: weddings, birthdays, holidays, promotions, and even Ho Chi Minh's birthday, organized by a physician not happy with the U.S. involvement in Vietnam.

The nurses took their meals at the officers club and often visited other military clubs in Vung Tau. The aviation battalion that flew Mohawk surveillance aircraft had a club, as did a signal battalion. Vung Tau was an R&R center, so many GIs visited often for their week of relative peace and quiet. The beaches were popular with them, and as often as possible the nurses joined them at the American Back beach, which was almost pollution-free and only a few miles from the Villa Dubois.

That was the pleasant side of life in Vietnam. Nursing was a different matter. It was a busy time and a tough time; little thought was given to recreation while on duty. Anne's first assignment was to a forty-bed orthopedic ward where the patients were mostly American, with broken limbs, sprains, or similar injuries. Anne had been on the ward only three weeks before she was pulled off to the ICU to give special care to a very ill wounded soldier.

The GI had been struck by a bee-hive round in the back. The bee-hive, an American weapon, had been fired at the enemy, but had reversed course and shot hundreds of tiny dartlike projectiles into the GI's back. They could not be seen on an X ray, so treatment was difficult. First the surgeons removed one projectile from the GI's abdomen and thought that he would be fine when he recovered from the surgical trauma. But he just became sicker. Anne nursed him along and worried when he was taken back to surgery and a second dart was removed from his kidney. He still did not improve. Another operation took place and a third round was found in his liver. He became weaker each day. Anne watched helplessly as the trauma of the surgeries, bleeding, and infection had their effect on the soldier's body. Shortly, he died, and Anne felt that a part of her died with him.

After this case Anne became assistant head nurse in ICU-Recovery. Since it had no running water, the nurses washed their hands in buckets of germicide and rinsed them in buckets of plain water. The ward, adjacent to the operating room, had thirty-five beds, and patients were taken there after surgery. They stayed until their vital signs became stable. Those who did not rally quickly or who had more serious problems were kept in the ICU, some for as long as six weeks. The nurses' station, which had the usual desk, chairs, medicine cabinet, and mobile chart rack, was in the center of the ward. From there the nurses could keep an eye on all the patients. Since each patient had two or more IVs, one to three chest tubes connected to gallon bottles, and usually a nasogastric tube, the nurses worked in a maze of tubes and machines.

The ward was beastly hot despite three air conditioners that ran constantly. The nurses never felt that the ward was air conditioned until they stepped outside into the blistering heat.

Anne's patients were of many nationalities. There were Americans, Australians, New Zealanders, and both military and civilian Vietnamese. Her patients included a Malaysian photographer who worked for the BBC in England; a Chinese merchant seaman; and a number of Laotian, Cambodian, and Montagnard (highland) soldiers and civilians.

The patients were in the ward for reasons that ranged from what

Anne called the ridiculous to the horrendous. One GI who had sucked on a package of Kool-Aid had to have an emergency tracheotomy because his throat swelled so severely. Two GIs played catch with a live grenade and lost limbs. A group of naval aviators were struck by lightning while installing a TV antenna on the roof of their quarters. A merchant seaman had drunk methyl alcohol; he died.

Most of the patients, however, had been injured in the fighting or by mines. The hospital at Vung Tau was the burn center for Vietnam, so that division was always busy with a great number of burn victims. Other patients included those who were injured in vehicle accidents and helicopter crashes and those with nonbattle ailments such as appendectomies and hernias. Also, since the ward was closest to the female latrine, all of the ill female nurses were hospitalized in post-op.

Anne says that in Vietnam some of the nursing techniques for patient treatment were primitive compared to those of today, but others were ahead of their time. Antibiotics, usually penicillin, were placed in the intravenous bottles and the solution was infused over an eight-hour period. The nurses didn't know then that the antibiotics lost their efficacy after an hour. However, they ambulated patients much earlier and more vigorously than nurses in the United States did at that time.

Anne remembers that one of the toughest times for all the nurses was when a group of Australian soldiers were wounded by a mine. Several had head injuries and were evacuated the first night. One had wounds to his buttocks, testicles, and penis, but the most severely injured was John. He had wounds to his face and he lost one eye, one leg below the knee, the other above the knee, and one arm. He also lost some fingers on the other hand. Anne dubbed John a "train wreck," saying that his body was so savaged it was miraculous he survived.

The nurses found that caring for any of the seriously wounded was upsetting. At first the injured expressed surprise and joy at finding themselves still alive. Then a pattern of four stages of grief emerged: denial, bargaining, anger, and acceptance. Because this group of Australians had been so ill, and because their evacuation home took much longer than that of the Americans, the nurses worked through all of the phases of grief with them. They found the anger, which was mostly taken out on them and on the corpsmen, difficult to bear.

John caused constant concern. After a few days he was returned to surgery for revision of one of his amputations. Within a week he became ill again. He was taken back to the operating room, where his gall bladder, which was riddled with infection, was removed. In all, he went back to the operating room seven times.

Anne said that sometimes he was so ill that the nurses were sure he would die before the end of their shifts. On one occasion the nurses were gathered around their station and Anne was complaining about the silver nitrate they used to treat burns. Not only did it dye their skin, but the chemical made holes in their uniforms, which each day deteriorated a little more. Anne commented that she wouldn't be a bit surprised if one day her whole uniform just fell off. At those words, John looked up from his nearby bed and said, "I sure hope I'm here that day." With that, Anne and the other nurses knew he had turned the corner: he would live.

Another of Anne's memorable patients was Dum, a Montagnard soldier who had suffered fourth-degree burns. His legs had been literally burned off.

"He was a mass of infections when he arrived at our hospital," Anne says. "Spitting and shrieking, he made caring for him almost impossible. He spoke a dialect that no one in our area spoke or understood. He cried out 'lah' for hours on end. It took days of quiet talking in English and tender loving care to calm him. He was a patient of ours for many months. His proudest day was when he graduated from post-op."

The nurses had seen so much of the misery and devastation that combat could cause that they were not at all reluctant to help some of the men avoid future fighting. One patient who was almost completely recovered from his wounds realized that if he had one more week of hospitalization, he would be sent back to the United States to be discharged from the army. If he was released sooner he would be sent back to his combat unit. The nurses decided to "lose" his papers in the bottom drawer of their desk. They shrugged their shoulders when asked about the soldier, and then on the proper day, they found the papers, which were promptly forwarded to authorities, and the patient was on his way back to civilian life.

In November Anne was promoted to captain and became the head nurse of a hundred-bed medical ward. Here the patients had malaria, hepatitis, and parasites, among other medical problems. On some days there were only one or two nurses and two or three corpsmen to take care of all of the patients. It took most of the day to distribute the medications.

The months passed and the routine was fairly constant in the medical ward—until February. The nurses had planned to celebrate the founding of the Army Nurse Corps on Groundhog Day, which was also the Vietnamese Tet holiday. The order was given to dig out the nurses' white uniforms for the occasion. Anne was in for bad luck. Her uniform had remained wrapped, forgotten under her bed, and undoubtedly deteriorated from lack of exposure to the air. Her white shoes, which had been none too clean when they were put away, were now hard and green with mildew.

The Vietcong began their Tet celebration early. The evening before, they launched their offensive of 1968, shooting and rocketing the hospital area. Immediately in Villa Dubois the doctors and male nurses brought out the cache of weapons they had collected and hidden in their rooms. They patrolled the halls, ready to repel any direct attack with their grenade launchers, bazookas, machine guns, and M16 rifles. The nurses realized they faced the possibility of not one but two dangerous situations.

Anne recalls, "We were in a total blackout and as we inched our way down the halls to move from one room to another (mostly in search of scotch) we would bump into each other and the men. The potential for one of us being shot by one of our protectors posed a real threat. At 5:00 A.M., after a sleepless night, the sergeant of the guard told us to fall out with steel pots and flak jackets. By the time we arrived at the hospital, patients were lined up all down the hospital streets. The theater was full of litters. My first task was to empty my medical ward of patients and send them somewhere else—to the Sixth Convalescent Center in Cam Ranh Bay or Japan. The paperwork was completed by the nurses, who signed for physicians. By

10:00 A.M. the surgical patients began to arrive from the recovery room. By noon the entire one hundred medical patients were gone and the surgical beds filled rapidly."

So many surgeries needed to be done on the wounded that the chief nurse asked Anne to go to pre-op. She left her ward under the supervision of a U.S. Agency for International Development (US-AID) nurse who had just arrived after fleeing her headquarters when it was overrun by the Vietcong. Anne spent the rest of the day starting IVs, monitoring vital signs, and assisting the physicians. It was a rushed time as Anne and the surgeons inserted chest tubes and kept track of the amount of patient bleeding by marking the gallon bottles used to drain fluid from the chest. By 7:00 P.M. Anne's fatigue uniform was covered in blood. The call for white uniforms now seemed a rather sick joke.

The next day Anne returned to her own orthopedic/surgical ward. In the following weeks she and the other nurses saw very few physicians, who were busy in the operating room debriding and closing the patients' wounds. Anne's ward was far from the operating room, so surgeons seldom made rounds there.

The nurses were really in charge now. They decided when the patients needed to be returned to surgery, how long to keep them on antibiotics, and when they could ambulate; they made almost every decision. When it came time for the patients to be returned to the United States, the nurses completed the paperwork and forged the physicians' signatures.

The nationality of the patients varied almost daily. At one time a group of Laotian patients enlivened the ward. They teased the Americans unmercifully, especially the members of the 101st Airborne, the Screaming Eagles. The Laotians had discovered that the cone-shaped water cups, when placed over their noses, looked like beaks, and they knew how to make noises that sounded like chicken clucks. Any time they thought the 101st patients were whining or complaining too much, they went into their chicken act, and the American patients were shamed into good behavior.

Anne was given more responsibility. She was made hospital supervisor in addition to her job as head nurse. It sometimes cut into her sleep when she had to work nights, but somehow the pace was calmer. Plus, Anne knew she was to end her tour of duty soon. She had extended her time in Vietnam so that she would have completed her military service by the time she left instead of being assigned to a stateside post.

In June 1968, Anne left Vietnam, and on that day the Vietcong continuously rocketed the Long Binh airfield. Anne's plane finally made a hasty landing and departure.

Anne remembers the flight home: "The flight was very subdued. We flew over the pole. Our only stop was in Alaska and so the flight was much shorter than when we went to Vietnam. I remember virtually nothing about the flight except that when we landed at Travis Air Force Base no one cheered. I think we were all too tired."

Anne was surprised when she got off the plane in northern California that there were no waving flags, no strains of the national anthem, and no great signs of welcome. But after she had been home a few days she understood why. There were Vietnam War protestors everywhere. Anne was thankful that for the journey home she had packed her uniform in her suitcase.

Anne was restless; she found it difficult to sleep, and her days and nights were confused. She found that her friends who had expressed a positive attitude about her plans to go to Vietnam were now less than enthusiastic about her service there.

"People would ask questions and you could see them turn you off as you answered. Some of them asked the most incredibly stupid questions. 'Did you have fun?' 'How come with all those men over there you couldn't get married?' 'Did you see anyone die?' When my tan faded, I stopped telling people I'd been to Vietnam."

Remembering how little privacy she had had in Vietnam, with no escape hatch at all, when she heard about a job at a boys' camp in northern Wisconsin, Anne jumped at the opportunity for some time in isolation. It didn't turn out that way. The boys looked upon Anne as a substitute mother, and the demands on her time were relentless.

After that summer, Anne turned her sights westward. Chicago would be cold in the winter. She decided on California, where she was hired at the UCLA hospital as a nurse on a surgical ward. The weather was great, but otherwise the job was, as Anne puts it, "a disaster." She explains, "After a year of practically independent nursing practice I wasn't able to give an aspirin without a doctor's order. Physicians had to be called to start IVs and draw blood. Medical students who had been starting IVs for just a few days would argue with the nurses about the viability of an IV, and they questioned the nurses' judgment."

It was thoroughly unsatisfactory. The hospital residents weren't helpful either—they recognized Anne's skills, and to avoid inconvenience to themselves, they often called her from the operating room or from their homes and asked her to start IVs or draw blood. Soon she was doing their work and her own.

Anne decided that the only sensible course, given her training and her experience in Vietnam, was to rejoin the army, which respected the abilities of nurses. Within three weeks, on 9 February 1969, she was back in the army, at Sandia Base, New Mexico.

The following January she was assigned to the U.S. Army Medical Center at Camp Kue Okinawa, where she was again faced with caring for evacuees from Vietnam. Now she was head nurse of a forty-eight-bed orthopedic ward, and the pace was frantic. Three or more times each week, a large group of new patients arrived. It took hours to in-process all of them. Anne still shudders when she thinks of how hard the nurses worked then, the long hours, and the amount of nursing care that wasn't done.

Army life obviously agreed with Anne. She served twenty-two years before she retired as a lieutenant colonel, having traveled all over the world, and having obtained both a bachelor's and a master's degree.

After retirement she spent a year and a half in Saudi Arabia as director of maternal child nursing at King Faisal Hospital in Riyadh.

In the early 1990s she and her youngest brother secured a sports franchise in Bend, Oregon, and for two and a half years Anne worked there daily. Currently Anne edits a genealogical journal, does volunteer work, and is trying to decide what to do with the rest of her life.

Connie Christensen McCall Connolly

Connie Christensen Connolly was born into a navy family in Key West, Florida, and grew up there. In 1967 her father, Cyrus Christensen, a mine warfare expert, was in command of a navy minesweeper, the USS Ability, and swore Connie into the Women's Army Corps (WAC) on-board the vessel. She then entered the Army Student Nurse Program, in which she spent fifteen months. After Connie passed her nursing state boards, her father commissioned her in the Army Nurse Corps (ANC) in the living room of their home. She was discharged from the WAC one day and enlisted in the ANC the next. She had joined the army with the motivation to go to Vietnam. She attended officer training and an operating room nursing course, worked in a hospital air evacuation ward, and served at both Fort Dix and Fort Monmouth. A year and a half after her commissioning, in July 1970, she received her orders for Vietnam.

Connie boarded a World Airways plane for the trip to South Vietnam. With her were 212 men in various branches of the military and the stewardesses. It was a long flight—twenty-one hours, with ground time in Alaska, Okinawa, and Japan. The reality of what she had done did not hit Connie until they opened the doors of the plane and she stepped out onto the ground at Bien Hoa, South Vietnam. "There was an obnoxious stench in the air that I cannot find words to describe, but one that I have never forgotten," she says. This reaction is similar to those expressed by many of the American women who served in Vietnam.

Connie spent the next two days at the 90th Replacement Battalion, awaiting transportation to her assigned post—the 67th Evacuation Hospital in II Corps on the coast, in Qui Nhon, the fourth-largest city in Vietnam at the time. It was at the 90th that Connie was introduced to in-country facilities and conditions. The shower room was loaded with spider webs, lizards, and slimy greenish-yellow tree frogs. The floor was filthy, and the water was cold.

From the 90th Connie was taken to Da Nang in II Corps, and to the 60th Group for processing in the finance and personnel departments; then she was transported to the 67th Evacuation Hospital. She began work in the operating room and was shocked at the devastating injuries from land mines and booby traps, as well as the gunshot wounds and white phosphorus burns. Early in her duty she assisted in a triple amputation on a nineteen-year-old soldier. Almost daily she helped dispose of amputated limbs.

In such hospital work, Connie says she was deeply and permanently touched. "I lost a bunch of my youth, and a great deal of my sanity for a time. But I am a survivor. . . . We all were. My coworkers quickly became my family away from home, and mail was our lifeline to 'the world,' as we called home."

It was when she was working in the operating room one day that Connie learned that her father had arrived in the Mekong Delta. He had command of a major part of the naval river operations in IV Corps, which included three river bases. She received an unanticipated note, which simply said, "Con—the scourge of the VC has arrived. Your Old Man."

Less than a month later, Connie was transferred to the 3d Surgical Hospital at Binh Thuy, which provided medical and surgical combat support for the navy, army, and air force in the Mekong

Delta, including her father's river bases seventy miles south. Twenty Quonset huts connected by a central corridor formed the hospital complex, which was typical of combat support hospitals at that time.

The U.S. government did not know that both father and daughter were in Vietnam, because Connie had enlisted with the surname McCall, the result of a youthful, short-lived marriage. The army did not knowingly permit two members of an immediate family to serve in the same combat zone. If Connie's father were wounded, he would be treated in the operating room of her hospital. There was a grave possibility that the enemy might seek him out; the Vietcong had placed a $5,000 price on his head because of his outstanding combat leadership during his first tour in Vietnam in 1964.

Commander Cyrus Christensen carefully watched over his men, and more than once, he waited for Connie to tell him the news about a man who had been in her hospital's operating room. He and Connie saw each other almost every two weeks, but then an attempt on his life caused Connie's duty to be cut short for fear that she, too, might become a target.

Before she returned to the United States, she met some men of the U.S. Navy SEAL teams. They had great respect for Connie's hard work and dedication, and they had deep admiration for her father. They could not do enough for her, and of course, when any of them were wounded, she did the best she could for them. They were so grateful to her that they presented her with a plaque of thanks and appreciation before she returned to the United States.

Connie often worked thirty-six hours without a break. Even when she was tired, she found it difficult to sleep because of dreams about the mutilated men. Connie was profoundly affected by the overwhelming number of casualties and the extent of the injuries. "The people who died were people my age; the people who were injured were people my age." Though grateful to be alive, Connie says she went home "with a very angry spirit." It was March 1971.

• • •

Back in the United States, the attitude of the Americans disturbed Connie.

"I returned to a world that had no knowledge, concern, compassion, or understanding of what I had experienced. I suffered from guilt feelings, having left my friends and my father behind. Readjustment was difficult, and sleeping at night was even more difficult. Having gotten used to the ever present roar of a Dustoff helicopter rotor blade, it was now too silent to sleep."

Connie was stationed at Fort Stewart, Georgia, which was a small post. The hospital encompassed three wards of an old World War II hospital, with 125 beds, an operating room, pediatrics, and obstetrics. There was not much to do. Connie turned to skydiving, a sport that she pursued for the next seven years.

After fifteen months at Fort Stewart, Connie separated from active duty and joined the Individual Ready Reserve. She used the GI Bill for schooling at Richland Memorial Hospital in Columbia, South Carolina, to become a nurse anesthesiologist. She served with several different army reserve units, graduated from anesthesia school, and passed the boards. She spent six months on alert waiting to replace an anesthesia provider in the Persian Gulf during Operation Desert Storm, but in the end, she did not have to go.

On 14 October 1997, Connie marked her 30th anniversary of army service, as a lieutenant colonel. She moved to Florida and is still a citizen soldier in the army reserve; she is also the veterans affairs chair of the Florida State Council of the Vietnam Veterans of America. She currently works at a medical center in Florida as an anesthetist.

Of her army career, Connie says, "I am proud to wear the uniform of the United States of America, and proud of my fellow soldiers and sailors. It has all been worth it, and I would do it all over again. In two years I will separate from service and enter the retirement rolls. That will be a sad day, and one filled with reservation."

In 1998 Connie's illustrious navy father, who seldom had a sick day, suffered a heart attack and died suddenly. Connie was heartbroken. Among her fondest memories were those of the days she and her father spent together serving in Vietnam.

Also in 1998, Connie and Bruce Dyer—one of the Navy SEALs she had met in Vietnam, but hadn't seen for twenty-six years— met again, fell in love, and planned to be married in Key West in the spring of the following year. Connie's father would have been pleased.

Mary Dickinson

Mary Dickinson was born, raised, and educated in Pennsylvania. In 1966, in line with the "buddy system," Mary and a friend both joined the Army Nurse Corps and volunteered for Vietnam. They were assigned to Letterman General Hospital in San Francisco and were there for four months before they received orders for Vietnam, each for a different location.

It was 25 February 1967. Mary Dickinson left the United States on a Continental Airlines plane: destination Vietnam. On the plane she met the rest of the unit of doctors and nurses who would start a new hospital, the 91st Evacuation Hospital, at Tuy Hoa on the South China Sea coast.

The plane stopped briefly in Hawaii to refuel, and Mary caught only a brief glimpse of Diamond Head and the lush foliage of Oahu Island. When they finally reached Vietnam, they all knew they were in enemy territory because tracers lit up the sky around the plane. Mary realized she had arrived in a war zone. The people on the ground firing at the plane wanted to kill her!

The next day the unit boarded a cargo plane, a C-130, headed for Cam Ranh Bay. Because there were no seats on the plane, they all sat on the floor. The pilot shouted back to them, "Hang on!" when he was ready to take off, and again when they were about to land. They did hang on—to one another.

For the last leg of the trip they took a Chinook helicopter. As they flew over Vietnam, the crew brought out a bottle of champagne from an ice chest, and they all sipped it from paper cups. Mary relaxed.

The hospital in Tuy Hoa had just been completed, and Mary spent her first weeks painting and preparing the emergency room to which she had been assigned. Shortly after the hospital began full operations, the nurses worked twelve-hour shifts, from 7:00 A.M. until 7:00 P.M., for a minimum of six days a week.

The first mass casualties in the new ER were twenty-five to thirty Vietnamese, mostly women and children. A Vietcong had wired a young child with explosives and sent him into a polling area where a free election of town officials was being held. Mary learned quickly that "such was life in Vietnam."

The ER staff faced victims of not only violence, but also disease. It was in the ER that Mary saw her first case of the plague. When the doctor gave the diagnosis, Mary was so distressed that she backed away from the patient. She acted the same way with a leprosy case. It was also from the ER that Mary witnessed her first murder of the war.

"We got a call from the medevac chopper that they were bringing in several Korean casualties and a Vietcong suspect. When the casualties did arrive, they brought in a little guy in black pajamas under armed guard. I was too busy to care about the VC, but the one thing that struck me was the fear in his eyes. He could have been an innocent farmer or a VC—I had no idea what he was, but he was so frightened I almost felt sorry for him.

We got the casualties cared for, and shortly after that, a Jeep pulled up in front of the ER and two big ROK [Republic of Korea] soldiers got out. I was surprised that they were so tall. Koreans were known for their savagery. The reasoning was that since their country was torn apart in a similar situation, the ROKs hated the communists. So they took the little shivering fellow out and put him in the back seat of the Jeep. One of the Koreans pulled out a pistol and shot the man in the head. The little guy slumped over and the soldier got in the front seat and drove off.

When I reported this to the head nurse the only response was that this is the way the Koreans do it, and the Koreans are our allies, so forget it."

The nurses had been in-country only three months when it was considered necessary to send several of them to Japan for psychological consultations. As a result, the chief nurse decided that everyone needed a change of scenery. Mary was taken off the ER and assigned to the surgical intensive care unit (SICU). Here she was in full charge of eighteen patients, helped by two capable and willing young corpsmen. It was physically, mentally, and emotionally exhausting work.

Mary took a shine to a little girl who had been wounded in the fighting in the area and spent much time that first day caring for the child—perhaps too much time, since she had seventeen other patients who also needed attention. But Mary felt a sense of satisfaction that evening as she went off duty. The little girl had made good progress. Mary knew that her intensive care had made a difference.

In the morning when Mary returned to the SICU, she received a shock: the child was in poor condition. The corpsmen reported that she had seemed to respond well during the night. Then she had begun crying for her mother. She had cried for some time.

As Mary recounts the incident, "The nurse who worked the night shift that night was a former psych nurse. The army in its infinite wisdom put a psych nurse on a surgical intensive care unit in the middle of a damn war. He was so stupid he almost seemed retarded and lazy. Both corpsmen told me that her crying really bothered the dummy and he went to the narcotic box and drew something up in a syringe and injected it into that child. Nothing was ordered, no syringe should have been used anywhere near that child. When I reported it I was told it was his word against mine—forget it—even though there were two witnesses. She died; she was just a gook."

Many times Mary faced emotional situations involving children. One night after she had finished her usual twelve-hour shift on SICU and was on call for ER, a boy who was about ten years old was brought in with a large group of casualties. As usual the enemy had launched rocket attacks after dark. Mary was especially concerned about the boy because he had a rare blood type, one that could not be found anywhere in the hospital. She went off ER at 6:00 A.M. At the mess hall she drank a cup of tea, then reported to her regular shift in the SICU at 7:00 A.M.

Mary's gut reaction about the boy, that he "was going to go bad," became reality. The surgeon was on the unit at the time. Mary had become friends with him—although she did not know why, because he was a difficult man to get along with. Mary and the surgeon started to resuscitate the boy. After about a minute the doctor looked at Mary and then simply turned and walked away. Mary remembers:

"I didn't catch on at first and I didn't know where he was going. He walked slowly to the end of the ward, climbed up on a bedside cabinet, put his elbows on the partition, and rested his head on his hands and just looked at me. When I saw the expression on that man's face, I started to shake and I wanted to cry. He was gone, in another world, and it really scared me because I wasn't sure how much more of this insanity I could take without going looney tunes. I think they sent him to Japan on a psych. I'm sure fatigue played a part, a big part in this, but I've never forgotten the expression on his face.

"If I had to describe Vietnam in one word it would be insanity. To me it was a year of total and complete insanity. Nothing was ever gained; nothing made any sense. There was a constant stream of mutilated bodies, and for what?"

Mary had watched her coworkers relieve their tensions by drinking alcohol, and she determined to get drunk. Mary normally did not drink, but now she persuaded the bartender at the officers club to give her three triple drinks in one hour. She thought if she got drunk she could escape some of the pain, but it didn't help. All the alcohol did was make her feel rotten in the morning.

The pressures of the daily trauma of the wounded built constantly. She decided to ask for a transfer from SICU, mainly because of what had happened to the surgeon, she said. "If it could happen to him, it could happen to me. I would have even been willing to work the POW ward. I just wanted off of SICU. They refused to take me off, so the next day I put in for a transfer to any other unit in the Republic of Vietnam. I didn't care if they sent me to Hanoi. Within forty-eight hours I got orders to the 71st Evac in Pleiku."

Pleiku, in the central highlands of Vietnam, was sheer luxury compared with the 91st Evacuation Hospital. It had real mattresses instead of canvas cots and had real flush toilets. Mary was assigned to the orthopedic ward, and although the pace was slower and the responsibilities fewer than at the 91st Evacuation Hospital, the hours were longer, and the casualties at times seemed endless.

In the battle for Dak To in November 1967, the casualties at the 71st alone were more than 1,800. Mary recalls, "It went on for over three weeks. It was just horrendous, even worse than the Tet Offensive. There just was no letup in the casualties and they seemed more intense than usual. Just to show the stupidity and insanity of the whole situation, after all this carnage, after all those decent kids who died trying to take that stupid hill—all the pain and suffering that was endured—lives that would be forever changed—not to mention that many were caused by our own artillery—after all this, after we finally took the damn hill, we promptly vacated it so that it would have to be fought over again at a later date. What was the point? The whole war made no sense at all. If you could stay alive for twelve months then you were a winner."

All the nurses did during the Dak To battle was work and sleep. The ER crew had been working around the clock for such a long time that they finally requested volunteer help from other units in South Vietnam. Two female operating room nurses and several male technicians and anesthetists answered the call. They helped out for some time before they were able to go back to their own hospitals. The 71st team was so grateful that they threw a party in honor of the volunteers. Mary saw the two nurses patiently waiting for transportation out for several days because their flights were repeatedly cancelled. Finally one day a Jeep came to take them to the airport. Mary saw them off and then went back to her quarters.

Having fewer casualties at the hospital released some of the tensions experienced by the nurses and doctors, and on the spur of the moment they decided to have a poker game. Nobody took poker very seriously. Mary says, "It was just a lot of loud fun. It's the only fun thing I can remember in Vietnam. The game was going strong with a lot of loud laughing and joking when the chief nurse came into the room."

They invited her to join the game, and she declined and just stood there quietly. Then she spoke up and said that the volunteers had finally left to return to their own units—which they all knew. She continued, "The plane crashed and all onboard were killed."

The chief nurse turned around and walked out the back door.

Mary says, "There was dead silence. Our reaction was so strange. We all reacted the same, by not reacting. We all just looked at one another. Nobody said a word and we went back to playing cards, very quietly. It was not exactly a healthy reaction. The psychic numbing that occurs when you live in an atmosphere of death and destruction is incredible. We suppressed so much that year."

And they survived so much, too. The Vietcong launched rocket attacks at least twice a week, including every Friday, and always after dark. Mary began to hate to see the sun go down because she knew the hospital would be attacked. In the early morning hours of 20 January 1968, the orthopedic ward where Mary was working took the brunt of enemy rockets.

The night supervisor walked into the ward, where they had just received a number of patients from post-op. She hadn't been there a minute when the first rocket flew over. Mary took her flak jacket and gave the supervisor the helmet, and they started putting the patients under the beds and covering them with mattresses. Everyone was down and covered when a rocket crashed through the roof and landed very close to a small Vietnamese child—but it did not explode. The little boy crawled out from under the bed and started running for the front of the ward. Mary took chase, because she knew that if he got out the door she could not go after him; she had to stay with her patients. Unbeknownst to Mary, her corpsman started chasing after her.

Chaos followed. "I heard the second rocket and I knew it had us. It was right there and I knew we were going to take another direct hit. I remember thinking how upset my parents would be when they learned that I had been killed. This incredible feeling of sorrow overtook me—it probably was just a millisecond, but I remember it distinctly. The sergeant had gotten up to chase after me. He had to have heard that rocket. Just as he got to me the place exploded and we both went flying. I was blown down the middle of the ward into the far wall. I don't remember the explosion. The next thing I remember, I was crawling to the front of the ward because several patients were screaming, 'Medic!' There was so much dust and dirt in the air—I remember tasting it as I was crawling."

On checking, Mary found it unbelievable that there were no serious injuries, just minor fragment wounds. The nursing supervisor was buried under a large chunk of roof; she had been hit by falling debris and pipes. Mary began yelling for help when she saw that two of the new post-op patients were running off the ward with their IV tubing dragging on the ground. Mary considered the whole scene ludicrous.

The staff moved quickly. They evacuated the patients immediately.

Flames had already engulfed the oxygen tanks, and the oxygen hissed and fed the fire. The tanks could explode at any minute, as could the unexploded rocket that had first landed. Luckily, corpsmen from other units in the hospital came to help. They cleared the orthopedic ward and got the patients to an empty overflow ward. They carried or dragged some; others, more able, hopped. Some screamed. There were now explosions everywhere, and hundreds of tracers came in. Rockets flew just over their heads. Mary thought back to the national anthem and the line, "and the rocket's red glare." The red glare here provided a horrid, frightening night.

Miraculously, there was only one death—the young Vietnamese boy who had tried to run out of the ward. He disintegrated completely in an explosion. About fifteen patients were wounded, and the night supervisor, Maj. Pettrina Meade, received a concussion. The helmet she was wearing had a deep dent in it, four inches long and two inches deep.

Mary and the corpsmen hastily restarted IVs, checked dressings, and tested circulation on cast patients. It was only after she helped complete the nursing duties that Mary noticed that the sergeant was limping and in obvious pain, and she persuaded him to go to the

ER. Then the strain caught up with her. Suddenly she felt lonely. She says, "I was tired of being scared. I wanted to feel safe again, but I knew I never would."

The only time Mary can recall actually crying in Vietnam was when an old friend came to the hospital in his helicopter. When he saw the damage to the orthopedic ward and did not immediately find Mary, he became tremendously upset. When at last he saw her in the mess hall, calmly drinking a cup of tea, he was so relieved that he became angry and started yelling at her. Mary began to cry. He hugged her in comfort, and all Mary could say while sobbing was that Sergeant Ramsey had gotten hurt while trying to save her.

The doctors and nurses worked even longer hours to tend the ever-increasing casualties as the tempo of the war stepped up. The red alert siren indicating incoming rockets frightened Mary, and now the ground attack siren began to wail for the first time. The North Vietnamese Army (NVA) and, in Mary's words, "the little guys in the black pajamas" made efforts to breach the barbed wire fence. Mary admitted to being even more scared. "I didn't know why I was more afraid of coming eyeball to eyeball with someone who wanted to kill me than an impersonal exploding rocket. Dead is dead, either way the end result is death, but every time the ground siren blared it was extremely frightening."

If the North Vietnamese Army troops broke through the barbed wire fence, it was logical that they would initially attack the nurses' quarters, which were on a hill in an exposed area right next to the fence. The nurses were instructed to run to the hospital wards for safety at the first sound of the ground attack siren.

After the orthopedic ward was destroyed Mary went to work in the ER where one night during a rocket attack the communication radio crackled. Mary listened: "A panicked voice was shouting that there were hundreds of NVA troops in the field between the airbase and the hospital. The ground attack siren immediately blared. I was sure the NVA would try to take the airbase, but the voice on the radio began screaming, 'It's the hospital, they're going for the hospital!'"

Mary began to shake; that seemed to be her first reaction in any frightening situation. She could not think what the hospital had that the North Vietnamese troops would want. They had no weapons, no planes, and nothing of value. The consensus was that they would overrun the hospital just to destroy the morale of the men in the field.

The enlisted men in the ER snatched their weapons and ran outside. One of the patients who had been lying on a litter got up, grabbed his rifle, and headed for the door. He lay down outside, guarding the ER. Mary yelled at him to come back inside, but he ignored her. Secretly, she was glad; he would be their protection.

Several nurses rushed in the back door of the ER, ran through the ward to the hallway of the X-ray room behind the operating room, and lay down on the floor. A discussion took place: would the X-ray room with its lead-lined walls be the safest place or the most dangerous? One nurse announced that she was going to be sick. Another told her to use her helmet, saying that was what it was for. Mary crawled away from the women, afraid that she too was so frightened that she would be ill. Then the ground attack siren stopped.

Mary's friend Jim, who had come in his helicopter when the orthopedic ward was destroyed, now came to Mary and insisted that she take the pistol he offered her. She refused. They exchanged angry words, but when he left he took the pistol with him.

Not long after that, the rocket attack siren sounded again. Mary, who was in her room—the first at the front of the nurses' quarters—rushed to relative safety under her bed. The ground attack siren added its wail. Mary proceeded to follow the rules by quickly heading for the hospital wards. As she skittered out from under the bed she heard the front door of the building open. She froze. An NVA!

"I listened and I heard nothing. Again I was sure I was going to die. I backed up under the bed as far as I could go, with my back up against the wall, and held my breath. He walked to my doorway and stopped. I swear my heart stopped beating and I just held my breath waiting to die. I was so stupid not to have taken the gun. I didn't want to die; more than anything I wanted to live. If I had that gun I know I would have fired every bullet into the shadow at my doorway. Then a very quiet voice asked, 'Is anyone in here?' I couldn't believe it—he was one of our men."

Mary came out. The young man had been terrified. He had been in-country for only three weeks and had been sent to the nurses' quarters to run with them to the wards. He was a lucky man; in the room next to Mary was another nurse who did have a gun and was just waiting for him to come to her door before she shot him.

The enemy rockets poured into the hospital compound; the sound of explosions seemed to be everywhere. The ambulance drivers went wherever they were called without question. One night when Mary worked in the ER, they brought in a big black sergeant on a litter. A skinny young white man walked alongside, constantly asking, "He is going to be all right, isn't he?"

Both of the soldiers had been on guard duty when the sergeant had raised his head to see which direction the rockets were coming from—just as one exploded. Mary could see that the whole right side of his head was gone. His friend must have seen this, but he kept asking the same question over and over. The doctor went over to him, put his hand on the buddy's shoulder, and said softly, "I'm sorry, but your friend is dead."

Mary was shocked at the young man's reaction. He threw himself on the concrete floor and repeatedly smacked his head against the floor. It took four of the ER staff to hold him down so he would not damage himself. Mary prepared medication to calm him. Her hands shook badly as she inserted the needle into the vial. The noise of the explosions outside grew louder, but the guttural sounds coming from the dead soldier's buddy sounded even louder, like a pained, hurt animal. He continued to roll on the floor until, a short time after he was sedated, he slept peacefully. The staff put him in a straitjacket, and the next day he was air evacuated to Japan for psychiatric evaluation. Mary often wondered what happened to the young soldier. "What price did decent, caring people pay in a senseless war?"

The next morning after duty, Mary went back to the nurses' quarters—the hooch—to sleep. She fell asleep while, outside, the unit prepared to hold a memorial service for the black soldier who had been killed. Mary awakened and heard the sound of "Taps." At that, she panicked. Had she finally cracked because of all the insanity? She ran to the back door and looked out. There a small group had

gathered, and she saw a man blowing a trumpet. Mary was so relieved to know that she had retained her sanity, she almost collapsed. To this day she hates the sound of "Taps."

When it was time for her to rotate home, Mary had mixed emotions. She was delighted to get out of what she called a hellhole but
miserable at the thought of leaving her friends behind to see the
devastation of the severely wounded and the men with shattered
lives, to hear the sounds of rocket explosions, and to live in constant
fear. She would be safe at home, and they would be among death
and destruction.

Mary left Vietnam on 25 February 1968.

Mary's reception in the United States was mixed. She became
friendly with the soldier sitting next to her on the plane, so when
they landed in Seattle they decided to wait together for their con-
nections to their home cities. As they walked down the concourse of
the airport, several young people coming toward them began
yelling "baby killer." Mary felt that the accusation was addressed to
her friend, although ironically, he had spent his time in Vietnam behind a typewriter. Mary felt a pang; it was only a month before that
the Vietnamese child had been blown to bits.

Fortunately, Mary said, the incident "wasn't confrontational, just
mouth, and they kept on walking."

The story was different when Mary landed in Philadelphia. Her
family greeted her happily, warmly, and proudly. And what a surprise awaited Mary when they reached their own neighborhood. Although it was midnight, it seemed that everyone in the area knew
she was coming home, and they turned out to give her a rousing,
supportive welcome.

Mary needed to serve six more months before her army duty
would be completed. Several of her friends were going back to Vietnam for further tours. Mary knew that if the army tried to send her
back, they would have to drag her kicking and screaming every inch
of the way. Luckily she was assigned to Valley Forge General Hospital in Phoenixville, forty-five minutes from Philadelphia. Mary
worked in the neurosurgical ward and only wore her army uniform
in transit, because she had learned of the general antiwar atmos-

phere in the country. In her white uniform it was impossible for anyone to identify her as a Vietnam veteran, and she did not communicate that fact to anyone, because she did not want to be exposed
to the hatred so many felt for the Vietnam War and those who
served there.

However, while she was at Valley Forge she received unwanted
publicity as a Vietnam veteran. She was nominated heroine of the
year by a patriotic veterans' organization. A story about her appeared in the *Philadelphia Inquirer.* It distressed Mary.

She says, "I really wasn't ready for all the publicity. I just wanted to
forget Vietnam. I was very uncomfortable being identified as a Vietnam veteran. Most of my patients were in wheelchairs and would be
for the rest of their lives, and the newspaper article was trying to
make a hero out of me. The whole damn world knew I was a Vietnam
veteran. It wasn't so easy to hide anymore. I moved to south Jersey,
and I knew at the time that I was running. It was very important to
me to go somewhere where nobody knew me, where I could get a
fresh start without Vietnam being in the picture. It worked; nobody
knew I had been to Vietnam and I was able to start over."

Mary was married after a brief courtship. She left nursing when
her first child was born and joined her husband's gas service business. Today her oldest child is in the Peace Corps in Paraguay, her
second daughter has a degree in chemistry, and her son is a
teenager who helps out in the company during summers.

Mary successfully put her Vietnam experience behind her
through a procedure she adopted: she kept her service there "a
deep, dark secret." She says, "I know I never really faced anything
about Vietnam. I never talked about it. Never really came to terms
with it. I took that year and buried it as deeply as I could and I swore
I would never let myself think of it. That worked for twenty years,
but it eventually came back to haunt me."

About ten years ago Mary contacted another nurse who had
served in Vietnam, whose wartime story had appeared in a local
newspaper. She lived only five miles away. Mary dropped her a note
and the nurse telephoned as soon as she received it. She asked
where Mary had served. When Mary tried to answer she found it dif-

ficult to remember. Was it the 71st Evac? The moment Mary decided the answer was yes, she began shaking.

"Just like Vietnam, I couldn't believe it! Here I am standing in the kitchen of my own home in a very safe Cape May County, trembling. Up until that time I thought I was a happy, well-adjusted person. That just started the whole ball rolling. My head was in Vietnam constantly. I started crying everywhere. I'd be driving and have to pull over, I was crying so hard."

Mary was shocked that although she was forty years old and a registered nurse, she had no idea what depression was—until then. She didn't know what was happening to her, and neither did her husband, but she did realize that it had something to do with Vietnam. It had started the day the nurse telephoned. Mary called her and told her about her emotional downturn. In return she learned about post-traumatic stress disorder and the veteran centers that could help her.

At that time, she didn't even know that she qualified as a veteran. When she had returned to the United States from Vietnam, she had tried to join the Veterans of Foreign Wars (VFW), but they didn't accept women, and the Vietnam Veterans Against the War didn't want her. She didn't know what one had to do to be considered a veteran. She just knew that she had "damn well been to war."

Mary went to a veterans' center and there began the long road back to emotional stability. The staff, many of whom had served in Vietnam, were able to provide psychological counseling. Mary had several months of individual counseling; it was during her second session that she remembered the Vietnamese child who had been blown away the night her ward took the direct hit. She had forgotten about that child. Now it all came back. Her son was the same age as that young boy had been those many years ago.

A talk group at the center followed the counseling. The men—a medic, a lab technician, a combat medic, and many wounded—all welcomed her warmly; they remembered how the nurses had cared for them. Slowly, Mary put the pain of Vietnam behind her. And it was deep pain.

"PTSD [post-traumatic stress disorder] is the pits. I've never in my life been in such pain as I was then. I think Vietnam the second time around was worse than the first because the psychic numbing that occurred in Vietnam is gone."

By 1990, when one of the group asked her to be the medical support for a "last patrol," she felt whole again and willing to help. The New Jersey Vietnam veterans marched from the Vietnam Memorial in Washington, D.C., with names of New Jersey veterans rubbed from the wall and placed in a polished box. Their destination was the state memorial in Holmdel. Mary joined them as the medical aide for part of the march. The courage and persistence of the men, many with disabilities, and the warm reception they received in the towns and villages throughout the state impressed Mary. She felt proud to be part of the group.

Today, although finally at peace with herself, Mary still feels that "nothing about Vietnam is easy for me, and I guess it never will be."

Carolyn Tanaka

Carolyn Tanaka spent her earliest years in Guadalupe and Dinuba, California. When she had finished the first grade, in July 1942, she and her family, along with other Japanese-Americans, were herded onto a night train to Poston, Arizona, and placed in a camp behind barbed wire. The family of six lived in one 30 by 30 room in a tarpapered building for the next three years. On their release, the family moved to Fresno, California. After high school, Carolyn won a full three-year scholarship to the Fresno General Hospital School of Nursing. Her classmates there were angry when, after graduation and emergency room service at the hospital, Carolyn volunteered for Vietnam.

She was inducted into the Army Nurse Corps on 3 October 1966 as Hisako C. Tanaka, Captain, serial number N2328873. After six weeks at boot camp at Fort Sam Houston in Texas, and service at Fort Ord in Monterey, California, on 12 February 1967 Carolyn boarded a plane for the seventeen-hour flight to Vietnam.

Carolyn found the flight tiresome, without movies or a radio, and knowing no one aboard. She felt alone as the only female on the plane with about 180 GIs, all going to a war zone. When the pilot approached Bien Hoa he announced that he was going to begin a nose-dive landing because the airbase had been mortared the night before and there were still enemy in the area. The swift, plunging dive landing frightened Carolyn and, she was sure, all the men aboard.

As she got off the plane, oppressive heat assailed her—a dramatic change from Monterey, with a registered high sixty-degree temperature, and Anchorage, which had been minus six when the plane landed there en route. Bien Hoa was 120 degrees in the shade. The men had fried eggs on the pavement that afternoon.

Carolyn asked a nearby sergeant how to identify the enemy. He told her they all wore black pajamas. As the bus drove through the town on the way to the 90th Replacement Center in Long Binh, about six miles away, all Carolyn seemed to see were Vietnamese men wearing black pajamas.

After much confusion and many changes, Carolyn's final orders placed her at the 24th Evacuation Hospital in Long Binh, about twenty-two miles northeast of Saigon, the largest army complex in South Vietnam. A year before, this ten-mile area had been swamps and rice paddies. The army bulldozers had leveled the land and filled in the holes, and the base was now home to many units, in addition to two hospitals: the 93d and 24th Evacuation Hospitals. It also held the Long Binh Jail, or "LBJ Ranch," and a huge ammunition dump which had been routinely blown up by the Vietcong until the army strung lights around the area. To Carolyn it looked like the Bay Bridge at night. In the army's judgment, since the Vietcong knew where it was, there was no use hiding it. The enemy would find it difficult to sneak in and blow it up in the bright light.

On Monday, 20 February 1967, Carolyn started her duty as a staff nurse in the emergency room of the 24th Evacuation Hospital. For the next month her shift changed weekly. Carolyn settled in and fit easily into the ER routine. She found daily living pleasant, though simple. Town was off limits, as was Saigon farther away, so shopping and even sightseeing were difficult. Carolyn asked about going to a Buddhist temple, but word of the great personal risk involved dissuaded her. She began to attend the base chapel. She was relatively happy with the food, especially since the nurses received rice two or three times a week.

The local Vietnamese found Carolyn an unusual sight: an Asian in a U.S. Army uniform in Vietnam, and a *daiwi* (captain), with short curly hair, to boot. As an Asian, Carolyn occasionally found herself suspected by the authorities. She remembers one incident clearly.

"One day I was riding on the back of a deuce and a half [two-and-a-half ton] truck with other men and women on our way to visit an orphanage. As we approached Saigon, the MP pulled the driver over and asked, 'What is the Vietnamese civilian doing on an army truck?' The chaplain explained that we were nurses on our way to visit the orphanage. The MP would not take the chaplain's word, and I had to produce my ID as proof I was an army nurse."

Carolyn's remark at the time was that the MP had better believe her, because they all outranked him.

At the orphanage, the seventy children ranged in age from two to about twelve, and at the sound of a whistle blown by the superintendent, they all stood at attention to greet the nurses. They sang songs, then left for lunch as the nurses began to tour the facilities. They found sad, deplorable conditions. All the rooms showed decay and neglect. One child, about two years old, was asleep on a metal cot with no mattress. Carolyn noted that many of the children had sores on their heads and bodies. The orphanage officials served tea to the nurses, and then the children returned to bow good-bye.

On the way back to the Long Binh compound, the missionary couple who had driven the final lap to the orphanage took a route through the narrow streets of Saigon, past the slums. Children were running around naked, and pets and animals roamed everywhere. Live ducks with their feet bound waited for buyers. The fish were sold live and the meat was hung up, covered with flies, or laid out on the ground to broil in the hot sun.

The nurses stopped for lunch at a first-class restaurant, the Fuji, then for supplies at the Cholon PX, in the Chinese section of Saigon. At the PX, goods ranged from nickel candy bars to diamonds, furs, and even brand-new automobiles, which could be delivered to the United States. When Carolyn and the others returned to their home base, she was tired, hot, and grimy, but oddly refreshed from having had a day away from "home."

Spring brought a surge in neurosurgical cases. Day after day of head injuries was discouraging, even for the most dedicated nurses.

By 1 April they had an unusual number of casualties. The 1st and 4th Divisions and the 199th Light Brigade were, Carolyn wrote, "getting zapped." Carolyn was too tired from caring for the stream of patients to clean up and go to a party that night. At the end of the week the hospital received casualties from Navy SEAL Team One and Dust Off Crew 283 (helicopters). The next day Admiral Ward came to visit his men of the SEAL Team, and later General Eckhart, commanding general of the 9th Infantry Division, came to see his men, followed by an air force general. After several days, General Hollingsworth of the 1st Division came to see his men. Carolyn says she had never seen as much brass come and go as she did during that short period.

That spring more and more nurses arrived on base, and the sound of pounding and hammering attested to the preparation of new quarters. Some nurses had been housed temporarily in the laundry room, and some in the site of the new beauty shop. The hospital had expanded to become the neurosurgical and maxillo-facial center of Vietnam. Carolyn saw that these patients were increasing so much that the chief nurse had a hard time finding nurses to take care of them. In addition, Saigon prepared to close one of its hospitals. The patients would come to the 24th Evacuation Hospital, which was now also taking care of the Vietcong casualties, Vietnamese civilians, and pediatric cases in the area. At this juncture the hospital staff had six children, and it was hard put to find baby food and diapers, since those were not army issue items.

Life outside the Long Binh army compound fascinated Carolyn. The Vietnamese she met were kindly but uneducated. The doctors who went out to the villages despaired of helping the local people, who traded their pills for ones of more interesting colors or sold them to the Vietcong. They seldom used the supplied soap to cleanse their wounds.

She enjoyed some of the amenities of the more sophisticated Vietnamese culture. She remembers a luncheon at the Jungle Inn near Bien Hoa, to which the military advisors of the 95th invited four of the nurses one Sunday. Carolyn learned that the Vietcong were said to eat at the restaurant and that Ho Chi Minh was said to be a frequent visitor. It was considered one of the finest restaurants in Vietnam.

The meal was something to write home about—and Carolyn did. "Barbccued wild boar . . . in a spicy sauce . . . chopped wild deer meat with nuts . . . curried antelope . . . doves cooked in a savory sauce . . . served in halves with the head still on the lucky half." Carolyn ate a lucky half's head, but felt compelled to spit out the eyes. Then she had more deer meat with vegetables cooked on hibachis, as well as tacos in hot sauce, washed down with Baum Ni Ba beer. For dessert they had green bananas, deep fat–fried puffed rice cookies, and tea.

After lunch, back at the 95th headquarters, recreation consisted of archery, pool, and dice games. The war came close to the compound. One night the enemy mortared the 11th Cavalry, three miles up the road, and a fire fight took place in Bien Hoa. After that, Carolyn threatened to carry her helmet to work and vowed not to travel the roads after dark.

Toward the end of April the nurses became extremely busy. Carolyn reported, "One evening we received thirteen litters all at once and wound up with twenty-one admissions and two KIAs [killed in action]. The next evening we received a female Vietnamese worker from the mess hall who had OD'd [overdosed] on CP [chloroquine-primaquine—for malaria] pills. She went into cardiac arrest and died in the ER. It doesn't take many of these pills to cause a cardiac arrhythmia. Many of the prisoners in the stockade stockpile their CP pills and OD when they get tired of prison life. Another evening we had five Vietcong patients with multiple fragment wounds and one Vietcong who had half his face blown away. Being the maxillo-facial center for Vietnam, this type of injury is common to us. Most survive the injury unless they have other serious injuries or commit suicide later on. Many of the nurses who worked with patients who had lost their faces are still haunted by the remembrances."

The next morning when Carolyn awoke she heard the sound of a chopper landing. The helicopter stayed on the ground so long she knew something unusual was happening. She got dressed and headed to work, even though it was her day off, thinking that the ER would be full of new patients. But that was not the case. The helicopter was there to transport patients to the 36th Evacuation Hospital to make room for the expected battle casualties.

The chief nurse asked Carolyn to open up a new ward as a minimal care unit for the incoming overflow patients. Carolyn did, and then was assigned to work there. The ward turned out to be a far cry from minimal.

"My minimal care ward filled up with fresh post-op patients with horrendous dressings, half of them with IVs, and some I would classify as needing intensive care. I was alone with the corpsman to handle this load. I had never felt so disorganized in all my nursing career. Needless to say, I worked my tail off for ten straight hours without breakfast or lunch to make it through the day. Every patient was a new admit, and I had thirty-one by day's end. Just the paperwork for thirty-one admissions was enough to drive me bananas, not to say anything about vital signs, dressing changes, or reinforcements, changing IV bottles, and other routine care. I made it through the day, but went to bed right after dinner with two pills and a swig of Joe's rum."

Carolyn did not spend all of her hours working. She managed to find recreation to relieve the strain of long hospital duty. She spent many evenings at the chapel with Jo, the physical therapist, who played the handmade wooden organ while both of them sang hymns off key. They also played Scrabble in between "singspirations" at the chapel.

Carolyn also made Medcap (a program for civilian aid) visits to neighboring villages. In May some of the nurses were scheduled to go to the villages behind Bien Hoa, but this plan was cancelled because Bien Hoa had been raided. The next day, since they had the time and a driver, they went to two villages, Bien Tau and Tan Trien. The trip was notable. Carolyn saw her first case of fish skin disease (ichthyosis), and the nurses had a harrowing ride back to base. The hour was late, the skies were dark, and rain was cascading down when they started home. The Jeep's brakes were deficient, if not nonexistent. The enemy was still in the area, so one nurse rode shotgun and the driver held a .45-pistol. Carolyn felt lucky to arrive safely back at base.

The next day Carolyn hitchhiked by plane to Qui Nhon to see her boot camp friend and future sister-in-law, Phyllis. The 250-mile ride via Pleiku and An Khe took a full day, but it was a needed respite from the almost constant hospital routine.

Toward the end of May, Carolyn helped the day shift take care of five Vietcong patients. "Two of them were a deep purple in color. They were tunnel rats. They had been flushed out of a tunnel with a chemical that turned them purple. Even their urine was cranberry colored. They were labeled VC #108 and VC #109, and their temperatures corresponded to their numbers. They had chemical pneumonia."

In the middle of June the 1st Division got hit and sustained 160 casualties, and the 24th and nearby 93d took these patients. In spite of having more patients, Carolyn found time to join the other nurses and the doctors in sports programs. She thrived on basketball, softball, tennis, and swimming.

At the end of the summer a whole crew of nurses and doctors left the 24th Evacuation Hospital. Carolyn was promoted to head nurse. The war heated up. All kinds of units were mauled by the Vietcong—not only American GIs, but Vietnamese Army and Thai soldiers. Many casualties arrived at the 24th.

Carolyn remembers well one American GI: "He had massive wounds to his buttocks and peritoneum, one eye gone, and his right hand mangled. When I got off duty, he was still in the OR and we had run out of A+ blood. I insisted on donating my A+ blood for him so that his surgery could be completed. He received thirty-six pints of blood in all, including mine, and survived."

On Christmas Day 1967, the hospital received an unusually large number of patients. Carolyn had sent the staff to see the Bob Hope show in Long Binh, and then from 6:30 to 9:00 P.M., the hospital admitted seventy-five patients with salmonella food poisoning. Carolyn taught a new nurse on her first day of duty how to start an IV, and the two of them crawled on their hands and knees from patient to patient initiating the treatment.

Patients came who had been hit by napalm bombs from U.S. Air Force planes. There were eight badly burned who arrived at the same time as eight with multiple fragment wounds. Carolyn wrote, "The severely burned patients walked off the chopper with their arms outstretched, burned flesh and clothes hanging from their arms, smacking their lips in thirst. The staff worked feverishly on these patients, and we got eleven of them out of the ER in thirty minutes—a feat no stateside hospital can match."

As the months went on, Carolyn became philosophical about the war. She was not completely sure what she believed. She wasn't convinced that it was a just war, but by the same token, she knew that the GIs, for the most part, were in full support of the campaigns, and that they did even more than the nurses to help the civilians. The nurses and doctors felt that they had come to Vietnam to serve the American GIs, and they were somewhat bitter about having to treat the Vietnamese population. The 24th was nicknamed the Vietnamese General, and the staff treated not only the civilian adults, but also the babies and toddlers whose homes had been mortared by the Vietcong. Carolyn felt that the medical trips to the villages were more for improving relations than for treating diseases. Most of the time on their visits to outlying areas there were no doctors, so the nurses and corpsmen took stethoscopes, made some sort of diagnoses, and treated the patients as best they could.

In January 1968, the army gave Carolyn a thirty-day leave as a reward for extending her tour for six months. Thus she missed the slaughter of the Vietcong Tet Offensive of February 1968. The last six months of her duty in Vietnam passed quickly for Carolyn. She was led to remark to acquaintances and friends back home that not all of war was hell. She had two R&Rs in Thailand and Japan during her eighteen months, and acknowledged that she did enough traveling to satisfy her desire to see the world.

As she was preparing to return to the United States, Carolyn thought of the patients who had almost broken her heart. One such had been in-country for only ten days.

"He arrived in the ER with no face. It had been blown away by an exploding rocket. He had no eyes, no nose, no mouth, no tongue—only a cavity that used to be a face. His brain was functioning, and he gestured with his hands in an attempt to communicate. I held a clipboard with a piece of paper in front of him and handed him a pen with which to write. Without being able to see, he wrote the words, 'no face.' I could not think of any words to comfort him. I remember putting my right hand on his right shoulder and feeling how muscular he was.

"I also took care of a young soldier from Madera, California, who suffered massive internal injuries when the bunker where he was standing guard duty caved in on him. He survived through surgery, and I went to visit him post-op. We both sensed his impending doom. I held his hands and listened to him tell me about his love of life. . . . He died in my arms, and I wept then and when I wrote his parents to share with them his last words.

"We nurses lived with a lot of guilt feelings for sending patients home with such devastating injuries, or for not doing enough for the ones we couldn't save.

"My very last day in the Army Nurse Corps in Vietnam was quite a send-off. I worked a thirteen-hour night shift, patching up over thirty GI prisoners from the Long Binh Jail. They had rioted and beat each other up. I was late getting off duty and almost missed the freedom bird home."

When Carolyn packed to leave, her chief nurse went to her room to tell her to put a civilian dress in her carry-on bag, and to change clothes as soon as the plane landed in Oakland.

"She said that way I could avoid being spat upon and called a warmonger or baby killer. I could not believe that twenty-three years after the end of World War II when I spent three years in an internment camp, I would be coming home to the same reception by my fellow citizens."

Carolyn hurriedly left the ER after helping the battered rioting prisoners. "What a send-off," she thought again as she boarded the plane for home, ending her Vietnam service.

Carolyn was able to repress her experience in Vietnam after she returned to the United States.

"Unlike most nurses, I had a job to go back to, and while my coworkers were not interested in hearing my war stories, they welcomed me home with open arms. I put everything away in a closet and didn't talk about Vietnam until about 1980, at which time I was asked to do a class for new nurses coming to the hospital."

The class was called "Tricks of the Trade." Carolyn taught the nurses how to make do with what they had and how to reuse things being thrown away, as well as other ways to do jobs that were not taught in nursing textbooks. When her classes got too large, such as in the graduation periods of December and June, Carolyn pulled out her colored slides of Vietnam and showed them instead.

In addition to working, Carolyn played softball and basketball, but she said she was a couch potato as far as any community service was concerned, with the exception of some work with juvenile traffic offenders.

Carolyn's life changed drastically when she was asked in 1986 to become a volunteer for the Vietnam Women's Memorial Project. The couch potato vanished, and Carolyn became active in trying to educate the public about the nurses in Vietnam, and later, after Desert Storm, about the contributions of women in all wars.

She spoke and continues to speak on television and radio, to newspapers and magazines, and to any groups that wish to listen. To do so, she has traveled extensively. She has received many honors for her dedication to the cause of recognizing women's service to their country.

Diane Corcoran

Diane Corcoran grew up and went to school in a middle-class suburb of Rochester, New York. She went away to college in Wisconsin for a year, but since she had decided at the age of ten that she wanted to be a nurse, she returned to Rochester to attend the Genessee Hospital School of Nursing. In August 1965 Diane started her long nursing career. During her second year at Genessee she was chosen to spend three months in India, where she learned about life, death, dirt, poverty, and cultural diversity. Thinking of her future educational possibilities, she joined the Army Nurse Corps. Her initial assignment was at the Presidio in San Francisco, where she helped treat soldiers returning from Vietnam. She first learned of the antiwar feeling in the country when the flower children protested outside the hospital gate. In spite of not having volunteered, she received orders for Vietnam for 17 August 1969.

Diane Corcoran was the only female on a very crowded airplane as it circled over the Golden Gate Bridge in a good-bye salute. After what seemed like 197 hours to Diane, the plane landed in Vietnam, and the men all scrambled to the call of a loud voice. She was eventually left "the lone body in a crumpled ugly striped uniform in the middle of the tarmac." She waited for someone to claim her or at least tell her where to go. She had a trunk, two suitcases, and a duffel bag.

"The air was so thick you couldn't breathe, and it was hot and humid. I was exhausted and couldn't think of much else except a shower and someplace to get out of the heat, but I do remember thinking, 'What the hell am I doing here?' Eventually someone came and took me to the army hospital in Saigon where I was to spend the night before going to the replacement center in Long Binh the next day. I remember lying on some terrible bunk with a single light swinging overhead, fading on and off like a scene from an old movie. I felt like I was in a Bogart film. Tired and lonely, I was wondering how I had gotten there and what would come next. I drifted in and out of sleep. I could hear what sounded like bombs exploding far off. Between my exhaustion and the bombs, I really began to wonder what I had done. However, eventually I fell into a much needed sleep."

Diane waited for her assignment for a few days and then was driven about five miles to her new duty home, the 24th Evacuation Hospital neurosurgical center. She moved into a wooden hut with a tin roof covered with sandbags. She had a small room next to the bathroom that had just about enough space to turn around in. Diane went to work at the hospital almost immediately on arrival, and she found she was so tired when she went to bed that she was grateful to have anything on which to lie down. The women worked twelve hours a day, six days a week. The twelve often turned into fourteen. It seemed to Diane that all she did was work and sleep.

She worked on the neurosurgical wards, where there were about twenty or thirty beds on each of two connecting wards. Two nurses and several corpsmen worked each shift. One nurse did all of the IVs and the other did treatments, dressings, and medicines. "Each patient had two or more IVs, so it took all day to mix them and keep them timed correctly and then change those that needed changing, which we did religiously every three days. We all helped each other and it truly was a team effort. We had many very sick patients, and with the volume and reparation of injuries, we soon became very proficient at what we did."

Diane was thankful that she had had extensive nursing experience in India, where she had taken care of many patients, and also at Letterman General Hospital in San Francisco. Some of the nurses had never taken care of so many patients, and they were frightened and awed by the responsibilities given them. However, as time went on most of the nurses became so sensitive to the patients that they could almost predict when a change in condition was going to take place.

The long hours continued. Diane remembers being so tired that she did not think she could stay awake a minute longer—but she did. However, once she fell asleep standing up while taking a patient's blood pressure. Another time, after a fifteen-hour night shift, Diane went to bed, fell asleep immediately, and was called to the ward ten minutes later. More casualties had arrived and she was needed. She worked another seven hours, got to sleep for four hours, and then reported back for duty.

Taking care of so many patients with dreadful war wounds, Diane became acutely aware of how much the human body could be devastated and still live.

"I somehow thought of people being shot in one place. It didn't occur to me they could be shot in five places and have a leg ripped off in addition. I was also unprepared for the strange positions feet and legs can get into in crash situations or how they might have some piece of rock lodged in their head that was a part of a mine. I learned to deal with the blood, but I never liked the contorted body parts."

Diane still remembers many patients clearly. One was Mike.

"He had only been in-country for about two weeks. He was shot in the back of the neck accidentally by one of our own soldiers. He was unconscious when he came in, but they took him to surgery. One of the new neurosurgeons worked on him for hours, only to have him end up as a quadriplegic. He never would be going home, because at the time we did not have portable ventilators on the air evac system, and he could not breathe on his own. Most quads died of secondary infections in a few weeks. There were plenty of bugs they picked up in the rice paddies and the water.

"It was so difficult taking care of him, knowing we were just waiting for an infection to kill him. He was wide awake and very anxious about his condition. We should have let him go during his initial surgery. It was so much harder for both of us this way. We had to read letters from his fiancée and parents, talking about their future plans, when we knew there was no future.

"On one occasion the electricity went out; since Mike was unable to breathe on his own, I ran for a bag that I could use to hand-ventilate him and allow him to breathe. His doctor was standing near, waving at me to let him go, yet Mike was mouthing, 'Please help me.' I pushed past the doctor and started using the bag to breathe for Mike. I later said to the doctor, 'Don't ever do that again in front of the patient. You saved him and we aren't going to let him die screaming for help.'

"He eventually got a lung infection and we started to sedate him for agitation. He quietly slipped away one night. . . . It all seemed so wasted and so very sad and there was nothing we could do to help, except make him comfortable. It was during times like this that you really thought about the ability to allow soldiers to die peacefully and spare them the pain, suffering, and anxiety of knowing they were dying.

"There were many sad moments. Taking a young soldier off a respirator and watching him slowly give in to a journey to the other side. The young soldier who had his arm blown off screaming at God, and not believing there was anything positive to look forward to. Having a blinded Vietnamese child with a head and abdominal injury hang on to [me] and cry for her parents, who were both killed in the explosion. Many many sad moments that are not easily forgotten."

After six months in neurosurgery, Diane asked to be moved to pre-op and recovery, because it was busier and she thought it would give her new and different experiences and challenges. Without a doubt, Diane found it much busier. The nurses took care of the new casualties, pre- and post-op, and prisoners of war, and also did a regular operating room schedule every day, in which repairs, debridement, revisions, and emergency surgery were performed. Many times they did thirteen or fourteen regular cases plus any casualties, and on some occasions they kept patients who were very sick.

There were two nurses on days and one on nights, and Diane was constantly amazed at how much they accomplished. She knew they saved lives with outstanding nursing care and attention to details, and with their skills, they made a difference.

Much of what Diane saw stayed hidden in her mind for many years and then at times would pop out unexpectedly. Other incidents she has thought about again and again over the years. One that particularly bothered her happened on a rainy night. A Vietnamese patient had arrested six times in the operating room. He had been given sixteen units of blood and was what the nurses called a "horriblectomy." He was not expected to live. In the recovery room he arrested again, and a young doctor came running out wanting to give him more blood to resuscitate him. Diane and the other nurse refused to start the blood again.

"It was well past time to give up. This was a new doctor who thought we should try everything on everybody. He did not realize that we did not have the blood to give or the time to save them all."

The young nurse on duty with Diane, who had been fearful six months before because she had little clinical training, now said to the doctor, "You will probably be out in the morgue trying to save this soldier. It's time to work on others and do the best we can." Diane could not help but smile at the remark.

The decisions in pre-op were always tough. Which patient should go to the operating room first? Often it was up to the nurses to decide. Usually the choice was clear, but one night Diane got into a shouting match with a doctor over which patient had priority. She won. She said, "They would have had to roll the litter over me to get to the OR." She had always clung to the principle that the patient came first. Sometimes that basic tenet was hard to follow when the patients were Vietcong soldiers who spat at the nurses or tried to bite them while they were tending to their wounds.

"They would laugh and tell us through the interpreter that they had killed five or ten GIs before they got hit. It didn't make it easy. It was difficult to separate all our feelings. However, it was good practice for the years to come."

Diane was outspoken, criticizing even superiors when she thought criticism was due, for better care of the patients. She championed her principles and always fought for certain standards. She was intense about her patients. She realized that the differences in patients who lived and those who died had made her a believer in a master plan.

"We would frequently see some very healthy GI who should have 'recovered from his minor wounds die, and some malnourished Vietcong with TB and jaundiced with major problems, who should not have been able to live, would stay alive for days with no blood pressure. We knew we made the difference between some patients living and some dying. Yet there were always some patients who really shouldn't have died and it just didn't seem to matter. It was their time and the plan was going to be fulfilled. And we could only help make the journey softer.

"All things happen as part of a greater plan. There are some choices along the way, but I believe if it's really your time, little can be done to change that short of a miracle, and I know they exist.

"I still think of the many times we laughed, cried, and were just sad or angry over the situation. I have come to view the youngsters and farmers who were Vietcong somewhat differently now. I'm sure they were very tired of having soldiers of any kind ruin their villages and be involved in their country in any way. They had years of war, first with the French, then us. They were sick of it all and just wanted us all out of their country. They were fighting for themselves and their old way of life. They didn't want us protecting them from anything, and they were probably right."

In between bouts of fatigue, there were times that actually brought forth laughter. But there was, Diane said, little to do on off time unless there was a party or a get-together. And it was often hard to separate work from nonwork. "One day I was walking through the ward to get my mail. I noticed a nice-looking man sitting in a recovery bed with a blank stare and went over to just talk. I looked at his chart and noted he had been in a helicopter accident. He was not hurt badly but looked like his whole world had caved in."

Diane does not know why she stopped to talk to him, because she was not working, but she did stop.

"He just looked like he needed to talk. I asked what had happened, and he told me he had gone in to rescue some folks out of another copter that went down, and he had gotten everybody out but his best friend. He couldn't get to him. I knew he was a colonel, special forces, and they were supposed to be the real tough guys, but he clearly was in great pain. I'm not sure why these words came to me at the time, but I said, 'You know, it sometimes takes a bigger man to cry,' and with that, this man fell like a heap in my arms and sobbed and sobbed. I just held him and stroked his head, as there was little one could say to heal the pain of that loss and feeling of guilt at that moment. After a few minutes, he sat up, wiped his eyes, said thanks, and then, 'Where you from in the States?'

I knew that was my cue to go on with the small talk, and I just followed his lead. . . . I remember that day so clearly, and it's one of those days when you knew that your presence really made a difference."

Now, when Diane looks back at those days, she wouldn't trade them for anything. "I learned a lot about living and dying, friends, work, skills, and how very clear you must be on values, goals, and how short life can be. There were many sad times. Some really fun times, and some intense times, but all of them I believe I integrated in a way to make a better, wiser me. I was very lucky; I believed in my ability to help. I did not believe in the politics of the war. I was able to separate the two things and gain many things, some from negative learning. It was a year of caring and holding many young men. . . . We were all they had at that moment to cling to life. We cared for them and loved them and did all we could, which was not always enough. . . . One cannot truly understand the glory of life until faced with dying."

Diane left Vietnam in August 1970, not because she did not like the army, but because she wanted to go back to school. She went to San Antonio, Texas, and started working in the ER of one of the local hospitals. She used the GI Bill for the tuition for school. Diane was frustrated at work. Civilian nursing was completely different from army nursing. In the army she had made many decisions and was given much responsibility. In Texas, she felt that the nurses could not do the simplest thing without having to get a doctor's order.

School was difficult for one who had been a practicing nurse and was in the same class with new nurses. Diane persisted and got her degree and then went back into the army. She was assigned to the Redstone Arsenal in Huntsville, Alabama. There she was able to be in touch with other Vietnam veterans, and although they never talked about their war service, just the knowledge that they had been there made the adjustment from Vietnam easier.

Diane went on to Europe, where, at night school, she earned a master's degree in psychology; her next assignment was to be chief nurse and interim commander of the combat support hospital in Fort Campbell, Kentucky. In 1976, the army selected her to get her doctorate at the University of Texas in Austin. After many assorted nursing positions, she retired from the army in September 1992.

Today Diane works as a director of health for an international corporation. She also lectures countrywide on grief and is involved with television and workshops about near-death experiences.

Diane thinks often of her Vietnam experience. "I learned a thousand lessons that year, some of them difficult ones; however, I would not give up that opportunity if given a choice. It was the best and worst of everything, and I choose to try and remember and concentrate on the best part of everything."

Navy Nurse Corps

Beth Marie Murphy

Beth Marie Murphy had been on duty at the U.S. Naval Hospital in San Diego for ten months when the chief nurse asked her if she would volunteer to go to Vietnam. Beth Marie had spent her impressionable teens in the safety of Massachusetts and had joined the Navy Nurse Corps in January 1968, hoping for a challenging military career. She knew very little about Vietnam, but she did know that many of the hospital corpsmen had gone there. Why shouldn't she go? It was not years, as anticipated, but weeks before she received her orders to the USS Sanctuary.

As the plane approached Da Nang, Beth Marie was frightened. Although she had been sure it would not, the aircraft survived a vicious storm after its Guam stop. Now it was faced with incoming enemy fire as it circled over the airport. It was then, Beth Marie recalls, that she "spaced out." She can remember little about the landing except that the passengers were rushed off the field and into a hangar.

There Beth Marie and another nurse who had received orders for the USS *Sanctuary* found each other, but they had no idea how to get to the ship. Two men in a Jeep, seeing that they looked lost, offered to take them to the U.S. Naval Hospital in Da Nang, where, they assured the nurses, transport to the ship would be available.

From the hospital a Chinook helicopter took the nurses out into the South China Sea, headed for the *Sanctuary*. The chopper was extremely noisy, and as it took off, one of the crew began to man the machine gun. It occurred to Beth Marie that someone might shoot at them. It was a disconcerting thought, and seemed out of place as the Chinook flew over a countryside that looked so green, lush, and peaceful. The white speck in the distance proved to be the gleaming hospital ship, with large red crosses painted on the side and on the smokestack. (Later, Beth Marie would often think about what good targets those red crosses on a shining white background would make for the Vietcong.)

Beth Marie opted for duty on the forty-bed orthopedic ward, which was on the B deck along with a twenty-four bed, three-crib international ward for Vietnamese women and children; a twenty-bed urology ward; and the ear, eyes, nose, and throat ward, also with about twenty beds. Here on B deck the wounded taken from the choppers were brought for triage—an examination and decision about what should be done for them.

Sanctuary hovered close to the coast of Vietnam, constantly moving about a mile offshore. Thus it was in easy range of the helicopters that brought out the wounded—most of the time right from the field. The nurses had to learn to cope with the constant motion of the ship and the noisy arrival of the choppers day and night. Beth Marie found there was little variety to the days: get up, go to work, walk around the decks, eat, talk to a few people, go to bed, get up, and start the routine over again. Sometimes during the evening on time off, Beth Marie let the Vietnamese children teach her how to fish from the deck; sometimes she was able to get off the ship to go to another navy vessel or to an officers club on shore so that the men could have feminine company.

Otherwise, many hours were spent in the dining room, playing cards, or watching very old movies with the other nurses or the doctors and ship's officers. They were forbidden to fraternize with the enlisted personnel. At the time, Beth Marie told herself she had nothing to complain about; she had a clean place to sleep, and it was even air-conditioned! Although they were not shelled nightly, as some land areas were, the nurses often openly joked that the red crosses were a great target—a matter Beth Marie had already thought about. Beth Marie knew that they all joked aloud to cover up their real anxiety that they might indeed be attacked. Most days it was work and sleep and work some more.

Beth Marie found the daily sight of desperately wounded men, both American and Vietnamese, extremely depressing, and her heart went out to the severely injured Vietnamese children. Today, she can still recall the terrified eyes and the frightened silence of a little Vietnamese girl, about seven years old, who had been brought to the ship. She had had both of her legs blown off by a mine. There was no room for her in the ICU, so Beth Marie spent a great deal of time taking care of her in the ward. But there was always the nagging thought: what would happen to her after she left the ship? The Vietnamese would certainly consider her worthless, since she would not be able to contribute to society in any way. The most she could do would be to beg. There was talk on shipboard about trying to get her fitted with artificial legs, but there were no facilities to fit her.

Some of the Vietnamese interpreters believed that she was a Vietcong, but that seemed impossible to the nurses. They tried to contact her parents, and one day, after a number of months, they succeeded. The ship at that time was near the demilitarized zone. The parents came, and although the doctors and nurses said she needed more surgery to close up the wounds on her stumps, her parents insisted on taking her with them. They promised to bring the little girl back in a week, but they didn't. The nurses and doctors never saw her again. As Beth Marie says, she was probably killed because she had become friendly with the enemy. Like a recurrent nightmare, the vision of the little girl still haunts Beth Marie.

Another patient particularly distressed, and impressed, Beth Marie. He was a clean-cut young man who came aboard the ship one day with ninety-nine other men who all had malaria. He looked and acted like an all-American boy—the "boy next door." When he had almost completely recovered from his malaria he began to go down to the international ward to play with the young children, and he often joined them at meal times and helped feed the very little ones. Beth Marie thought he would make a great dad someday. But the day after he was discharged he was returned to the hospital ship.

He had stepped on a mine and had lost both legs, one arm, and an eye. Beth Marie was sickened; she had gotten to know the young man as a person with family and friends back home—and now he would never be the same again. Years later, Beth Marie cannot even remember his name, but she can clearly remember how shocked she was when she saw him with his dreadful injuries. She often wonders whether he made it back home, and whether the doctors and nurses did him a favor by having great technology at their fingertips. Beth Marie says, "We did what we could, but it was never enough."

So many men came through the orthopedic ward that Beth Marie could not even estimate how many there were. They would come in one day, and then in a few days would be stable enough to be air evacuated out. Others would be kept for days on end; they were the ones who would never make it out of the ICU alive. At night, when on duty, Beth Marie could hear them breathing and groaning. She wished that she could do something to make it all better, but she could not. One day as she bent over a new casualty who had lost a leg to a mine, the soldier told Beth Marie that his leg hurt dreadfully. When he saw the look on her face, the soldier grabbed her and said, "It is there, isn't it?" Beth Marie had to tell him the truth. That would not be the last time that she had to tell a young healthy fellow that life was going to be very different for him.

Beth Marie was struck by another patient on the ship: "One of my most distressing memories is of a fellow lying in the hall outside of triage with a punji stick through his eye, sticking out about six inches. I knew it was in his brain. I did not remember this until very recently in a bad flashback. I still shudder thinking about it."

Day after day went by as Beth Marie and the other nurses did the best they could for the wounded soldiers. Although they had worried about the red crosses on the ship, they had no real concern for their own safety. Then that summer Beth Marie read in *Stars and Stripes* about Sharon Lane being killed. "She was," Beth says, "a young nurse who had been in the wrong place at the wrong time. She was killed in a mortar attack. Until that time I never let myself think that we could be killed—we were nurses, and nurses didn't die in combat." Now Beth Marie realized that indeed, she could be killed.

For the next few weeks Beth Marie worked in the operating room and the recovery room. It was during this period that the bloody battle in A Shau Valley took place, and the choppers brought in casualty after casualty. Beth Marie recalls working all day and far into the night. She ran from one operating room to another and then to the recovery room. She had a head wound in one room, an eye wound in another, and a wound to the heart in the third room. She knew that the man in the third room would never make it. Yet an orthopedic surgeon and another surgeon were trying to save him, in spite of the fact that he also had a bilateral amputation of the legs.

Beth Marie kept checking to see if the doctors needed anything. She rushed into the first room with the head wound and asked if she could do anything. The neurosurgeon obviously sensed her tension, and he spoke up: "Why yes, could you release the tourniquet?" As Beth Marie recalls, she bent down to do just that, and everyone in the room burst out laughing—tourniquets were not for heads but for limbs. The laughter and the silliness of the incident served its purpose: Beth Marie relaxed.

Relief from caring for the war casualties came one day when one of the GIs brought a baby to the nurses. He had found her in a garbage can, and he wanted to adopt her and take her back to the United States when he left. The baby was about a year old and weighed only ten pounds. The nurses fell in love with her, and they took over the job of bringing her back to good health. They kept her in their quarters and got their friends to send them beautiful baby clothes. Then one day the commanding officer of the hospital ship told the nurses they had to discharge the baby because now there was absolutely nothing wrong with her. The nurses knew that was true, but they were reluctant to discharge her because they also knew she would be placed in one of the many orphanages. They circumvented orders. They discharged the child but readmitted her under a different name, and eventually they found a good orphanage, which kept the baby until the serviceman was able to take her back to the United States with him. Beth Marie always longed to see that child again, but she never did.

When Beth Marie was first in Vietnam she thought it was good that the Americans were there—to protect the Vietnamese from the "ravages of communism." But as time passed she began to wonder whether her government was telling the truth. She would read in the *Stars and Stripes* about the great progress of the war—yet that was not what the men were saying. She and the other nurses heard about a decrease in casualties, yet that was not what they were experiencing. Beth Marie was disturbed. What was true?

As Beth Marie was questioning the validity of the war "facts," she became ill with an intestinal disorder. She lost twenty pounds and developed high blood pressure. Finally, she got her physical condition under control, but she found that she did not want to go back to work. Beth Marie was surprised; this was the first time she had had such negative thoughts. Years later, in hindsight, she can sense that this was the beginning of her depression.

Then, perversely, as it became close to the time for Beth Marie to leave, she decided she wanted to stay. She would extend her stay for a year. She was told that she could not, and today Beth Marie credits that decision with saving her life.

Vietnam had been intense, and there she knew that what she was doing was important—would stateside nursing make any sense?

The last month in Vietnam was a blur in Beth Marie's mind, as was the trip home. She remembers pulling away from the hospital ship in a boat, and then the cheers that went up when the plane cleared Vietnamese airspace. That is all. She had decided she would take an antihistamine and sleep her way back to the world, and she did just that.

When she arrived in the United States, Beth Marie headed to North Carolina, where her sister was studying at Duke University. When they met on campus there was no welcoming hug, but the sudden demand: "Get that uniform off before someone shoots at you." That was how Beth Marie learned about the huge protest against the war. It wasn't cool to be back from Vietnam, her sister told her; in fact, she said, it was dangerous. At home, Beth Marie found that neither family nor friends wanted to hear about Vietnam.

When Beth Marie went to her new duty station, a Seabee base in California, she could not adjust. The hospital was small, she argued with the chief nurse, and she was angry all the time and did not know why. She also cried a lot, and she did not know the reason for her tears. She felt she wanted to leave this hospital and go back to Vietnam, where she had done nursing that had mattered. Here, she felt she was "babysitting people who weren't really that sick." She remembered the cases in Vietnam: amputations; removal of shrapnel; repair of shattered bones; chest, abdominal, and all kinds of wounds—all caused by war. Some lived, some died, and some would never be the same. The doctors and Beth Marie had done the best they could for them.

Beth Marie knew she had to change her situation. She joined the U.S. Air Force Nurse Corps, went to flight school, graduated, and received orders to fly medevac out of California's Travis Air Force Base. Now she was not at all sure she should go back to Vietnam. She finally decided to disqualify herself from flight duty because of knee surgery, but then went even further and left the air force altogether. Beth Marie entered a religious community.

With few exceptions, Beth Marie spent the next twenty-four years changing and moving almost every other year. She took various religious training, taught school, spent a year in a house of prayer in Denver, lived in several different religious communities, and by the late 1980s was in school studying to become an Anglican priest. She was ordained and moved to Canada.

However, new surroundings did not help. Her depression grew, and Beth Marie had little energy or motivation to tend the parishes she was given, although she loved being a priest. Then, in 1993, Beth Marie heard about the dedication of the Vietnam Women's Memorial in Washington, D.C., and knew that she had to go. She did, and at the celebration she attended a conference on post-traumatic stress disorder. Beth recognized herself as a victim of the disorder.

The next year she attended a weekend gathering of nurses who had served in Vietnam, and she cried the whole time she was there. It was, she realized later, as if "the finger came out of the dike." She had panic attack after panic attack, she could not really work, and by the summer of 1995, she was so depressed that she did only what she had to do in the parish. She knew she needed help.

She entered the Women's Trauma Recovery Program run by the Veterans Administration in Menlo Park, California. She admitted she had post-traumatic stress disorder and completed the four-month program, straightening out her medication, learning some excellent coping skills, and coming to terms with her Vietnam experience. It was a beginning. Toward the end of the program, Beth Marie became angry about what Vietnam had done to her, and she determined not to let it destroy her anymore. Since then, she has always believed that the Women's Trauma Recovery Program saved her life.

Beth Marie moved again, to Saskatoon and the prairies in Canada, to start over once more. She is still in therapy and on medication, but she is determined to make life in Canada different and says, "I hope by God's grace and hard work I can." Perhaps she can put the sorrow and grief of Vietnam behind her.

Kay Bauer

Kay Bauer grew up and was educated and trained in nursing in Minnesota. A lack of finances for college propelled her to the military, which would pay for her education, and chance had her in the navy's recruiting line instead of the army's. In the Navy Reserve she served in St. Albans, Long Island, then spent a year in Japan, where she applied for and received a regular navy commission. She was sent to Guam for a year, and this was followed by more than two years with the naval hospital at Great Lakes, Illinois. Kay Bauer's ambition was to become a teacher and a missionary. At the navy's suggestion she applied for missionary nursing within the navy and received orders to Vietnam. When he heard the news, Kay's father worriedly shouted, "Doesn't she know there's a goddamn war going on over there?"

In January 1966, Kay Bauer stepped off the air-conditioned TWA troop transport, which had landed in Saigon, and found herself in sauna country. Taking a breath was almost like breathing under hot water. Kay had been exposed to East Asian heat before, but its intensity struck her anew. Saigon was only a temporary stop on the way to Rach Gia, in the Kieng Giang province of South Vietnam, where Kay would be stationed.

Kay was a member of the group called the 2d Forward Navy Surgical Team, which would work in the Vietnamese hospital there. Its mission was to provide surgical capabilities. The presence of the U.S. medical team, with its equipment and skills, would enable the hospital to offer extended surgical care to both military personnel and civilians in the area. About fifty local nurses worked in the hospital, but there was only one Vietnamese doctor, who was also the chief of medicine for the whole province of two million people.

The American team consisted of seven members, all male with the exception of Kay, who was a general-duty registered nurse, and Bev, the operating room nursing supervisor and instructor. The commanding officer of the group was an orthopedic surgeon who had been a pilot in the RAF during World War II before he immigrated to the United States. He had joined the navy only a few days before the team was organized.

In Saigon, the group reported to the U.S. Army, which had military charge of the area. There they were treated as soldiers, not medical personnel. The army issued each member a one-man tent, a fatigue uniform, an undershirt, undershorts (Kay declined the undershorts), a helmet, a helmet cover, a heavy plastic rain cape, boots, a canteen, cups, a knife, a digging shovel, and a belt to hold it all. The army also gave them M16 rifles with clips and bandoleers of ammunition. Kay weighed only 105 pounds, and when she tried to carry the total load of supplies, she actually fell over. They all laughed, but Kay decided then that she did not need the gun and ammunition. Bev took them for her.

Bev proved to be extremely knowledgeable, and during their stay in Vietnam she taught Kay many unfamiliar nursing procedures. She had been born in Chicago, but had grown up in Scotland and England. She had taken her nurse's training in a five-year program held in underground shelters during World War II and had returned to the United States in the 1950s.

On their second day in-country Kay learned that they really were in a combat zone, although it was not officially listed as such. By regulation, the navy did not send females to combat zones. (The men on the team were classified as being in a combat area—an odd bit of gender discrimination.) On that second day, Kay went with Bev to the U.S. Navy Hospital in Saigon, which was then being turned over to the U.S. Army. There she heard the disturbing news that only a few weeks before, during a mortar attack on the hospital, eight of the navy nurses had been wounded and had received Purple Hearts.

After a few days, the medical team boarded a navy C-130 headed for Rach Gia, the provincial capital city with a large population. It was so little known that when Bev later wrote her reports for the director of the Navy Nurse Corps, the director was puzzled. Where was Rach Gia? She could not find the city on the map.

When the team arrived at the airport they saw no aircraft, only five shy children. Any pilots who landed did so by sight alone, since no one manned the tower; there were too many Vietcong in the area. The commanding officer was confident that someone would come for them, so they trooped with their luggage into a small, dusty, unfurnished building to wait. Shortly an army captain arrived and took them, in two Jeep trips, into town.

In Rach Gia they were housed in a two-story white building with doors, windows, and screens, but no running water or telephones. A large generator supplied electricity—on occasion. On the plus side, the house came with an accomplished married couple who looked after them. They were called Betty Crocker and Westinghouse, so named by the previous navy team. The couple lived only a short distance from the house, and they came early and stayed late. They cooked, cleaned, did the laundry, and really were in charge of everything.

The men shared the downstairs, while Kay and Bev had the upstairs. The rooms were primitive but adequate, and most important, the beds were equipped with mosquito netting. All ate well. At first they relied on supplies from Saigon, but more often than not, these never arrived. They ate mostly the local foods, prepared by Betty Crocker. These foods were delicious and healthy: fruit, vegetables, chicken, fish, eggs, and rice. Kay had never before eaten octopus, eel, or shark. The army offered to sell the team some C rations at $30 a box, but they declined.

The house faced a canal, and beyond that a local shipyard where the Vietnamese Navy made its Junque boats for coastal patrol. A long row of large grass houses with dirt floors stretched out behind the house. A short distance away, across a dirt road, was the hospital, which had been built of stone and concrete by the French in the early 1900s. It had primitive doorways and windows without glass or screening, which could be covered at night and during storms by wooden louvers. A sluice ditch from the ocean flowed through an open courtyard in the hospital's middle section. The Vietnamese used the ditch to wash their clothes, as a toilet, and for food preparation when rainwater was scarce. There was no running water in the hospital, and the electricity was hooked up only to the emergency and operating rooms.

The 2d Forward Team's first job was to improve the facilities the first team had established—the operating room, the central supply room, and the post-anesthesia room—and then to set up an intensive care unit. The two female nurses helped with these efforts and also taught nursing education classes to the local nurses. The Vietnamese nurses had had only a two- to three-month on-the-job training period. The nurse midwives, however, had eighteen to twenty-four months of training, and they delivered most of the babies because there was only one doctor in the province.

After Kay and Bev had lived with the men for several months, they decided to move, since they preferred not to share the common bathroom, kitchen, and living room with men. They rented a house about four blocks away, across the canal from the hospital. There was enough room for two U.S. Agency for International Development (USAID) nurses to move in with them. There the women did the cooking in a large kitchen, which had one half of the roof open to allow rain to fall into a huge cistern. It also allowed all kinds of creatures, including birds, to fall into the cistern until the women found some screening and had it installed.

Their days at the hospital began with making rounds with the Vietnamese nurses and then again with the doctor, when he was there. Kay and Bev taught classes two or three days each week. They taught specific medical terminology, job descriptions, the uses of the various parts of the hospital, and general nursing care. As for the physical care of the patients, that was done by the extended families that came to stay in the hospital with the patients. The only unit where most of the care was done by nurses was the ICU that the team established. There were two interpreters at the hospital. One,

Mr. An, had fled with forty members of his family from North Vietnam to escape the communists. By the time they reached Rach Gia, only twenty of them had made it through the war-torn countryside.

Both Kay and Bev did dressing changes and dispensed medicines at times, usually when they were demonstrating something they were teaching. If they were to do so on other occasions the local nurses might feel that their work was being criticized. The pediatric nurses were, Kay discovered, the easiest to get along with and be at ease with. They joked and discussed nursing often. Kay found that impromptu sign language and some amateurish drawings bridged the culture gap. As she says, children and adults cry, smile, and laugh in the same language the world over.

Kay and Bev checked on the diets that were given to the patients and found that there was just one regular diet. Those who could not eat it were given a liquid diet, liquid left over from the regular diet, or just rice with the liquid. Rice was the staple. For breakfast it was rice with fish; lunch and dinner were rice with fish and vegetables and at times some fruit. The lack of refrigeration was a blessing in disguise—everything was fresh. Rach Gia was in a delta where fruits and vegetables flourished, and the fish catch was always good and fresh. Of course, many of the patients had their prejudices and scorned much of the food. They wanted only rice and would eat only certain types of fish. Food was plentiful in the hospital, and the nurses had to watch the pediatric ward at mealtimes carefully to see that the parents did not eat the children's food.

The children in the hospital suffered from many problems. Some of them died from tetanus, diphtheria, worm infestation, or malnutrition, and the infants died when they were born prematurely. Sight was destroyed by infections from flies. Polio, TB, and bone cancer were common. Burns were frequent because the Vietnamese cooked with kerosene stoves, which were often dangerously close to the mosquito netting.

Kay and Bev tried to teach the local nurses about the beneficial use of painkillers, but pain medication was generally ignored. There was no need to lock up the Demerol, morphine, and similar drugs, because no one was interested in stealing them. But that was not the case with antibiotics, which had to be kept under lock and key.

Most of the patients with injuries received them as a result of Vietcong firearms and explosives. The Vietcong set up mines on the roads between cities. The survivors who came into the hospital were covered with mud as a result of being blown off the buses or whatever conveyances they were in and into the rice paddies. Before anything could be done to help them, they had to be washed down with basins of water from the cistern so that the wounds could be treated.

One day Kay was cleaning the back of a small boy when she saw a piece of his body—she thought it was his tongue—sticking out. Then she realized it was part of his lung. She quickly tucked it back into his chest, secured the tear well with tape, and had an X ray taken. It was hard to believe, but he did not have a collapsed lung, and he was healed and sent home in a few days.

Other patients had hands, feet, legs, and arms blown off by the land mines. One woman came into the hospital with a wound from a rifle. The spiraling bullet had entered just above her temple on the right side and had traveled beneath the skin under her eye, over her nose, and under the other eye, exiting just above her left temple and leaving only superficial damage. Dressings on wounds were seldom changed unless Kay and Bev suggested it, and they were never changed during the period from Friday to Monday. Maggots were used to clean the wounds. Surprisingly, they did a good job.

Traction for limbs presented a constant challenge because rods and sandbags, rigged with ropes over a series of pulleys, created the traction device.

The sandbags inevitably developed pinholes and never lasted more than a few hours.

The team conducted dentistry, another challenge, in the back part of the courtyard, where an old dental chair and broken equipment had been discarded. Since anesthesia and pain medication were used only in the operating room, those who had teeth extracted had no pain relief. Often patients scheduled for dental surgery escaped during the preceding night rather than face the ordeal.

The Vietnamese nurses worked normal day shift hours, from 8:00 A.M. until 5:00 P.M. with time out for siesta. The night shift at the hospital consisted of one nurse outside of obstetrics. Kay described the night scene: "It was impossible to find a patient after dark as the mosquito nets went over all beds and families slept under and around the beds, making each ward a solid mass of netting. The hospital was a secure area, so household animals such as pigs and goats, children, and entire family possessions were brought to the hospital as well as all extended family members." It became quite a crowded affair.

There were some Americans in Rach Gia, including army personnel as well as civilians working for U.S. construction companies. They came to the Vietnamese hospital when they were hurt on the job, when they had been injured by Vietcong firearms or explosives, or when they were ill. Most of the time they were treated for medical disorders such as trench foot, colds, and leech infestations. One American army pilot and one air force pilot helped in the defense of the city. Each flew a two-seater plane, observed enemy activity, and called in the bombers when needed. The planes were small, but they had rockets under their wings which could be detonated by the pilot or a passenger.

Pronounced gender discrimination existed within the hospital. Kay found working with the local medical staff difficult. The men were always in charge, no matter how much or how little training they had. If a new male nurse arrived, he automatically took over. The director of nursing was male. Whether he knew what he was doing or not, a male nurse distributed the medications.

Once, some students from Saigon University came to talk to Kay and Bev. Instead of requesting information as the women expected, they had come to harass the American nurses. They asked why Kay and Bev were in Rach Gia when poverty and ill health existed in the United States. Kay acknowledged that the United States had its problems, but explained to the students that their quarrel should be with their own government, which had invited the Americans to come to the hospital.

Each day brought something new to ponder or to decide. One day the Vietnamese asked Kay and Bev to see the Vietcong prisoners. Kay hadn't known that there were any in the hospital. Five men and one woman were crammed into a small cubicle with a wrought iron doorway and no windows. Built-in benches lined both sides of the meager space. The Vietnamese doctor and the local nurses had decided that they could not see the prisoners, because somehow that would mean losing face. Kay and Bev went to the cubicle and dressed a pus-draining knee wound of one very young man and checked on a nursing mother with a healing chest wound. An older man had a severe cough, which the American nurses suspected was TB.

Kay and Bev also worked outside of the hospital. Shortly after they arrived the Vietnamese asked them to treat Army of the Republic of Vietnam (ARVN) troops and their dependents. They agreed to do so if a clinic was set up. This was done, and the nurses went there once a week. The clinic was well patronized because the Vietnamese knew that it had access to a wide variety of medications.

Sometimes the Vietnamese asked the two women to leave their immediate area to take care of people who were afraid or unable to come to the hospital. Kay often worried about these trips, because she knew that the Vietcong were all around them, but the local army sergeant in charge assured her that a scout party would precede them and that they would be escorted by troops heavily armed with rockets and multirounds for their M14s. The women always went to the same place—a low, long, green building with a large red cross marked on the white roof. There the nurses routinely treated the most common problems, ringworm and internal parasites. It was discovered that the Vietnamese nurses had an average of eleven to thirteen kinds of intestinal parasites—and they were among the healthiest of the population.

Kay and Kathy, one of the USAID nurses, took a trip that was long remembered. At the request of the ARVN they went to an island to vaccinate against an outbreak of the plague. One of the ARVN command advisors, a U.S. Army captain, went with them. They left on an ARVN Junque boat filled with passengers who were vomiting because of the diesel fumes. The boat stopped after about an hour and a half when they saw land in the far distance. Rowboats came alongside, and the crews told the women to take what they could with them and jump into the rowboats. The rest of their supplies would follow them. When the rowboats reached waist-high water, Kay and Kathy got out as directed and waded to shore. The nurses set up in front of a school, sterilizing their syringes and needles in water boiled over a kerosene stove.

Their supplies consisted of a roll of cotton, an old whisky bottle filled with denatured alcohol, and numerous vials of plague vaccine. They found it difficult to convince the children to come forward and be vaccinated because the parents were reluctant to set a good example. But eventually the nurses succeeded. Kay and Kathy decided there was time left for a swim before they returned to the hospital. Since they had their bathing suits on under their fatigues, swimming posed no difficulty. The problem came later when the women discovered that they were to stay the night—in their wet suits and fatigues.

Supper was at an elder's home, which consisted of large pieces of corrugated metal stuck into the dirt, covered with strips of more corrugated metal to make a ceiling. Long, wide pieces of cloth divided the space into four rooms. Two beds were the only pieces of furniture. Kay and Kathy ate rice and fish with ground hot white pepper and nouc nam sauce while squatting on the dirt floor. Bedtime presented other problems. They were taken to the mayor's house, and here also, there were only two beds. The mayor and his wife took one and the captain took the other—to save face, he claimed. The women had the choice of the floor or the dining room table. They chose the latter. Who knew what bugs would be cruising the dirt floor? The nurses' wet swimsuits itched, and the table was a hard mattress.

Several months later the captain apologized for taking the bed and invited Kay and Kathy to his ARVN command for dinner and a movie, which he had commandeered along with a projector and a small generator. The movie lasted longer than the women had anticipated, and when they were ready to leave they discovered that it was very late and dark outside. They were in the village next to their own and were faced with running the gauntlet of patrols of troops from both sides in the war from both villages. It was obviously dangerous to be out of their own home and village.

Kay drove the Jeep as fast as she could over the dirt roads, and they arrived in their house just as the household crank-up field phone began to ring. It was one of the men from the ARVN command where they had just been. While they were watching the movie in the middle of the compound, the Vietcong had set up mortar explosives, which had detonated right after they left. The men were now taking the wounded to the hospital. One American sergeant had been killed, the captain and one of his men had been seriously injured, and many of the Vietnamese families and soldiers had been killed or severely wounded. Eventually the captain and one sergeant were air evacuated from the hospital, which treated and released the Americans. Some of the Vietnamese, however, were patients for a long time. Kay never saw the captain again; a new one was sent in to take over the command.

Someone else would now take Kay's place, too. Her tour of duty was over. Early one morning she left Rach Gia aboard a small plane headed for Saigon. She stayed there overnight, and within forty-eight hours she was en route to California.

Kay Bauer's Vietnam experience had ended. Now, as she thinks about it, she feels her view of the war was limited. She went to Vietnam to work with the Vietnamese, and that is what she did most of the time. "If I were to make a decision now about going," she writes, "I guess I would do the same as before except be a bit wiser and more accepting of things not changing."

The C-130 made no stops, and the trip home was long. Kay was still in her uniform when she took a bus to the airport in San Francisco in the late evening and got aboard a Northwest plane bound for Minneapolis. Kay tells what happened next.

"Almost as soon as I was seated, I was surrounded by the stewards and stewardesses, who wanted to know if I had just come from Vietnam. Deciding that it was probably best, I admitted that I had. They immediately brought out steaks and ice cream and champagne and helped me fix the seats so I could stretch out and get some sleep. They continually asked if there was anything I needed or they could do for me. When others recount their horrendous homecoming experiences, I have always been appalled. Arriving at the Minneapolis/St. Paul airport, my parents met me and I was treated as a hero."

Kay's superiors in Washington asked her if she would go on recruiting duty, and she was delighted to do so. She chose Quantico,

Virginia. To her, after the primitive conditions in Vietnam, living in Quantico was like living in a paradise.

"Running water, showers anytime. Telephones that did not have to be cranked. Clean, dry sheets, no mosquito netting. Screens. Electricity. Soap. Drinking water from the tap. Radios that had English spoken. Television. Taking care of the marines was wonderful. They were so appreciative of everything we did for them. Most of them, of course, had returned from Vietnam with nothing much more than their Purple Hearts. We learned quickly to awaken the ward by turning on overhead lights because tapping anyone on the foot might evoke such a strong response that weights and traction would come undone and sometimes surgery had to be redone. Being a vet myself helped to some extent, but I could not talk with them about what I did because I had been with the 'gooks,' and all 'gooks' were enemies."

After ten months in Quantico, Kay was asked to do recruiting duty in her home state of Minnesota, and she accepted.

Kay expects to retire from the navy in two years, but for now each day is overflowing. She has her navy duty and two part-time jobs, as an ICU R.N. and a college instructor. She has a husband she describes as long-suffering, children, and grandchildren. She does volunteer work and is president of both the Minnesota State Department of the Reserve Officers Association and the seven-state area chapter of the Association of Military Surgeons of the United States. She has started on a master's degree in vocational education and manages to find a little time for daily exercises, relaxation, and visits with friends and neighbors. A full life indeed.

Air Force Nurse Corps

Monna L. Mumper

Monna Mumper lived, studied, trained, and worked as a nurse in Pennsylvania before she became a member of the U.S. Air Force in June 1956. Monna served in the air force for eleven and a half years before she began flying aeromedical evacuations out of Southeast Asia.

On Christmas Day 1967, Monna Mumper flew with six other flight nurse volunteers to Japan's Yokota Air Base, home of the 56th Aeromedical Evacuation Squadron. Flight duty began almost immediately. The nurses spent only a short time settling into their nearby living quarters at Tachikawa Air Base, in a suburb of Tokyo.

Living accommodations were more than adequate, but the women found little enjoyment in the apartments because they flew one flight after another in the C-141s, ferrying the wounded. The planes, each of which carried two flight nurses and three medical technicians, flew many different routes. Since physicians were rarely onboard, the full responsibility for the care of eighty patients rested with these medical personnel.

The plane might fly from Yokota to Vietnam to pick up the casualties in need of further treatment in either Japan or the Philippines, or it might ferry them all the way to the United States if the doctors decided they were up to the trip. The plane usually stopped en route at Elmendorf Air Force Base in Alaska or Travis Air Force

Base in California. If the nurses were lucky when they stopped at Elmendorf, they stayed overnight and a new crew took over. The flight originating at Yokota enplaned the wounded who earlier had been brought to the hospitals near Tokyo from Vietnam or the Philippines. The plane then took them on the long hop to the United States.

Monna never knew what was going to happen on a flight. Several times she and the other flight nurse had barely signed into the bachelor officers' quarters at Andrews Air Force Base in Maryland when they were alerted that they had to return to Southeast Asia because both they and the aircraft were needed there.

Monna found that many of the trips were not easy, physically or emotionally. Nothing prepared any of them for the extent of the injuries they saw—men who had double and triple amputations, who might also be blind, with head injuries, fractures, and severe abdominal conditions. The average age of the fighting men was nineteen years, and most of the wounded Monna saw were that age. Some of the medical crew were not much older; they were in their early twenties. In a way, Monna and the other older nurses felt lucky, because they coped better than most of the younger women.

The stress of caring for men with severe multiple wounds was often compounded by the lack of adequate rest. Monna admits that at times some of the nurses burned the candle at both ends, through too much alcohol or too little rest time between flights. This was especially true during the Vietcong Tet Offensive and during other attacks when the medical crews were unable to get the normal rest that was standard for flight crews.

A typical flight into Vietnam from the Yokota home base began early in the morning, typically at about 6:00 A.M. The nurses picked up their supplies and medicine kits and went to the aircraft. They drank coffee and chatted with the crew; then, after boarding, they read or slept until it was time to land. Normally they did not get off the airplane after landing in Vietnam, but supervised the medical flight technicians and hospital personnel as they loaded the patients, either litter cases or ambulatory, onto the C-141. The flight crew learned to spend minimal time on the ground because the plane was shot at several times on landing or takeoff.

Aboard, the nurses worked as a team. One was responsible for the general care of all patients, while the other had responsibility for giving all medications. They assigned seats or litter spaces for the patients and were provided cards that identified each, including name, diagnosis, medications, and any treatment to be given during the flight. All ambulatory patients fastened their seatbelts before takeoff, and straps confined the litter patients at all times.

With a full load at takeoff, the nurses sat on canvas stools at the sides of the aircraft, and that was usually the last time they sat down until just before landing. A full complement of eighty litter patients demanded constant attention.

The least severely wounded and those who needed little care during the flight lay on the top tier. Patients with more severe medical problems lay in the middle and bottom rungs, where they were easily accessible to the nurses. Blood pressures were taken without listening with the stethoscope because the C-141 noise made hearing impossible. The nurses pumped up the blood pressure cuff and felt for a pulse in the area of the arm for a beginning and ending beat.

Monna remembers specifically one nineteen-year-old on one of the trips. He had lost both legs and one arm, was blind, and had reduced hearing. Since bed sores could begin even on an eight-hour flight, they had to turn the patients and straighten the sheets. Monna still remembers the cries of this young man as they lifted him on his litter. She often wonders what happened to him. Did he ever get home? Some patients who had IVs needed constant watching. Some needed help in eating their dinners. Others needed help smoking or using bedpans or urinals. The nurses changed or reinforced dressings when necessary.

The wounded were always grateful for any attention they received. Monna remembers one trip when she had to tell the men that they did not have any of the regular hot TV dinners and could only offer them C rations, cans of nourishing but not too tasty food. They heard groans from all parts of the aircraft, but the complaints did not last long—the men were too glad to leave Vietnam.

Unlike the arrival of a C-141 in the United States, where the plane landed and then taxied to a distance from both the terminal and the runway, in Vietnam the aircraft usually parked close to the buildings, an area which, it was hoped, was safe. Although the general rule was to take off quickly after the patients boarded, sometimes the medical crew stayed in Vietnam for hours or even days, depending on how many flights were needed and how many C-141s and crews were available.

The same situation existed at Clark Air Base in the Philippines, at Travis Air Force Base in California, and at Yokota. Monna never knew how long the stay would be. When they stayed over at Clark, she lived four to a trailer, and if they knew they would not fly for twenty-four or forty-eight hours, the nurses could leave the base as long as they were available by phone at all times. Sometimes they went to the officers club for a meal—a good change from the aircraft fare.

At Tan Son Nhut in Vietnam, if they had to wait for a flight out they stayed over in a two-story wooden building, two bunks to a room, and Monna invariably got the top bunk, which almost abutted a ceiling fan. Here, when mortar attacks came the nurses donned their flak jackets and helmets and either hid under the beds or ran down the steps to a nearby bunker, which was a hole dug in the ground. It had a dirt floor and accommodated ten people.

Tan Son Nhut was shelled several times when Monna was stationed there for a week to work on the patient in-flight scheduling by seat or tier. She took the advice of the regular staff on duty there as to whether to stay put and get the patients under the beds or go to the bunker. Monna did not envy those whose duty kept them continually in Tan Son Nhut.

On the flights from Yokota to the East Coast of the United States, the C-141 always flew over the North Pole because this was the shortest route to the East Coast. Flying time to Elmendorf was between eight and nine hours. If a medical emergency came up and the plane was less than halfway, it could return. The nurses had learned to perform lifesaving procedures such as tracheostomies (opening an airway by cutting into the trachea) if necessary, but Monna's crew was lucky; most of their emergencies occurred over land, and they called a military hospital to receive advice on procedures.

When the nurses stopped over at Elmendorf Air Force Base, they usually arrived late at night, around 10 P.M. As they departed the aircraft, the Red Cross came on board, bringing refreshments and good cheer. If a flight surgeon was needed to judge a patient's fitness for further travel, the surgeon also came aboard at this time.

A bus came and took the medical crew to a building where they locked their medicine kits, and then they were dropped off at the bachelor officers' quarters office to get rooms and leave their clothing bags. The nurses were usually hungry, so they walked to the officers club for a snack or meal. Alaska was cold, and Monna can remember one winter night when the wind was wild and they hung onto each other's parkas so that they wouldn't get separated and lost during the blinding snowstorm. If the weather was good and they had more than eight hours on the ground, sometimes they went to Anchorage for drinks and dancing. However, many times they were too tired to do anything but eat and sleep. When they had to depart depended on how many crews were staging at Elmendorf and how many flights were scheduled to accommodate the flow of the wounded.

Monna usually spent her time in Vietnam on the flight lines at the Cam Ranh Bay, Tan Son Nhut, or Da Nang air bases. Often her medical crew stayed overnight while waiting for the next mission out. One day while waiting for their next mission from Cam Ranh Bay, they went to the beach, a rare pleasurable occasion. However, when Monna stayed at Tan Son Nhut, she often went to the bunker, since the Vietcong attacked the base frequently, sending in mortars.

In July 1968 Monna experienced a frightening event that is still vivid in her memory. When her medical crew flew into Cam Ranh Bay, they were assigned a secret mission to the Royal Thai Air Base in Udorn, Thailand. After they arrived there in the afternoon they learned that they were to wait for the arrival of the first prisoners to be released from Hanoi in North Vietnam. The base had no available rooms, so the flight and medical personnel decided to stay with the C-141, which was parked about a mile from the terminal. Most of them stretched out on three seats to get some sleep while they waited. An airman armed with an M16 weapon stood guard just outside the plane. The senior medical technician, SSgt. John T. Walsh, was also on the alert outside. Around 10:30 P.M. the sergeant came running onboard, shouting that someone was firing at them.

The unidentified enemy successfully hit the plane. As Monna grabbed her shoes and ran down the crew steps in the front of the plane, she saw flames shooting up from one of the engines on the left side. She recalls, "Everyone scrambled in all directions. Someone yelled, 'Get down! Get down!' But I thought I was too close to a burning aircraft that could explode. I did get down and lie flat on the runway. While lying there tracer bullets were flying overhead. As skinny as I was, I felt awfully big lying there. Before long I heard shuffling feet coming toward me. I didn't move a muscle, even when the person hesitated when he got close enough for me to touch him. He hesitated a moment, then continued on to my left. Since I did not move, I could not look up and see what he was wearing, but it sounded as though he wore sandals rather than shoes. I did not know, but there were aircraft beyond me and I heard explosions."

The guard had been busy shooting at the enemy, and the sergeant had the quick thought to turn the spotlight off of their airplane and direct it into the hills, making the C-141 less visible. Monna lay on the runway for about forty-five minutes listening to the firing and explosions before one of the airmen came up to her and directed her to a Jeep to which the other flight nurse, Louise Stroup, had been sent. Both returned to the terminal, and after about two and a half hours all of the flight and medical crews turned up. The pilot and the flight engineer had been hit by shrapnel, and although Sergeant Walsh, the senior medical technician, cared for these two men, the flight engineer later died from his wounds.

The next day the crews inspected the C-141 and found it completely inoperable because of the shooting damage. Inside, Monna checked her belongings and found that the two new dresses she had bought when she went to Hawaii from a West Coast mission were still hung up in the aircraft. They were riddled with bullet holes.

The flight and medical crews secured another plane, in which they flew to Clark Air Base in the Philippines. The prisoners never came to Udorn Air Base.

Monna did not want to frighten her parents, so she did not report this harrowing mission. She believed that what they did not know would not hurt them. Then a letter arrived from her mother. Indignantly, she asked her daughter: did Monna think that McKinley was still president and that they didn't get any news? The story had been printed in the hometown newspaper. Monna hurried to explain.

Another disturbing flying time came as a result of the weather. Surprisingly, it was in the United States. One day when the C-141 was carrying a full load of forty litters and about twenty or thirty ambulatory patients, it flew through a thunderstorm on its descending approach into Andrews Air Force Base in Maryland. The aircraft seemed to be bouncing all over the sky. Everyone was buckled up. When Monna heard bolts and screws fall to the floor from the ceiling, she became alarmed, but the plane landed without incident, although with several shaken passengers. One sailor remarked that he was a sailor, definitely not a flyer.

As the date for her return to the United States approached, Monna had some time off to climb Mount Fuji and to have a whirlwind week of R&R, visiting Hong Kong, Kuala Lumpur, Singapore, Bangkok, and Taipei. However, she felt sorrow at never knowing the final fate of some of her patients. Especially paramount in her mind was the young soldier with the amputated legs and arm, who was also blind. Caring for patients only on flight evacuation precluded knowledge of their future fates.

It was March 1970 when Monna Mumper left Southeast Asia and Vietnam behind her.

When Monna was sitting in the San Francisco airport waiting for her flight home to Chambersburg, Pennsylvania, an awful sense of doom came over her. She thought, "Dear God, I've been through a war and now I feel I may be in an aircraft accident." When she arrived home she found out her father had unexpectedly died in his sleep at that same time. It was an eerie experience.

Monna was too grief-stricken over her father's death to notice the hostility toward Vietnam veterans. She went to her new assignment, three months at Sheppard Air Force Base in Texas, then entered a six-month nursing service management course at the same base. Monna stayed in the air force through assignments in Spokane,

Washington; California; South Carolina; and Elmendorf in Anchorage. She retired in 1981 and returned to Chambersburg. She had filled fourteen assignments in twenty-five years of air force service. In summarizing her air force career, she says, "There was not much I would change if I could. It was a good life."

Monna now lives in the house in Chambersburg that she bought in 1978. She traveled a great deal with her mother until she died in 1995 at the age of ninety-two. Since retirement, Monna has volunteered in many areas: tutoring illiterate adults, manning a contact help line service, and delivering for Meals on Wheels. She is secretary-treasurer of the local Retired Officers' Association, a member of the local VFW, and a member of the Military Order of the Cooties, who visit veterans at a West Virginia hospital. She plays golf several times a week. Monna obviously enjoys her busy retired life.

Eileen G. Gebhart

Eileen Gebhart was born, raised, and educated in Pennsylvania. She received a scholarship to attend the St. Luke's Hospital School of Nursing in Bethlehem. After graduation in 1959, she completed an obstetrical nurse intern course and worked in a hospital labor and delivery department. She stayed there only a short time before she took the leap to California, where she worked for a year as a medical-surgical staff nurse in a small hospital. Then, to cure the wanderlust that still assailed her, she joined the U.S. Air Force Nurse Corps. Eileen did not, however, feel professionally challenged, so when the call was out for nurse volunteers for Vietnam, she responded. When her parents learned of her Vietnam assignment, her emotional mother cried for four days and would not watch the news, and her practical father wondered what she was going to do with all her possessions.

In February 1966 Eileen and eleven other nurses—the first female air force nurses to be sent to Vietnam—left California, bound for Hawaii in Class A blues, stockings, and heels.

"After a twelve-hour flight from Hawaii," Eileen recalls, "I finally exited the airplane to set my swollen legs and feet on the flight line in Saigon. We were immediately directed to a tent for processing. After the paperwork was completed, we were taken by bus to a hotel in Saigon. This hotel gave us mats to sleep on in a room large enough to accommodate all twelve of us. The next morning we were flown in a C-130 to Cam Ranh Bay."

When the aircraft touched down the entire base personnel was there to greet them. A young lieutenant stepped up and asked if they had taken their pills. When the officer saw the nurses look at one another in disbelief, he hastily added, "Monday is malaria pill day." The men had been preparing for the nurses for some time. They had erected tents for living quarters and had built a washroom, shower, and four-hole latrine, which was a shed over "honey buckets"—large metal drums of used engine oil. When filled, they were easily ignited.

The nurses' quarters were wooden-floored tents, with four cots and a single suspended light per tent. These would be home for the first six months; after that the nurses would move to hooches—wooden-slat dormitory structures with a bunk bed per room, community showers, and a latrine with conventional toilets.

The Air Force Medical Corps mission at Cam Ranh Bay was to support army, air force, and civilian personnel while they were constructing airfields and shipping docks and setting up air evacuation capabilities. They also supported an Air Force Tactical Air Command fighter wing of F-4Cs that flew bombing missions into North Vietnam. Unlike the army nurses, who faced the physical and emotional stress of working on the front lines, air force nurses, usually in support positions, faced the stress of daily inconveniences and frustrations interspersed with hours of boredom.

The 12th U.S. Air Force hospital at Cam Ranh Bay consisted of several wards. A ward was two adjoining tents on wooden floors. Beds were cots. The surgical suite was a hooch with plastic covering the slat windows to keep the ever-blowing sand out of the building. Living at Cam Ranh was like camping on a sand dune with constant blowing sand. The fine sand clogged equipment, got into and under wound dressings, was always in food, and clung to the skin. Wounds rapidly developed infections.

Patients typically had work-related injuries or medical conditions such as malaria, hepatitis, gastroenteritis, venereal diseases, alcohol and drug problems, or mental health problems.

Patient food was usually dehydrated or dried foods sprinkled with fine sand. Any fresh vegetables were sterilized by soaking them in bleach. Refrigeration was unreliable or nonexistent. The Sunday evening meal was C rations because it was the cook's night off.

Most of Eileen's nursing care consisted of listening to the men talk about their experiences in the field.

"Many wept under the cover of the night's darkness. Sometimes I wept with them.

"Caring for the patients was a daily exercise in creativity and innovation. Our drinking water was housed in a 'water buffalo' that sat in the sun. It was highly chlorinated and very difficult to get past the nose. Hence, forcing oral fluids and brushing teeth were major problems. We used Fizzies and Kool-Aid to hide the odor of chlorine. Substitutes were sodas, strong coffee or tea (sun-brewed), or beer—whatever was available.

"Wound care was dependent on availability of supplies and solutions. We worked with what we had. Managing a malaria patient with a fever of 105 degrees in a tent of the same temperature without a cooling blanket or ice consisted of sitting with the patient under a lukewarm shower and forcing fluids until the crisis subsided."

The original hospital tents were later replaced by air-conditioned, windowless metal Quonset huts, which allowed the use of up-to-date equipment and hospital beds. The hospital area and the living quarters were near the flight line, where planes were constantly taking off and landing twenty-four hours a day, making conversation and sleep difficult at best.

For the first six months the nurses walked everywhere; there were no paved roads or bus service. They wore the heavy GI-issued combat boots, and they never strayed far from their quarters because there were no latrines for the women on the base except near their tents. Eileen eventually stopped taking the malaria pills because they gave her diarrhea and it was often difficult to get to a latrine in time. Flexibility and innovation were necessary to survive. Those who could not adjust were sent home before their tours were completed.

Eileen was exposed to sexual harassment in the military. "I was harassed in some form almost every day I was in Vietnam," she says.

"Sexual harassment comes in different degrees, such as minimal with deliberate invasion of what little privacy we had." Eileen says there were as many excuses to come into the nurses' quarters as there were men. Covert harassment included, for example, the GIs stealing the nurses' underwear from their wash lines to hang up in their own tents. More obnoxious were peeping Toms who tried to sneak peeks on the sly. It took the nurses some time to catch on to the trick: the men strung lights down the middle of a nurse's tent so the outline of women moving about inside could be seen on the tent flaps. It took the nurses quite a while to learn that many men were spending their evenings watching them dress and undress.

Solicitation of sex was the most outright offense. There were times, Eileen says, when she thought the enemy was the American GIs, not the Vietcong. The approaches and lines asking for consensual sex were too numerous to count. Some type of harassment occurred almost every day. On a far lower scale were the minor irritants, such as the lack of necessary female supplies. When Tampax finally arrived on base, the GIs bought them to clean their M16 rifles, leaving the nurses without them. Eileen handled most harassment and irritants by simply ignoring them.

The nurses were lucky, though. Their base was never attacked while Eileen was there. An attack was an ever-present threat, but the Vietcong seemed to respectfully avoid the Republic of Korea marines who protected the area. "We could see night flares and hear gunfire across the bay, but fortunately, we never had to run to the bunkers in fright or seriously think about using the M16 we knew little about."

For recreation the nurses played cards with the GIs. There was almost always a game of poker, hearts, or pinochle. They planned cookouts when they could trade with someone for the meat; they wrote letters; and they talked for hours with one another, making fast friendships—Eileen says these friendships have not been equaled in intensity since then.

The nurses never really knew who the enemy was. The Vietnamese who worked on the base had no loyalty to either side. "They stole our medical equipment and medicines and sold them to the Vietcong while giving enemy troop movement information to our people. Supplies earmarked for U.S. troops often landed in the Vietnamese black market or Vietcong hands."

Eileen's mama-san, hired to do the cleaning and laundry, routinely stole the nurses' personal belongings and then took a proprietary attitude, as if they now rightfully belonged to her. Because of cultural differences Eileen could not ask for them back.

A men's choral group was formed on base, sponsored by the chapel. Eileen, who had an extensive musical background, having started piano lessons at the age of nine, was cofounder of this group and keyboard accompanist. The first sixty men to sign up were the members, whether monotones or not. Eileen thoroughly enjoyed these sessions, and they filled her off-duty time nicely. By the fall of 1966 more nurses had arrived on base, allowing female voices to be added.

The group sang for special events and holidays on base and in-country. When Ed Sullivan heard of these Choraleers, he sent a television recording crew over to tape a few of their songs for his Christmas show, which aired that December.

The choral members became a closely knit group. After practices, many of them just sat around and talked. All of the members looked after one another and they became like a close family. Some of the Choraleers died in combat over North Vietnam. Eileen says this choral group "was an important emotional part of my Vietnam tour and a source of pride."

Later, when the chapel finally received a Hammond organ, Eileen and a sergeant alternated playing for church services. Eileen felt that "practicing the organ was a way for me to 'escape.' It helped me keep my sanity in this insane environment."

The nurses were restricted to base unless they were sent on temporary duty to help other medical facilities, on medical missions to the Vietnamese villages, or on R&R. Periodically they relieved the nurses at the Tan Son Nhut Air Force Base Dispensary in Saigon. It was not particularly pleasant duty, since the dispensary was located next to the morgue, which was heavy with the smell of formaldehyde. During the day Saigon seemed like any big city, but at night it definitely became a war zone. From the balcony of their quarters, the highly sandbagged and guarded Hotel Rex, the nurses could watch and listen to the war until the closeness of the firepower forced them indoors.

Then suddenly Eileen became a short-timer—the term used for someone who has about thirty days left in Vietnam duty. Eileen says, "This was a very ambivalent time. I knew I was saying farewell to people I had grown to love, and would probably never see them again. On the other hand, I was returning soon to the land of milk and honey with a new appreciation of life."

It was time to go home.

"Happiness had become sleeping in a sand-free bed, getting jungle boots for your birthday, a hot shower or bath, fresh milk, pizza, a letter from home, a box of homemade chocolate chip cookies, friends, clean clothes, and a true sense of what it is to belong. I gained more than I lost from this experience, and was eager to share what I had learned with others. But when I returned home, no one wanted to listen.

"When returning stateside, there was no time to readjust and no buddies to readjust with. In just twelve hours I flew from war-torn Saigon to Hawaii, with flushing toilets and McDonald's hamburgers. I thought the flight back would be a twelve-hour celebration, but it was one of the most somber trips I have ever taken.

"When our plane landed at Travis Air Force Base, I did not expect a band, but I did expect at least a 'Welcome Home' sign, a hug, or a free cup of coffee. Nothing happened. I went through customs and all of a sudden I found myself in a phone booth wondering whom I should call first and saying to myself, 'Is that all there is? So I'm home. Big deal!'

"I was not aware of the hostility toward the war and the military until I returned. I did not experience the overt hostility that some of the nurses I served with did. They reported being spat on, refused service in restaurants, and called baby killers. But I did experience covert hostility. I rapidly became very much aware of the anger the public had toward Vietnam veterans and the military in general. I learned not to speak of my Vietnam tour. Even in 1975 while attending school in Denver, I was advised to remove any military insignia from my car and dress in civilian clothes when off base to avoid conflict with civilians."

In a typically Alphonse and Gaston scenario, without any basic underlying cause, Eileen's family did not ask her about Vietnam because they thought she did not want to talk about it. And she didn't talk about it because she thought they did not want to hear about it. It was an uneasy and unfortunate situation. Her parents died without ever asking her about Vietnam, and only in the last ten years have some family members expressed an interest in hearing about her Vietnam experience.

Since an early age, Eileen had always been involved with some kind of musical endeavor, either vocal, brass, or keyboard. Wondering if this hobby could become a profession, she decided to take the chance. At the end of her original four-year enlistment in 1968, Eileen separated from active duty and moved back to Sacramento, where she worked in an emergency room in a small hospital while playing keyboard with two musical groups—"one for money and the other for a chance to be creative."

Eileen had learned not to burn all her bridges behind her, so before she left active duty, she joined the Air Force Reserve Medical Air Evacuation Unit at McClellan Air Base in Sacramento. The reserves sent her to flight school in Texas, and then for her two-week summer tour she was assigned to Yokota Air Force Base in Japan, where she flew with an air evacuation unit that was transferring Vietnam patients to medical facilities in the United States. During this tour Eileen sensed how much she missed the security and familiarity of the military.

In March 1970 Eileen realized she could not make her living from her music, and it was not as much fun as she had anticipated, so she returned to active duty. The air force sent her for further formal training that allowed her to rise up the nursing hierarchy until finally, after twenty-three years of active duty, Eileen retired in September 1988 as a full colonel.

Eileen attended various ceremonial events for Vietnam veterans in Washington, D.C., in the succeeding years, and one of her most emotional experiences was to be warmly welcomed home by male Vietnam veterans. The first time it happened—the first person ever to welcome her home from Vietnam—was an ex–Navy SEAL who had been in Vietnam for two tours. He gave her a hug and said, "Welcome home." Eileen cried all the way home, at first not knowing why.

"At one time no one wanted to hear about Vietnam, and now this newest generation is intrigued by it." Eileen has been invited to speak time and again, and she is glad to do so. She now does volunteer work at the Biloxi Veterans Administration Medical Center. She is also still involved with music, playing keyboards for a singer specializing in oldies.

"It took me about twenty years to realize the anger I harbored toward the people who treated Vietnam veterans so unfairly," she says. "I have replaced that anger with disappointment; I am working on replacing that disappointment with understanding. Would I volunteer for Vietnam again knowing what I now know? In spite of how the American public felt about this unpopular war, my answer is yes."

Donna J. Cunningham

Donna J. Cunningham, one of seventeen children, was born in a small coal-mining town in Pennsylvania. After high school, Donna believed that she could either marry or work in a shirt factory. Instead, she opted to attend a small miners' hospital school of nursing. In spite of being told that she did not have "enough brains" to be a nurse, Donna graduated as a registered nurse after three years at Pennsylvania Hospital, Philadelphia, where the nursing class transferred when the miners' school closed. Donna worked at the hospital for a year, then joined the Air Force Nurse Corps on 20 February 1963. She trained in Alabama, worked in Nebraska, successfully attended flight nurse school in Texas, and served her next tour in Turkey. At the end of eighteen months she headed for the United States, stopped briefly in Thailand to visit her sister, then enplaned again on the military space that was available, en route to the United States for reassignment.

As an air force flight nurse, Donna flew into Da Nang in September 1966 in a civilian aircraft contracted by the military. Donna received her first glimpse of Vietnam. Before landing, the pilot told the passengers to close all window blinds and not to attempt to look out. Although Donna was curious, as were the others, she saw only a military airstrip similar to all the other airstrips she had seen, except that everything was camouflaged and barbed wire was placed almost everywhere.

"I vaguely remember the dirty, weary, dead-tired, vacant-eyed group of soldiers who boarded the plane. After we were airborne a short time the pilot announced that we had just left Vietnam. The entire plane erupted in a roar of cheers, clapping, whistling, and re-lease of tension. I didn't understand any of it at that time. I de-parted that plane at Clark Air Base, Philippines, and after ten days of waiting and begging, I finally made it back to the States as the only passenger aboard a C-141 filled with cargo. I realize now that the plane probably carried bodies of dead American soldiers. En route I landed at Yokota Air Base, Japan, Elmendorf Air Force Base, Alaska, and terminated my flight at McGuire Air Force Base, New Jersey. Little did I know then that two years later I'd be making that same trip every month."

Back in the United States, Donna was assigned to the infectious disease ward at Lackland Air Force Base in Texas, and after a year and a half of service there, in September 1968 she transferred to the 56th Aeromedical Evacuation Squadron stationed at Yokota Air Base. In Japan, Donna lived in the bachelor officers' quarters at Tachikawa Air Base, which was about thirty miles from Tokyo and twelve miles from Yokota. After she was checked out in the flight routine, she began almost daily flights for the evacuation of wounded and ill men from Vietnam. There were usually more than forty litter patients and thirty to forty ambulatory patients aboard, and each man had a flight tag that listed his diagnosis, medications, and treatments.

The schedule called for four C-141s to fly empty into Da Nang, Tan Son Nhut, or Cam Ranh Bay in Vietnam four times daily, and the evacuation trip varied, with landings in Yokota; Clark Air Base in the Philippines; and bases in Alaska, Illinois, the District of Co-lumbia, and New Jersey. Severe burn patients traveled to Kelly Air Force Base in Texas.

The medical crew for an evacuation flight consisted of a charge flight nurse, such as Donna; a medicine flight nurse; and three medical enlisted technicians, called corpsmen. The procedure sel-dom varied. The loading crew put the patients aboard, patients in litters were strapped in, and ambulatory patients' seatbelts were fastened. The plane cruised at thirty-three thousand feet, everyone received a hot TV dinner, and the nurses routinely checked the patients, gave back rubs, tended IVs, and reinforced dressings. (They never changed them in flight because conditions were considered unsanitary.) The charge flight nurse functioned as the final authority about each patient. She could order the pilot to divert if a patient needed immediate care, or she could request a surgeon to accompany a patient in flight to his destination if he was critically ill. She could refuse to take a patient if she believed the patient was not stable enough to make the long trip.

The nurses were always busy; it was only after the patients were offloaded at the destination that the flight nurses could rest.

Since the C-141 was basically a cargo plane, if it was "deadheading," or flying empty into a base, the women, carrying blankets and pillows, fanned out and found places to sleep atop the cargo crates. The plane's bunk for the flight crew, equipped with a comfortable regular mattress, provided a superior facility compared to the wooden crates. If none of the flight crew intended to occupy it, they might allow a medical crew member to use it. Donna accepted that favor one time. She slept peacefully until she felt a body all over her. Donna says, "One of the male flight crew members had other thoughts than sleeping, and assumed that I would be eager to accommodate him. I grabbed my pillow and blanket and left hastily. I never took advantage of the chance to sleep in the crew bunk again."

The nurses took turns at nurse of the day (NOD) duty, which meant one full week in-country in Vietnam. Donna always requested Da Nang. She did go to Tan Son Nhut and Cam Ranh Bay, which most of the nurses preferred because they were close to Saigon and the beaches, received fewer rocket attacks and lighter casualties, and enjoyed a good party life. However, on Donna's first visit to Cam Ranh Bay she was warned not to walk alone on base because of the danger of rape. Donna initially thought the Vietnamese or the Vietcong were the dangers, and she could not figure out how they could get on base. But she discovered that the caution referred to the American GIs. In Da Nang she never feared rape; she knew the GIs there showed respect for the nurses.

Da Nang received frequent enemy attacks. Donna learned the importance of having readily available candles and of knowing at all times where she had put her flak jacket and helmet.

On other trips, NOD duties consisted of visiting military hospitals and checking the patients who were scheduled to fly out the next day. Donna assessed their wounds and whether patients wore casts or needed chest tubes, IVs, or any special equipment for oxygen, suctioning, or blood transfusions. She noted each patient's condition and needs and called that information in to the air base headquarters, where any needed equipment was put onboard the plane. Orders were cut, and then Donna made up the load plan for the litter and ambulatory passengers. Certain patients had to be placed in certain layers of the litters for easy accessibility.

After the work for the plane was finished, the nurses were free to either go to bed and sleep or go to the officers club and relax with other officers. They got up early the next day to load the patients for the flight. After the plane left, Donna, as NOD, could go back to sleep.

During Donna's orientation week in Da Nang, she was visiting with the in-country troops, most of them pilots, at the officers club when a rocket attack occurred. "To my surprise," she later remarked, "no one did anything different. Everyone continued to eat or drink; no one put on a flak jacket or helmet. Later I learned the rocket landed near the NCO [noncommissioned officers] club, but no one was injured."

Aside from the NOD week, the life of a flight nurse constantly changed as flights were made into different bases. Donna's stay at her home base of Yokota was the only stable element. There she packed and repacked her suitcase, ready to go on the next flight. Donna needed two sets of clothes: one for cold climates (Alaska) and one for warm climates (the Philippines).

Sometimes Donna faced real danger. Once, Clark Air Base alerted her at about 2:00 A.M. for a flight into Cam Ranh Bay and then on to Yokota. The plane landed at Cam Ranh Bay and received a report from the NOD. Donna went out to the flight line, all of the patients were loaded into the aircraft, and the plane prepared for takeoff. Donna walked to the front of the aircraft to give her preflight briefing to the light load of men, about twenty on litters and fifteen who were ambulatory. Just as she arrived at the cockpit door, she says, the flight crew ran out.

"The flight crew came flying down out of the cockpit and out the door of the aircraft. They were running so fast I was taken completely by surprise. They nearly ran me down. I recovered quick enough to yell at the last man, 'Hey, where are you going?' He yelled over his shoulder without missing a step, 'To the bunker. We are under attack!'

"There was nothing I could do because I had never been briefed on what to do if under attack on the flight line. I didn't even know where the bunker was. I walked to the ambulatory section and asked my NCOIC [noncommissioned officer in charge] if he knew where the bunker was and he replied, in a stammer, 'Yes, ma'am.' He knew enough to be scared. I didn't. I told him to take the ambulatory patients to the bunker and return when the flight crew returned. He gave me no argument and ran off the plane.

"I walked to the rear of the aircraft where the litter patients were. The load master was in the middle of tying down the baggage and asked me what I wanted him to do. I could tell by the way he spoke that he was scared out of his wits. I had no idea what I wanted him to do. However, I heard myself quietly and calmly tell him, 'Loosen the cargo straps in case we have to shove the cargo out and unload these patients and then stand by.'

"In my mind I was thinking, *The flight crew deserted me and I'll be darned if I'll let this guy get away. He's staying right here with me.* I walked up to the litter patients and told them, 'We'll all just be very quiet and maybe they won't know we're in here.' I smiled since I was kidding and they all knew it. My calm professional manner, I think, reassured them. We were stuck, we knew it, we couldn't go anywhere, and I wasn't about to leave them. I walked back to the front of the aircraft and got a tray of chocolate milk. I passed it out to the patients and we talked. All I remember is being alone with the load master and litter patients.

"About fifteen minutes later an air force master sergeant came onboard and asked where my flight crew was. I replied that they were in the bunker. He told me he'd have the crew back here immediately. True to his word, the flight crew returned, along with the ambulatory patients and my NCOIC. The crew closed the doors, started the engines, and we were airborne within minutes. It was rapid and almost straight up. Everyone breathed a sigh of relief, more so this time than any other medevac I had ever taken out of Vietnam. The pilot announced when we left the territory of Nam and all the patients whistled, clapped, and cheered. It was the same response I had heard in 1966 when I first flew out of Da Nang."

When Donna reported what the flight crew had done after they landed in Yokota, they were grounded and given a letter of reprimand.

In the two years that Donna flew medevac, she flew eighty-two trips. Finally in September 1970 her service in airevac ended. Donna requested an additional year on that duty, but the request was denied and she returned to the United States. She received an assignment as the charge nurse of the obstetrics, labor, and delivery unit at Columbus Air Force Base in Mississippi. Donna worked at the hospital there for a year and a half, and had finally adjusted to the fact that she was no longer in charge when she was dumbstruck to be told that orders had been issued for her duty in Vietnam.

"I really believed I had done my time in Nam. Granted, I wasn't stationed there, but I had spent a lot of time there NODing and flying in and out. It was May 1972. I accepted the assignment to Tan Son Nhut Air Base, Vietnam, requesting a port call for November."

Donna arrived at Tan Son Nhut on 6 November 1972. Living accommodations were hardly first class. Around Thanksgiving time, the nurses moved to the hospital because officials said the base and the war would soon end. Donna lived in the OB/GYN office on one of the wards. The hospital consisted of Quonset huts joined together; each hut was a ward. The nurses lived in one ward. One nurse bunked in the linen closet. Everything was improvisation in Donna's room; for example, an army blanket served as her carpet. She could walk in and sit down or stand up and wash her hands in the small bath. She walked across the hall to shower.

On 5 December, the enemy attacked with rockets. The red alert sounded, and Donna put on her helmet and flak jacket and dived under the bed. Then she remembered her bare legs sticking out from under her short pajamas. She crawled out and grabbed her housecoat to throw over her legs, as if that piece of cloth would protect her. Each nurse kept a book, a flashlight, soda, cigarettes, a lighter, and an ashtray under the bed because they never knew how long they would be there.

A short time after this attack began, the nurses remembered that a new nurse had arrived that day. As old timers, they all climbed out from under their beds to instruct the neophyte in procedures. The new nurse couldn't get under her bed because it wasn't up on blocks, so the nurses all lifted the bed, and Liz, the new nurse, scooted under. When they let the bed down, the springs were about an inch from her nose. They gave her cigarettes, a lighter, and an ashtray, and then they all ran back to their own beds for cover. When the all-clear sounded the nurses dressed and went to work.

Later the same day the enemy launched another rocket attack. Donna was ordered to stay in the hospital because a pregnant Vietnamese woman had been brought over from the NCO club in labor. The nurses considered Donna the most qualified to handle the birth, and she did so.

At the hospital most of the American patients were drug addicts, and the war casualties were Korean. The marines no longer guarded the Americans; that duty had been turned over to the men of the Army of the Republic of Vietnam. Donna did not enjoy her work at Tan Son Nhut because, she says, she was not really taking care of war casualties as she had expected, but of "druggies" instead.

"I just felt it was such a waste of not only nursing and medical personnel but military personnel. Most of the medevac flights at that time were all drug abuse. You could sense the ambivalence toward the guys with a drug problem. A lot of them were arrogant, some were confused, and others appeared vacant or lost. What a waste. I don't think the war contributed to the drug scene, nor do I believe the military or war makes alcoholics. I believe those who got on drugs in Nam probably would have done the same at some time in their life no matter where they were. If the war caused drug abuse, then how do we account for the vast number of military personnel who served in Vietnam and didn't become addicts?"

Donna found the last part of December 1972 nerve wracking.

"It started 14 December with what we thought was a rocket attack at 5:45 A.M. The whole day proved upsetting. Land explosions kept going off, and we never knew whether it was a rocket attack or what when we finally received the all-clear word around 6:15. The nurses all got dressed and went to the dining hall in the hospital. We lived, worked, and ate in the hospital. I remember we were going through the serving line and this God-awful loud bang went off that shook everything in the building.

"Within seconds all of the occupants were flat on the floor. I was crawling toward the rack that held the trays, and I was bound and determined to get under that rack. The hospital administrator walked in and said, 'What are you all doing on the floor? It's only an ammo dump blowing up!' Only an ammunition dump! Well, to the sea of green bodies in that dining hall, it was more than an ammo dump.

"The ammo dump was about eight miles southeast of Saigon. All day, ammo dumps exploded. Everyone was on edge. Everyone was carrying a flak jacket and helmet. I remember debating with myself about wearing my jacket and helmet over to the chapel. I finally decided I'd rather be ridiculed than dead.

"Later we all talked and laughed about all the things we did. Marty, a male nurse, was in the shower when the first 'attack' hit. He said he was stark naked and dove for cover under his bed. Then he realized he was naked, ran to his dresser, and got the St. Christopher medal his wife had given him before he left for Nam. He put it around his neck and got back under the bed. He no longer felt naked."

Marty survived the war without a scratch.

Donna found the food at the hospital generally distasteful. The meat, she believed, must be some years old because it tasted like perspiration from the freezer. A dish of French green beans and bacon contained a big dead roach. The eggs were powdered and tasted like sulfur. The bread was made from rice flour and tasted awful. Donna ate her cereal with coffee because the milk had a grainy taste. Once in a while an officer would get steaks from some mysterious place and they would all have grilled steaks, an unexpected treat. The Vietnamese officers club had good Chinese food, and the nurses ate there often.

In December 1972 everyone was talking about peace. Gradually, Donna saw places close up; war activities began to slow down and fewer patients came to the hospital. Christmas came and went, but still no peace treaty was signed. The Vietcong hit again with rockets during Tet of 1973, but there were no American casualties. Then Donna received orders for her new assignment, in Thailand. She was to leave Vietnam on 18 March 1973.

Personnel left, and Donna became chief nurse at the hospital, now cleared of patients and turned over to the Vietnamese. The medical staff were held as hostages until Hanoi released all the American POWs. Every day in March, the nurses were scheduled to leave. Although they reported to the airport, they were never permitted to leave. They referred to themselves as POPs, which variously meant prisoners of peace, prisoners of the Pentagon, prisoners of politics, and pawns of the Pentagon. Sometimes when they reported they were told they would leave the next day. They would get packed and ready to go and have another going-away party; the next day would come and Hanoi would not release the POWs, so they would be held back again. One day they got to the flight line and sat there for hours, only to be told they were not going.

Finally, after playing the game of leaving day after day, on 27 March Donna and another nurse were told they would be leaving the next day. They arrived early the next morning and got to the flight line, where they waited and waited and waited. The plane actually left at 6:00 P.M.

Donna says, "We had finally made it out of Vietnam!"

Donna served in Thailand, where she thought the accommodations were fifty times worse than in Vietnam, but she left there on 30 November 1973 for Langley Air Force Base in Virginia. "I was happy as a lark to be home in the good old U.S.A. again," she says. Donna trained as a primary care nurse practitioner, served an internship in Alabama, and was assigned to Dover Air Force Base in Delaware, where she remained for five years before transferring to Plattsburgh Air Force Base, New York. She completed her B.S. degree, received her master's degree in 1984, and retired from the air force as a lieutenant colonel after twenty-two years, on 1 April 1985.

Donna believes that her time spent nursing the wounded of Vietnam was the mission she was given in her vocation of nursing. She never went through any trauma from Vietnam. She says she will always remember Christmas 1972, when Bob Hope came to Tan Son Nhut to entertain the troops and she and thousands of troops heard the singing of the hymn, "Silent Night, Holy Night."

One of the great rewards of her service came when she walked the parade route at the dedication of the Vietnam Women's Memorial in Washington, D.C. Donna's eyes filled with tears as she heard the calls of the male Vietnam veterans alongside the parade: "Welcome home, sister, thank you."

It was an emotional moment for Donna. "I served my country in the military because I wanted to. I was proud to serve. I never expected a thank you. However, it sure felt good to hear it."

Donna K. Buechler

Donna K. Buechler was born, raised, and educated in central Illinois. Following family tradition, she joined the military after graduation from nursing school in 1967. She chose the U.S. Air Force with the explicit purpose of going to Vietnam. She graduated from flight school in July 1968, then left for Vietnam on 5 January 1969 to serve at Cam Ranh Bay with the 12th U.S. Air Force Hospital and then the 26th Casualty Staging Facility. She next served with the 56th Aeromedical Evacuation Squadron at Yokota Air Base in Japan for two years. On that assignment she flew into Vietnam and took wounded patients to Japan, the Philippines, or the United States.

Donna Buechler was terrified from the moment she stepped foot in Vietnam on 5 January 1969. Everywhere she looked, she saw heavily armed men and fortifications against enemy attack. "As I viewed the wire and sandbags around and over the fence that marked where the nurses' compound was, I cried softly and said out loud, but to no one in particular, 'I've made a terrible mistake and I want my mommy and daddy.' I felt an emotional wall come over me as I entered the nurses' compound."

The events of her first night at Cam Ranh Bay unnerved Donna; the enemy rocketed the base. Donna was frightened, and her roommate tried to comfort her. She showed Donna where her helmet and flak jacket were kept and told her they were supposed to get under the bed. They could not do this, because the bed was too low, so they each hunched into a ball between the bed and the dresser. The sound and impact of the rocketing intensified Donna's fear, but her roommate tried to console her by saying that as long as she could hear them she was OK and if she couldn't hear them, it did not matter anymore. The base survived the rocketing that night without casualties.

The next day Donna took up duty on ward seventeen; there were between thirty-five and forty patients on the ward, with only one nurse, the head nurse, and several medical technicians. Donna noted that the nurse wore a white uniform rather than the fatigues she had been told to wear. "It made for a strange sensation, a sense of normality and calm and usualness in a situation that was bombarding me with new and threatening data." The nurse was changing a dressing on a young man who had multiple shrapnel wounds in his left leg. "His leg looked raw, with too many wounds to count; I was horrified and did not want to touch his leg but did not want to show my horror either, so I went ahead and did as she told me to do regarding how to care for him."

After Donna had been in-country for six months, she was transferred to the 26th Casualty Staging Facility, which was still part of the U.S. Air Force hospital at Cam Ranh. She had been there only a short time when, on 7 August, Cam Ranh Bay Air Base was overrun by the enemy.

"It was about 2:00 A.M. Things were actually pretty quiet. All of my patients were resting quietly, if not sleeping. I had the lights dimmed. The light between the Quonset huts was on, as I was preparing IVs for the upcoming day's flights that would take all of these men out of Vietnam. All of a sudden my friend and roommate Zap came into the ward from the outside. I had not called her and I did not need any help. She hurried to me, and even in the dim light I could see the blood had drained from her face.

"'They've broken through our perimeter!' I knew what the words meant, but they couldn't mean the same thing as what guys had told me about many times. Not here. This was Cam Ranh Bay Air Base. We got rocket attacks and mortars lobbed in. Walking them in, that's what I learned to call that activity. We even had bomb scares. Cleaning women sneaking them in and leaving them in our hooches. All of that had become routine. Amazing, we human animals, what we can become accustomed to.

"She told me again, 'The VC have broken through our perimeter and are heading this way. They have already gotten to the 6th and they lobbed grenades onto the wards. Some patients have been rewounded and some killed. We're locking you in here, taking your med techs. All lights have to be turned out. Do not turn a flashlight on, nothing!'

"In the time it took her to say that, my techs were gone; I had the lights out and had walked Zap to the door. She left, locking the door behind her. It was dead still and darker than I ever knew it could be. I held my hand up in front of my eyes and I could not see it. I huddled in a corner and tried to let my eyes adjust, but there was no adjusting.

"Then I started hearing the running going on outside. I could hear gear hitting against the running bodies. I could hear small arms fire, first in the distance, then closer. Someone would try to open the door, and I froze even more. I think my breathing stopped, I was so scared. I heard mortars coming in and they were no longer just routine. I could not help any of my patients even if they needed me. I silently willed them to stay asleep—to not know what was going on. They were always jumpy as it was. They did not like being without their weapons. They felt much too vulnerable. Everyone was totally quiet throughout that two- to three-hour ordeal.

"Daylight broke, and peace and routine returned to Cam Ranh. The enemy had done some significant damage to structures, but no one had been killed on the air force base. Two patients had been killed at 6 CC. A total of ninety-nine people were injured; fifty-four of them were patients at 6 CC [6th Convalescent Center]. The event was never talked about. I never remembered it until a few years ago, in treatment."

Later, when she was on assignment to ferry wounded patients out of Da Nang aboard a C-141, Donna had a strange experience that was to change the direction of her future service. She was a flight nurse on the plane, which was on the flight line, loading the patients, when one of the wounded men called for a nurse. "Please help me, nurse, please help me," he called softly, over and over. Donna was in the comfort station, checking to see if she had all the medications she would need for the flight.

"I heard him calling and started toward him. I could see, as I got closer, he was another triple amputee, nineteen or twenty years old. All four extremities raised at different times as I walked back. Two short stumps for legs and an above-the-elbow stump for his right arm. The uninjured arm just reaching out. He couldn't see I was coming to him. I'm glad. Because then he could not see when I froze in place. I was probably twelve to fifteen feet from the end of his litter; I literally froze in place. I could not force myself to keep going to him. He kept calling softly. All I could see were those three stumps wrapped in the gauze we used at that time. The whole back of the plane was filled with more wounded, and him calling for a nurse. I turned and walked away. And I buried that memory along with a lot of my other Vietnam happenings."

After this incident Donna knew she could not do any more patient care. She had begun fainting at the sight of blood. So she opted out of the military and went to school for one semester, and then went into psychiatric nursing. She knew she could no longer look at physical wounds, touch them, or tolerate even being on a hospital ward.

Donna continued in psychiatric nursing but knew she needed professional help to overcome her anxieties. Her startled response had heightened and she was hypervigilant and completely preoccupied about Vietnam, but she did not talk about it. She finally found a professional counselor to help her with what was obviously post-traumatic stress disorder. The counselor never asked about her military experience, so Donna did not mention it, although she knew that it was at the root of all of her emotional trauma. Then she stopped consulting the counselor.

By spring of 1977 she felt compelled to go back to military life.

She joined the active reserves as a flight nurse, since the idea of resigning her commission was abhorrent to her and she knew she could not go back into a hospital ward and could not pretend to do nursing care. She flew many missions during the next few years.

Donna progressed professionally without much thought about Vietnam until the spring of 1984, when she volunteered to be interviewed about her Vietnam experience for a student's master's project.

"The interview took three hours, was extremely painful, and was the first time I had ever talked about Vietnam in any detail. I actually realized I remembered very little; I could only see clean white linen with clean white dressings on the patients. It was very calm and quiet. I knew none of that was true but I couldn't pull any memories up. I just felt terribly sad, felt a deep need to cry but could not. I was afraid that if I ever did start crying I could never stop.

"From then on I had some nightmares and much preoccupation about Vietnam, but I would not talk about it for fear that I would lose my nursing license because someone would think I was crazy. The man who interviewed me gave me a book by a woman about her service experience in Vietnam and suggested that I needed to read it. I was terrified. I started again in individual counseling. I was asked about military experience in my sessions, but the counselor did not ask for any details about my Vietnam service, so I never volunteered anything about it. I figured that it must not be important if she didn't ask me any questions about it.

"I finally got over the feeling that I was crazy, but I decided that for some strange reason I was making something out of nothing. I decided to attend a one-hour program at the Vet Center about the Vietnam experience. All during the program I clenched my knuckles so hard that they turned white. When the program was over I went to my office and slammed the door as hard as I could and yelled 'I can't take this anymore,' and I cried uncontrollably."

Donna continued nursing in the military. In addition, she became involved in working toward the establishment of a women's memorial in Washington, D.C. She entered the Vet Center program as a team leader and attended the Chicago Welcome Home Parade for Vietnam veterans. There, the male veterans showed tremendous praise and appreciation for all the nurses. Donna had not realized how much she needed such treatment, but, she says, "I sucked it up like a starving person would eat food once it was presented. I cried and cried and cried. I thought I would be OK since I could cry now and I knew Vietnam had hurt me."

When Iraq invaded Kuwait, Donna's nightmares, anxiety, and panic attacks increased. When the United States declared war against Iraq in Desert Shield, Donna fell down on her knees and just screamed "No," then cried hard. The air force notified her that she and the other nurses were on alert to be activated, and they were to report within twenty-four hours when they were activated. That news terrified Donna. She started having panic attacks whenever she had to wear the chemical warfare gear, or when she had to ride in a car.

In March 1991 Donna was activated and went to Myrtle Beach Air Force Base in South Carolina as assistant chief nurse. She was afraid that she would not be able to hold up if she had to get on a plane with combat-wounded patients. However, she returned to Scott Air Force Base after one week because there were not enough casualties in the Persian Gulf for the nurses to be needed.

Donna continued with the air force reserves but continued to have severe PTSD symptoms, both on the job at the Vet Center and in her private life. She was scheduled to make flights with the air force, but since she was emotionally unfit to fly, she was removed as a chief nurse. Without that position, and unable to work in a hospital, she retired from the air force reserves in May 1993. Donna had served in the air force for twenty years and ended her military career as a lieutenant colonel.

She received medical and psychological help, yet in the summer of 1997, she experienced a "severe and most complete emotional re-experiencing of the August 1969 attack at Cam Ranh." She later participated in a Veterans Administration–Harvard research project studying the psycho-physiological responses of female military nurses who served in Vietnam. She was diagnosed with PTSD, depression and panic disorder. Her life has been painfully upset by her exposure to the war, which spawned tears, rage, sadness and irrational behavior.

Today Donna Buechler works with combat veterans as a team leader at the Springfield, Illinois, Vet Center. She has a master's degree in counseling and is a licensed clinical professional counselor. She was never able to return to bedside nursing after Vietnam.

Women's Army Corps

Karen Offutt

Karen Offutt was born in Arkansas but left when she was six. She lived in California for most of her life. She graduated from high school in 1967, when she was seventeen, then attended nursing school for a semester, dropped out, and the next year joined the army to attend training as a stenographer. She volunteered for Vietnam because she felt "it wasn't right for only our men to be sent over to risk their lives fighting communism," and because she wanted to see for herself what the war was about.

Karen Offutt remembers leaving California to go to Vietnam. She remembers a long flight, stopping only once, in Hawaii.

"I remember arriving in Bien Hoa and getting off of the plane with a lot of soldiers standing there cheering. At first I thought they were welcoming us, but then it seemed to me that they were cheering the fact that they were leaving, not that we were arriving. It was hot and the land was red. I was supposed to go to Saigon to work for Gen. M. G. Conroy at Military Assistance Command-Vietnam [MACV] headquarters. Instead, I was put on a bus going to Long Binh. The bus had chicken wire on the windows, and I asked an older man sitting next to me what it was for. He said it was to deflect grenades. I sat there in silence, but I remember looking back toward where the plane had been, thinking I'd made a huge mistake and wondering how I could get back on the plane.

"They put me in a room upstairs at the WAC [Women's Army Corps] barracks in Long Binh. The place reminded me of a fort or something, with a fence around it, I think. I recall someone telling me to have some items, like a canteen and a helmet, under my bed, even though I had not been given fatigues yet.

"At any rate, I was tired from the long plane trip and as I was drifting off to sleep, or perhaps had gone to sleep, the whole room shook. There was a continuous *bam, bam,* that tore through the night. With each sound, my bed shook. I asked someone what it was and they said that we were being rocketed or mortared. I remember thinking I was going to die my first night in Vietnam. I asked them what to do and they said that Charlie was usually a bad shot. The attack continued through the night, and I don't think I slept. I remember lying there paralyzed with fear. A girl told me also that sometimes the 'gooks' came inside the perimeter wearing explosives to blow themselves and us up.

"I can't tell you how long I was in Long Binh. I can tell you that it was July of 1969 and that I hated it. We were fired on all the time, and to me, it was a hell on earth.

"In addition, I couldn't understand why I was even in Long Binh when I was supposed to have gone straight to Saigon. I asked the older-looking sergeants in charge and was told I wasn't going to Saigon because I was nineteen and you had to be twenty to go there. I still had no uniform, and they put me to work cleaning a pool full of green water with huge bugs that were awful. I had shorts on and had to wade in there to clean the thing."

One day Karen was walking by an official-looking building, and she stopped in and told the personnel there that she wasn't supposed to be in Long Binh. She asked them to call Gen. M. G. Conroy in Saigon. Obviously they did, because Karen remembers that a few days later a sergeant major drove up in a black sedan.

"He asked for me, and I went to the WAC office. He told me to get my stuff. The WAC sergeant told him I wasn't going anywhere, and he said sharply to me, 'Get your gear!' I went to my room, got my belongings, and got in the car with him. From that day forward, he would always be special to me as he got me out of Long Binh.

This makes me sad because I can't remember his name. . . . He drove for a ways and I looked out the window at the red mud. Then we came across houses made with flattened beer cans and no doors . . . and children, half-dressed or naked, playing in the mud. I remember telling him that people don't live that way. He told me differently. The smell in Saigon is something I'll never forget. I remember feeling that I had been taken to another time and place, and it saddened me deeply."

Karen does not recall how she acquired her living quarters or how she knew where headquarters was.

"I don't recall any of that. I remember my room on the third floor, across from a day room at the Medford BEQ. I remember my roommate and that she gave me a military billy club that her boyfriend had given her. I still have it.

"I remember being trained by General Conroy's stenographer, a navy man named Jim, who was to leave soon. I stuck to him like glue. . . . I seem to remember something about his wife breaking up with him or wanting to. He was sad. He had a space between his front teeth.

"General Conroy was a short, kind man. He was very nice and treated me like a daughter. Mostly I took dictation and typed, and served tea for dignitaries, at which I was so nervous and always spilled. It was a standing joke with the general and me about me always burning someone with tea.

"I remember going into downtown Saigon to pick out a material that would be framed, to be given to a high-ranking ARVN [Army of the Republic of Vietnam] general, perhaps the highest-ranking general. I had to find out how to say 'happy birthday' to him in Vietnamese.

"Children were on the street trying to sell their sisters for their services. Girls would say to the men, 'GI, I love you three months, forever.' A mama-san next door sold hot Cokes to us."

Karen had only been in Saigon for a short time when the headquarters newspapermen approached her to pose for a pinup as "Bunker Bunny of the Week." She didn't want to, but they kept nagging her, and finally she gave in and agreed. The paper's staff took her several different places to pose, and she hated it. "Everyone was looking at me all the time anyway and taking pictures of me, children and women touching my face and eyelashes. At first it was flattering, but then it began to feel smothering."

Among other spots, they took her to a park downtown. She had to wear something of her own, so she chose a dress. Then they took her to a TV studio and told her to wear her fatigues, but only the top and the underwear.

"I had to hug a huge camera. I was humiliated and felt stupid and used. I was so young though, and I had been taught to obey, so I did. At least when the pictures came back, I got to choose which one they could print. I chose the dress pose.

"In October I had to go to the States for my grandfather's funeral. I took a flight out and ended up in Okinawa. I stayed there for about two plus days. They kept telling me they didn't have any flights for me. They were rude and hateful there. I got physically sick. I don't think they even had food there, but at any rate, I remember being angry. I had called my parents, and they were going to have to wait until I got there for the funeral.

"I talked to someone in charge at the airport and they gave me a really bad time. I remember swearing at them, and they threatened to call my superiors. I never swore, so I was surprised at myself and my attitude. I told them to call all they wanted. What would they do, send me to Vietnam? They told me finally they had a body plane for me to go out on. I didn't want to, but I said OK.

"I don't know what happened after that, but I remember the plane I was put on. I sat in the back of this huge plane, on the side, with this foggy condensation coming up all around me in the darkness. I don't remember bodies. Maybe they were there and maybe I've blocked it. I do remember how I felt being in the belly of that huge plane all alone in the dark. Finally someone came and told me I could sit in the navigator's seat. I did."

Karen somehow got to the city in Arkansas where the funeral was being held, but at the ceremony, she behaved strangely. "During the service I started crying, this loud, long, wailing cry. No one could hear the minister. People were looking at me. My parents tried to stop me, but I couldn't. I just couldn't stop."

Karen's grandfather was old, and she had seldom seen him after she left Arkansas, so her extreme distress seemed inexplicable.

Years later, when she recalled her hysteria at the funeral, the only reason for it she could unearth was Vietnam. "There was obviously something inside of me festering up."

Later, Karen's father took her to a doctor because she was still sick from her Okinawa stay. She was diagnosed with double pneumonia and told not to fly for two weeks. Karen tried to last that long, but she says, "I needed to get back to Vietnam. It was pulling on me. Here I was with my family, and all I wanted was to get to Vietnam. I don't have any idea how I arranged transportation or where I flew out of, but I went back as quickly as possible."

When Karen got back to her room, she found she had a new roommate, a woman nearly twice her age, and the room had been changed around. She draped a blanket across the wall at the end of her bed for privacy, making her world even smaller. She also bought a knife.

"I think it was a sword. I slept with that and the billy club. It wasn't bad enough I was afraid of the Vietcong killing me or capturing me (I'd been told what they would do to women, especially virgins), afraid of our own men, or afraid of being hit by a rocket, mortar, or sniper. It seemed as if I was safe from no one. And Vietnam is where I started to not sleep. I haven't slept since.

"No one was in charge of me over there. I was nineteen and was told I was the youngest girl stationed in Saigon, also the lowest-ranking WAC there. I don't recall anyone checking on me or me reporting to anyone. I was just there.

"I developed an eating problem over there too. I'd go down to the cafeteria at MACV for a sandwich. I remember taking the sandwich and drink to a table and trying to eat. My hands would shake so violently that I couldn't get a cup to my mouth. I'd have to use two hands. That was because there were all of these men staring at me. They would just sit and stare. Some were dirty, like they had just come in from the boonies, and they had old, sad faces.

"I started buying tuna in Cholon [the Chinese section of Saigon], even though we weren't supposed to go there. I'd go to the bathroom at MACV and eat on the floor with the mama-sans. They'd spread out newspapers and eat their fish heads and locust-looking things. I'd squat and eat near them. I didn't know but a few Vietnamese words, so sometimes we would communicate through gestures. Well, so I didn't eat much. Sometimes I didn't eat anything for lunch and had gone to work early, like around 5:00 A.M. I worked anywhere from eleven to fifteen hours a day, six and a half days a week. At one point, my fatigues no longer fit me, and I remember having to get new ones."

Karen also volunteered at an orphanage in Saigon during the half day a week she had off. She does not remember how often she went—whether she went only a few times or all of the time. She does remember that it was run by nuns and had a huge iron gate at the front of it, and that there were children of all ages in the orphanage. And she remembers how the children looked.

"They had scars, sores, shrapnel wounds on them. Their bellies stuck out. Some wore shirts but nothing else. They limped. They were so pathetic and I wanted to take them all home with me, if I ever got home. There were lots of tiny, tiny babies who looked like preemies. I fell in love with one little baby girl in particular. I wanted to adopt her but was told it was nearly impossible."

One little girl obviously needed medical help, and Karen and a friend took her to the hospital at nearby Tan Son Nhut. The staff would not treat her, because as an orphan she had no parents to sign for her. Finally they found a Vietnamese clinic that took some minimal care of the child. They took her back to her mat at the orphanage. Karen felt dreadful.

"I held her little hand and gave her a charm bracelet my mother had given me. I felt defeated and cried as I left. Most of the war I just felt helpless. I couldn't change things for anyone, couldn't fight, knew what was going on in the States with the protesters, and I got very mixed up. We had gunfire all the time around us. Sometimes it was from the hamlet next door and behind us, sometimes from the streets. One day I went to the Medford and they were dismantling a Claymore mine someone had planted in front of our entrance."

The Vietcong blew up a car on the street behind Karen's housing, and at another time, they planted fifteen pounds of plastic explosives nearby, which killed two Americans.

At least once, to do her stenographic job Karen had to fly to her assignment, and to do so she flew in a helicopter with open sides, with gunners hanging out. The experience, she says, "was scary. I thought we'd be shot down or I'd just fall out of the chopper." Later that year, on New Year's Eve 1969, when nearly all of the residents of the Medford were on the roof, a sniper began shooting at them. When the shooting started they all felt and heard the bullets whizzing by them, and they all hit the floor, according to a friend of Karen's. Karen herself has no memories of the incident, but she says that for years she has had "visions of a sniper shooting at me. I couldn't tell if it was something that happened or I had dreamed it."

Karen's memory of Vietnam events is selective. She remembers clearly that she lost her virginity in Vietnam. She had turned twenty on 26 October 1969 and had decided that she was not going to die without knowing what it was like "to be a woman." She explains, "I also thought that if I was captured and wasn't a virgin, maybe the Vietcong wouldn't want me so much." Karen went out with a man and got drunk, and they returned to the day room of the Medford. Karen saw him for a few weeks, and then he told her that he was married and had a little girl. That was the end of that romance.

Karen felt guilty and horrible about the whole incident. She went to the chapel at Tan Son Nhut and prayed fervently that if she was killed in Vietnam, she would be forgiven. Then she met an MP named Johnny, and they dated until she went home. Death was always on her mind when she was in Vietnam, and she feels that it has never left her since.

Karen remembers going to the 3d Field Hospital, right next to the Medford, to visit someone she knew who had been in a Jeep accident. "I stood there in the middle of the room full of broken bodies, men without parts of their faces, legs gone. . . . Awful. They looked at me and I felt so guilty, so helpless. All those men were looking at me with their pleading eyes . . . young men who were old." This experience returns to Karen in the form of a recurring dream.

During December 1969 Karen went to Cu Chi in a Jeep with two men to see the Bob Hope Christmas show. The general didn't want her to go down that particular highway because he believed it was too dangerous, since there had been a number of ambushes there recently, but she went. Karen has since learned that there are bridges along that highway, and she realizes that something untoward must have occurred on that trip, because she cannot cross bridges now without fear and hyperventilation. What happened? She does not know, and believes that she probably never will.

Karen finds it hard to recognize herself as she appears to others.

More than twenty-eight years ago, in Vietnam, she acted heroically without forethought. It was January 1970. While in her room she smelled smoke.

"There was a hamlet next to the Medford with makeshift houses on both sides of an alley. I could see smoke from my third-floor room. I warned the other people in the Medford and took off downstairs to the alley, with shorts on and barefoot. Flames were everywhere. There was a covering over this narrow alley that bridged the homes on the left and right. I ran down the alley with the covering falling down around me in flames.

"The Vietnamese were running back inside their homes to take out their possessions and pigs, chickens, and so on. The whole place was burning up as the flames spread rapidly through these cardboard/beer can houses. I pulled people out and would run back in to get more. Finally the fire department came. I went back up to my room. Actually, I think I had burns on my feet, but don't believe I got any treatment for this.

"I didn't think any more about it. Then one day, MACV received documents saying I had been the only American woman to risk my life in the fire. I was put in for the Soldier's Medal. Since I wasn't a man (I was told this was the reason), they gave me a certificate instead. I sent letters to the States asking for clothing for the fire victims, and I received quite a lot to give them."

Karen's memories of her year in Vietnam are shattered. There is so much she can remember of those days—and so much else that is buried somewhere inside her. She does recall that when it came time for her to go home, the trip was miserable. She cried all the way on the flight to the United States, "wanting to go back to Vietnam, and yet thankful I was still alive. I always felt guilty for not being a nurse there."

Karen's service in Vietnam changed her forever, yet an understanding of the effect of those days has eluded her. "For nearly twenty-nine years I've tried to fill in the memory gaps as to what happened—what I went through in Vietnam. It has been like a piece of me was removed, with nothing but fear, confusion, and distrust left to fill the void. I don't know why I can't remember people, people's names, events, and places. I have spent hundreds and hundreds of hours trying, but I am still left with much of that year as only a fog in my mind."

Paperwork shows that Karen Offutt served in Vietnam from 18 July 1969 until 10 June 1970. She found the adjustment back to life in the United States difficult. Her family did not ask about Vietnam, and she didn't talk. Only recently have Karen and her brother, Ray, talked about Vietnam.

"All I know is that when I came home and was temporarily assigned to Fort MacArthur, when someone dropped a book, I hit the floor—dress, heels, and all. If I went to the store and a can fell, the same thing. I was humiliated beyond belief. People looked at me like I was crazy. I felt like I didn't belong anywhere anymore. I don't often hit the floor now, but I still scream when a balloon pops or someone comes up behind me. People at work have given me weird looks but I can't help it. I can't sit with my back to a door and always sit near an exit. Those same people think me friendly, funny, intelligent, and responsible. Inside, I am glued together—barely."

Veterans Administration psychologists have diagnosed Karen with post-traumatic stress disorder five different times. She currently receives individual counseling and also attends group therapy. She is convinced that she was exposed to Agent Orange. She once saw a spraying map of Vietnam and was told that in the Saigon area, the heaviest year of spraying during the war was 1969, because Saigon was overrun during the Tet Offensive in 1968.

Now when anything out of the ordinary happens, or when Karen experiences a crisis, she goes numb inside. Her feelings, like those of thousands of Vietnam veterans, are the tragic aftermath of exposure to the war. She can articulate the feelings that assail her, but she has not as yet been able to overcome them.

"I basically feel dead inside. I get very little enjoyment out of life, yet am afraid of dying. I always have some psychosomatic disease going on. I drive my family crazy with it . . . always asking them for reassurance and yet not wanting to go to the doctor for fear of what the diagnosis will be.

"I used to want to skydive. In Vietnam I went often to the Medford's roof, four floors up. Now I am afraid of heights. If I even think about looking down from a high place or see it on television, I hold my breath and start to have a panic attack that feels like I am fainting or falling.

"I don't have anyone in my daily life who is a real friend. There are some who think they are, but they aren't. If they aren't Vietnam vets, I don't trust them. . . . I don't trust anyone. I only trust myself.

"I don't sleep well, *ever,* and yet I'm afraid of drugs so I don't usually take them to help me sleep.

"Sometimes I have flashbacks and they hit me just as if I am being knocked into a wall. My heart starts racing, the image appears, and I'm taken back in time. They say to remember is to be able to forget. How can I forget Vietnam when most of my memories, a year out of my life, has been sucked from me only to appear at random, unexpectedly? It's like buying a thousand-piece puzzle that has eight hundred pieces missing and you can't even tell what the picture is supposed to be.

"I guess another thought I have is that if you weren't a nurse in Nam, you weren't anything. Whenever someone finds out I was in Vietnam, they always assume I was a nurse. There were women there with the USO, Red Cross, and so on, but no one seems to know or care about them—us. Often when men find out I was in Long Binh or Saigon, they trivialize it and say that I wasn't in any danger. That I had clean sheets to sleep on. This only increases my guilt and anger. I have nightmares about Vietnam, and in those dreams I am in combat, fighting alongside the men, and always captured or shot. I guess it's my way of reconstructing my role so that my service there is validated.

"I've been through three marriages, with the first lasting the longest, sixteen years. I have three children whom I love to pieces: twin sons, Justin and Kevin, who are twenty-six, and a daughter, Kristin, twenty-three. All are from my first marriage. Justin was born with cancer. Kevin had ADHD [attention deficit hyperactivity disorder], and Kristin had grand mal epilepsy. Kevin and Kristin appear to have minor heart problems, while Justin has had severe problems and suffered a heart attack recently. I was told by their father that I caused them to have all of their medical problems by volunteering for Vietnam—as if I had known anything about Agent Orange.

"I've had several breast lumps removed and many premalignant colon polyps. My granddaughter, Megan, has ADHD now as well. I know so many of the women and men who served in Nam who have cancer or who have already died."

Karen lives in Tampa, Florida. She is licensed as a registered nurse in four states, but is not currently working. She says, "PTSD is taking its toll and it's hard to even think about working, being around the public, giving, giving, giving. I'm all given out. . . . They say hindsight is everything. I won't say that had I known how Vietnam would change my life and my children's forever, that I would not have gone. I feel betrayed though. We are the walking wounded. Many of us didn't die in Nam but it sure feels like it."

(The material on which the above chapter was based was written for the author, and is copyright by Karen Offutt. See endnotes.)

Claire Brisebois Starnes

Claire Brisebois grew up and was schooled in Maine. She joined the army at age eighteen to get away from the life for which she says she was destined: working in shoe shops and mills. Too independent to consider marriage, she knew she wanted to see the world. She chose the army because its minimum enlistment was only three years. Claire trained at Alabama's Fort McClellan and Georgia's Fort Gordon and spent the next few years working in communications centers in California, Japan, and Oklahoma. When the Vietnam War began to escalate, Claire volunteered for duty in Vietnam to find out for herself the facts of the conflict. She left Travis Air Force Base in California as an administrative member of the Women's Army Corps (WAC), and headed for South Vietnam on 25 March 1969.

On the plane, where she was one of two women, with more than one hundred men aboard, Claire wondered if she was doing the right thing. She concluded that she was. "I was young, and nothing seemed to scare me. This was to be just another adventure."

This adventure, at the moment, seemed to be taking forever. The plane made several stops to refuel, and twenty-two hours later the passengers spied the South Vietnamese coast.

Claire describes her reaction: "We had landed at Bien Hoa airfield in the early afternoon at the hottest part of the day. After having our orders checked, I and the other WAC climbed aboard a deuce and a half [two-and-a-half-ton truck], and we were off, a trail of dust following us. Though I was exhausted from the long hours in the air, I was wide-eyed as we drove through the town of Bien Hoa. This was my first glimpse of Vietnam. I looked into the dirty, bronzed, weathered faces that stared at us as we passed what seemed to be thousands of bicycles and so many different kinds of little motorized vehicles going every which way. It still hadn't crossed my mind that I was in a war zone."

When they arrived at the WAC detachment in Long Binh, the driver surrendered his .45 caliber pistol to the MP and they went through the gate. Claire signed in, received linens, and was assigned a room. In the room, there wasn't a soul, but there was an empty top bunk. Claire was so tired from the long trip, she climbed up onto the bunk and fell fast asleep. She awakened to the practical joke welcome of her three roommates: "Incoming," they yelled at the top of their lungs. Groggy, Claire fell out of the bunk. It was not an auspicious beginning, but they all became fast friends.

The next day Claire was busy sewing her unit, rank, and insignia patches onto her clothing. They were brown, black, or green—dull colors that would not catch the sun and sparkle, giving away position. She was also issued rubber covers for her dog tags so they would not make noise when they hit each other.

The WAC compound consisted of two long two-story buildings, with an orderly room and a supply room but no mess hall. The women ate at the 24th Evacuation Hospital or at the Loon Foon, the local restaurant across the street, or at a unit club. The WACs did not have a club, but they had a huge covered patio where they socialized and watched movies almost daily. Outside the orderly room was a refrigerator filled with beer and soft drinks, so in essence, the refrigerator became their club. Payment was by the honor system. With such facilities, Claire enjoyed life in Long Binh. Though the women worked long hours, they partied vigorously with the men, either on the patio or at one of the unit clubs, some of which had swimming pools.

The individual rooms were fairly spacious and could accommodate seven women, a maximum never reached while Claire was there. There were three double bunk beds and a single bed, a small window air conditioner that actually worked, and a small refrigerator for keeping food sent from home or any perishables acquired by chance.

The war in Vietnam was escalating, and eventually the women were restricted to the Long Binh compound; the outside area was now classified as unsafe. The small irritants loomed larger: mildewed clothes, large insects, excruciating heat, no hot water, and the almost nightly incoming whistling sounds and outgoing artillery booms.

In response to alerts, the women began spending more and more time in the nearby bunkers. They needed no other reminders that they were in a war zone. When the red alert sounded, signifying an imminent attack, the women gathered their gear and headed for the bunkers. Sometimes they received no alert and the sirens sounded after the first round was lobbed in. Once in the bunker, the senior enlisted person took roll call to be sure all the women were present. Then there was nothing to do but wait.

"We would spend hours in there, listening to the explosions outside. It was during those times that I felt helpless. All we could do was sit quietly, praying that a round would not hit us or near us. When the all-clear sounded—three siren blasts—we returned to the rooms and went back to sleep. Some nights we would have two or three alerts."

It was work as usual the next day. Claire was assigned to headquarters of the U.S. Army Engineer Construction Agency Vietnam as a clerk. The unit's mission was to "provide centralized management and control of engineer construction, real estate, base master planning, and real property maintenance functions of U.S. Army Vietnam (USARV)." Claire's role was to ensure that congressional investigations were being answered. In addition, her knowledge of French brought her extra work as a translator of lease papers between the South Vietnamese and the U.S. government. This latter job kept her fairly busy, since all official Vietnamese papers were written in French.

Claire was busy but unhappy. "Shuffling papers was not why I had wanted to go halfway around the world. The questions I had about why we were in Vietnam were not being answered. I also knew I had more to contribute to assist our guys who were spilling their blood for this country. Translating papers and ensuring that congressionals were answered just didn't seem enough."

Claire's thoughts about Vietnam were still unclear when she had a chance to visit the POW portion of the detainee hospital compound of the 92d Evacuation Hospital. Perhaps she would find some answers here.

"I had so many questions. As I walked down the aisle, I could feel the eminent stares and the hatred these North Vietnamese and Vietcong had for what I represented. Finally, I found one who spoke French. It turned out that he was a South Vietnamese doctor who had been educated in France during the French colonization of Vietnam. We spoke for a short time. I asked him why he fought for the North. Out of real patriotism, he informed me that someday his country would be free of all foreigners and there would be only one Vietnam. This was his dream. He had never known true freedom.

"I asked him if he thought that communist China was free, to which he replied that the Chinese were still not united and thus would never be free until reunited. He was talking about Taiwan. He explained that Ho Chi Minh had to be a dictator to accomplish the mission of uniting Vietnam; once the unification occurred, he would see to it that his people would get the freedom they had fought for so hard and for so long."

Claire thought about these explanations and admired the man's patriotism, but she says she felt a twinge of sadness "knowing of his belief that communism would bring the freedom he so much craved for. He was right, though, when he said that someday the Americans would give up, that we didn't have the stomach to continue a war for as long as it needed to win. It was like a prophesy. . . . Their will to win was astonishing."

In July 1969, a change of job assignment took Claire out of Long Binh. The WAC commanding officer announced that the headquarters in Saigon was looking for someone for a special assignment, and of those who volunteered, Claire was chosen. She didn't know what she was going to do, but she was joyous that she would be leaving Long Binh, even at the price of extending her tour of duty in Vietnam.

Claire reported to headquarters of the Military Assistance Command Vietnam (MACV) in Saigon on 1 August 1969. Her new assignment was to help revolutionize the methods used for the newspapers and magazines of the various in-country military units. Up to this time all the units had sent their copy to Japan for typesetting and printing—and it cost an exorbitant amount. Now command decided that MACV would do all the typesetting in-country and only print in Japan. To accomplish this, MACV would hire Vietnamese women; Claire and two men, one an Air Force E-9 and the other an Army E-6, would train and supervise them. The three were assigned to the command information office of the MACV. This office also published the official command newspaper, *The MACV Observer*, and ran the Armed Forces Vietnam Network radio and television stations.

Claire and the two men, along with the four Vietnamese women whom MACV hired, set up in the newspaper office. The equipment was extremely complicated; command decided to send Claire and the men to Honolulu's IBM office to learn the new system. It was a good break.

One of the Vietnamese women was fluent in French, so Claire taught her the operation, and she passed the knowledge on to the other women. Thus they introduced a new system of newspaper production to the Republic of Vietnam. Claire started to seriously learn Vietnamese. Soon she was able to hold conversations in the local language.

She also began to learn the reporting and writing side of the newspaper trade. She received blanket in-country travel orders, which allowed her to come in contact with the Vietnamese population, American military troops, and Allied forces. She was exactly where she wanted to be. She had independence and the opportunity to see firsthand the devastation the war was creating in Vietnam. By July 1970 she had been promoted to staff sergeant and had changed her MOS to public information specialist.

Claire's new position, with its contacts with people throughout South Vietnam, brought her mixed feelings about why the Americans were there.

"Though I had made some wonderful Vietnamese friends, I could see that our involvement there was fruitless." Everything she saw made her question "why the U.S. became involved in the first place."

Near Da Nang at an Army of the Republic of Vietnam (ARVN) fire base, Claire witnessed an example of how the South Vietnamese treated their prisoners. A dreadful stench was coming from some conex containers. Claire wondered whether the rumor that the Vietnamese army baked captured enemies inside these containers was true. She saw a scared young North Vietnamese boy dragged from one of them for interrogation. Claire thought he could not have been more than fifteen years old. With an American advisor, she sat through part of the interrogation, which indicated that the prisoner was guilty of enemy action. She never knew what happened to him.

Many matters puzzled Claire.

The U.S.-instituted program of "capturing the hearts and minds of the South Vietnamese" was not working. Although planes dropped thousands of small notices each day offering the enemy safe haven and money to come over to the Allied side, few of the enemy defected.

"It took a while to make true Vietnamese friends. You couldn't trust anyone—the enemy was unknown. They were your friend by day, something else by night. For the cause, they sacrificed their children, sent them with grenades and such into a crowd of foreigners. And the children always surrounded you, groping, pawing, begging.

"But what was happening at home during this time was more incomprehensible to me. Nothing seemed to make sense anymore. Jane Fonda had visited Hanoi and reportedly pledged her allegiance to our enemy. I had lost so many good friends. Though I was questioning some of our government's decisions, I could not bring myself to admit that my friends' deaths were in vain. It seemed to me that at this point we had to win this thing, and soon. All of this nonsense had to stop, here in Vietnam and at home.

"But I kept doing my job to the best of my capabilities. For this, I received a second award of the Joint Service Commendation Medal in January 1971. But all these medals didn't make up for what we had lost and still were losing. I took a second R&R to get away from it all, this time to Taiwan."

In Saigon Claire lived at the Medford Hotel, where enlisted men lived on the first two floors and the women of the army, air force, and marine corps lived on the top two floors.

"The building had a Vietnamese guard by day and an MP by night. There was a concrete wall about eight feet high on the street side, from which chicken wire extended to above the second floor. This was so if someone lobbed a grenade, it would roll down. Sandbags were also piled in front of the wall."

Claire's room, number forty-eight, was small—twelve by fourteen feet—and she shared it with an air force tech sergeant. There was a small kitchen across the hall, where Medford residents socialized. Many made their dinners there; otherwise, they ate at the MACV snack bar or at local restaurants. Since the American food made by the Vietnamese was appealing to the eye but appalling to the taste, Claire began to eat and like Vietnamese food.

Room number forty-eight had one window, below which the poor Vietnamese settled by the hundreds in shacks made of scrap wood and flattened Budweiser and Coke cans. The livestock— chickens, pigs, and other animals—shared the living space with the people. Smells and sounds came blasting up through the window. There was constant noise: talking, laughter, honking, sirens, gunfire, and the whop-whop of the helicopters bringing the wounded to the nearby 3d Field Hospital. Through this local noise, the women could hear the sound of the American troops firing their weapons and the sound of incoming rockets.

Claire says she finally resigned herself to the prospect that they might get hit. "Well, so be it, it was meant to be. I slept like a baby, with my boots nearby. Funny, mama-san always seemed to know when we would get incoming. If I found my boots on the bed, it meant stay alert. If the boots were under the bed, I slept soundly."

Claire's day began at 5:00 A.M. She left the Medford at 5:30 and did not return until 6:30 or 7:00 P.M. There was no regular work week. The work had to be done, and it was. Everyone seemed to know his or her job. When Claire had to drive to Long Binh, after much ado because carrying weapons was forbidden for WACs, she was armed. She carried an air force .38 caliber pistol. To Claire and her supervisory colonel, it seemed ridiculous not to have a weapon for protection. After all, the WAC training had included a weapons familiarization course on the .45 caliber pistol, the M16 rifle, the M60 machine gun, and the M79 grenade launcher. The colonel made sure Claire was armed.

The days were full and busy for Claire. She helped to produce *The MACV Observer* and to distribute it throughout Saigon and Cholon. Driving a pickup truck, Claire faced the full jam of Saigon's streets, with cars, pedicabs, bicycles, motorcycles, Jeeps, military trucks of all sizes, and pedestrians all vying for street space and going every which way. Horns blared and animals wandered among the vehicles. Claire says, "Traffic jams were everywhere; it was complete chaos."

Not far from MACV headquarters was the racetrack, but the women were told to stay strictly away from it because it had become a meeting place for the Vietcong. Claire did not know whether this report was true, but she stayed far from the racetrack. However, she visited much of the rest of Saigon. She visited the bars along the waterfront where live music was provided, mainly by Filipino bands. The Vietnamese bar girls, fascinated by the women with the "round eyes", often temporarily left their soldiers to talk to the American women. Claire can still remember some of the favorite songs of the day: "We've Got to Get Out Of This Place" and "The Green Green Grass of Home". Now Claire realizes how foolish she and her friends were to patronize the waterfront bars; it was dangerous to hang out there. The floating restaurant on the Saigon River was a favorite target of the Vietcong.

Only twice did Claire get hurt in Vietnam. One time she was battling with a Saigon cowboy—a thief on a motorcycle—over her government-issued thirty-five-millimeter camera. As he raced by, seizing the camera, Claire hooked the strap on her arm. Both of them fell down, and Claire was dragged on the ground. He finally fell off the motorcycle and ran away with the camera, which by this time

Claire realized must be smashed. Claire had his sandals and motorcycle. But she was banged up from being dragged and spent several days at the 3d Field Hospital.

The next time, Claire was riding with others in a deuce and a half truck when someone began shooting at them. Just as Claire was jumping out, the truck accelerated. She lost her balance and landed awkwardly on her leg.

She was given emergency treatment but refused further aid because she was scheduled to leave the next day for R&R in Taiwan. She left, but she spent a miserable five days with extreme pain in her leg and hip. On her return to Saigon, Claire spent several weeks in therapy to heal her leg.

When Claire could not get a vehicle to drive to Long Binh, she hitched a ride with the military. Before sunset, the ride from Saigon was safe, but at sunset the road was closed to all traffic except convoys. Claire often rode in a convoy, usually in a V-100, an armored vehicle on wheels. In the convoy no lights were used. When Claire rode in the lead vehicle she felt uneasy. She and the gunner watched for anything that moved on the road. One night they saw something moving. The gunner trained his mounted .50-caliber machine gun in its direction and was about to fire when they saw that the movement was caused by an old man on a bicycle on the side of the road. He probably never knew how close he came to being shot.

One morning Claire awoke and heard the news that American troops had gone into Cambodia. Claire recalls the jubilation: "Everyone felt it was about time, since they all knew that Cambodia served as a sanctuary for hit-and-run attackers. But the reality of the reaction stateside slapped me in the face like cold water. I was so overwrought with anguish when learning that college students were demonstrating against the offensive that I fired off some letters to university newspapers. It was a rather long letter in which all of my emotions were made bare. One university printed the letter word for word. They sent me the following issue in which were the students' responses to my letter. I was devastated by their logic. I became bitter. I was bitter at our government for not explaining things better and letting the media pick and choose what there was to explain. I was bitter at our people for not supporting our soldiers, their own countrymen."

In October 1970 Claire was in Da Nang, scheduled to go to Hue, when suddenly she changed her plans. She had a feeling she should go back to Saigon. She waited all day for a plane out and finally hitched a ride on a C-123. She was exhausted when she reached her quarters. It was supper time, and the women told Claire to go ahead and eat; she could wash and change later. Claire had just begun to eat when the mama-san appeared and said the chaplain was waiting downstairs to see Claire. Claire said later that she knew instinctively what he was going to say. Her mother had died.

"Before I knew it, I was on the plane going home. I had not been home since Christmas 1969. I was still in dirty fatigues since I had no time to change. I'm sure I didn't smell too good, either. My uniform was packed. I had been told that I could wash and change at Travis Air Force Base. However, when I got there, I found I had to leave for San Francisco immediately so as not to miss my flight to Boston. After what seemed like hundreds of hours, I walked totally exhausted into my aunt's house at 3:00 A.M., still wearing the fatigues and boots I'd had on in Da Nang. I stayed up all night, making decisions for this and that, since the funeral was early the following morning.

"What a trip this had been. Antiwar sentiments were stronger than ever, and my run through the San Francisco airport scared me more than being in Vietnam. I was in jungle fatigues, wearing jungle boots in San Francisco. A group of people began following me, yelling, 'How's the war, Sarge?' 'Killed any babies lately?' If it hadn't been for an airline attendant who hurried me onto the plane, I probably would have been beaten to a pulp that day. I was running, listening to their jeers, and was about to turn around and stand my ground. But here I was being seated next to what seemed to be a hippie girl, and away we flew. She turned out to be quite cordial and inquisitive. Once we were airborne, the flight attendant asked me to come to the rear of the plane. Several soldiers had already congregated there. We were told that we could request anything we wanted, compliments of Pan American. I was home."

Claire can barely remember the funeral. She stood in the rain in her army uniform beside the grave of her mother.

"Mom would have wanted me to wear my uniform. She was very proud of me. The next thing I remember was waking up and seeing my aunt smiling. I had slept for three whole days. Being concerned, she had called the doctor. He told her to let me sleep—that my body would tell me when it was time to wake up. And so it did.

"My time home became a time of mixed emotions. I felt like I was in a dream. I couldn't sleep—too quiet. The time change [thirteen hours behind Saigon time] also ravaged my body. I'd walk in the cold to a small all-night restaurant at 3:00 A.M. for breakfast. My life was turned upside down. One night I was reading *Life* magazine and read that a dear friend of mine, Henri Huet, had been killed in Cambodia. He was a French photographer on assignment with *Life*. Even at home, the war was reaching me. Was I really at home? I became emotionally drained. I had nobody to talk to. My aunt, though she tried, could not completely understand. I didn't want to return to Vietnam.

"But my time wasn't finished, and I had to return for three more months. *How ludicrous,* I thought. Things had changed. I was depressed. My life had taken a sudden turn. I would be returning home for good, but not to what I expected to return to."

Claire went back to Vietnam. She finished up the job she had been assigned. Now they employed eight Vietnamese people and were doing twenty-one in-country service newspapers and six magazines. Personnel had changed, and Claire found that many of her friends from Saigon had left the country while she was gone. She had become disillusioned with the whole effort.

"Our military forces were beginning to lose ground. It seemed like the whole world had gone crazy. I was proud of what I had accomplished and am still proud of my service. But I was going to keep it to myself."

Claire flew back to the United States in March 1971.

After she returned to the United States, Claire never wore her uniform in public again. She was assigned to Fort Monroe, Virginia, as noncommissioned officer in charge of the public information office there. She left the army in 1973 but continued to do the same job as a civil servant. Also in 1973, she married Edward Starnes.

Then the inevitable happened. In the spring of 1975, South Vietnam began to be conquered completely. Saigon fell. Claire was stunned. She watched the television news day and night. She couldn't tear herself away.

"This had to be a dream. But the screen kept giving me live images. I watched the refugees crowding toward Saigon, the helicopters leaving the American embassy's roof pad, complete chaos in the streets of Saigon. How could this be happening? How could we just let it happen? I tried frantically for days to call the refugee hotline, hoping that I could find some of my girls. But I kept getting a busy signal. When I finally got through, I couldn't find my close friends, Mrs. Phong and her husband, who was a South Vietnamese officer, or any of my friends. It wasn't until much later that we read about what had happened to those brave South Vietnamese who had given their allegiance to the Americans. My heart still skips when I think about our abandonment of South Vietnam and its people.

"My husband and I went to work at Fort Bliss, Texas, where we stayed for eleven years. A son was born in 1975 in Virginia and another son in 1977 in Texas. While in Texas, I fulfilled my dream of obtaining a college degree. In 1986 we returned to the East Coast, where I was editor of the *Ordnance* magazine of the U.S. Army Ordnance Corps at Aberdeen Proving Ground.

"I retired from civil service in October 1994 and worked with the public school system in Maryland for three years, and now am completely retired. . . .

"Vietnam? Right or wrong? There still is no answer for me. But finding old friends has made it easier to think about."

One of Claire's early roommates in Vietnam persuaded Claire to go with her to the 1997 dedication of the Women in the Military Service in America (WIMSA) Memorial in Washington, D.C. For Claire it was balm for her feelings about the war. At the ceremony they found thirteen of their former friends from Long Binh and one from Saigon. It had been almost thirty years since they had seen one another. Somehow the renewal of Claire's friendships that had been formed in the disturbing Vietnam years released tensions and rekindled "many memories, memories that I now feel I can share."

Suddenly, she says, "after so many years we're talking again. Life is good!"

(The material supplied by Claire Brisebois Starnes is under copyright in her name and is used with her kind permission. See endnotes.)

Linda S. Earls

Linda Earls grew up on an Illinois farm, attended a two-room country grade school, and went to high school in Westville, Illinois. The Cuban missile crisis occurred during her sophomore year, and from that time on, inspired by the military talk of the teachers, all Linda wanted to do was join the army. In August 1964 she did; she trained in Alabama and Kentucky and then served in a Texas hospital, where she stayed for three years as the Vietnam turmoil was escalating. She determined to go to Vietnam, and finally received those orders. She flew off aboard a TWA jet from Travis Air Force Base with three other Women's Army Corps members (WACs) on 30 April 1968.

Linda Earls boarded the plane in her green cord uniform and heels. After the nineteen-hour trip, with refueling stops in Honolulu and Okinawa, her feet were swollen from sitting so long. She and the other WACs looked as though they had slept in their uniforms. As they neared Vietnam, the pilot announced that the approach would be extremely short to lessen the risk of shelling. It was startlingly short, but they landed safely at Bien Hoa, where soldiers gathered to board for flights home.

The WACs rode in an old rusted bus through some partly destroyed villages to a processing point, and by Jeep to the WAC detachment at Long Binh. They settled into the barracks, learned about bunkers and alerts, and received their first malaria pills. Before the first week was out, Linda started work as a clerk-typist in the comptroller's office in army headquarters. She soon discovered that she had a ringside seat for the war; from her desk she had a window view of the valley below, which constantly received rockets from helicopters and bombs from jets.

Linda easily adopted the routine: reveille at 6:30 A.M., breakfast at the 24th Evacuation Hospital near the barracks, a military bus to headquarters, and work from 7:30 A.M. to 7:30 P.M., seven days a week.

Linda observed the almost daily attacks on the valley as she worked at headquarters. "I could see jets fly in, go down low, drop their bombs, and then go straight up. I could see the fire flash and the smoke." In spite of the war around her, Linda found that the days went by in a rather routine fashion, highlighted only by such events as getting paid (more than she received in the United States because now she did not pay income tax) and hitching rides on choppers to shop at neighboring PXs. She was also busy helping her roommate take care of a newly adopted dog, Reddy. In everything they did, they all faced the torrential monsoon rain.

New experiences tumbled one over another, juxtaposing depressing and exhilarating events. Linda visited the Vietnamese orphanage and saw hundreds of children of all ages there. She said, "Most of them have sores or a rash. They lie in metal cribs on straw mats and flies swarm over them. They look pretty pitiful." Linda's heart ached for all of them.

In contrast, her first chopper ride proved to be wonderful. The men of the U.S. Army Special Forces picked Linda up for a party in Vung Tau in a helicopter, the only viable mode of transportation. On the trip she sat beside the door gunner and had a great view of the ground during the forty-minute ride to the beach.

However, Linda had been in Vietnam only a month and a half before she expressed her dissatisfaction with her assignment. She said, "I would do anything to get out of this office job. I hate sitting behind a typewriter all day. What I want to do, a woman can't do, such as be a chopper pilot or door gunner."

There was little variation in off-duty hours. For entertainment Linda and other WACs often went to some of the clubs at night, or sat outside the barracks drinking beer and talking until bed check at midnight. Linda shared her packages from home, which usually contained bubble gum, candy, and nuts. They all constantly fought the bugs.

Toward the end of the summer, the war activity accelerated, becoming noisier and more frequent. Linda described the situation: "The jets have been bombing in the valley closer than before. They go down very low, drop the bombs, then come straight up, circle over the headquarters, and do it all over again. Everyone stops work to watch. One night there was a horrible blast that woke us up. The buildings and our beds shook and dust was so thick we could hardly see. At 5:45 it started again. We didn't have our reveille formation even though it was an inspection morning. We found out the big blast was Charlie hitting the Bien Hoa ammo dump. There are a lot of casualties coming into the 24th Evac Hospital every day."

Army life in general was not boring for Linda. One fall night she had noncommissioned officer duty; she coped with a drunk WAC and with girls who were outside the gate with their boyfriends long past the time when they were supposed to be inside. She put them all on report. Mortars and artillery boomed in the background. Linda did the bed check at midnight and got wet from the drenching rain. Reddy followed her through all the barracks until the dog spied a cat. Then she took off in chase.

Another night, tear gas drifted over to the outside of the barracks, leaving a thick fog. The next morning a small plane flew overhead broadcasting the *Chiue Hoi* program from a loudspeaker, urging the Vietcong to give up their fight. Another night, the Cobra gun ships shot rockets in a steady stream at a good-sized element of Vietcong trapped down by the river.

Thanksgiving came, but it didn't seem much like Thanksgiving to Linda, since she worked all day in hot weather. December brought R&R in Bangkok, Thailand; Christmas; and a move to new barracks. Martha Raye, Bob Hope, and Billy Graham came to perform. And on Christmas Eve Linda received a promotion to staff sergeant.

Throughout her letters home, Linda revealed little snippets of her feelings. She missed clear water and clean-smelling towels. This year, she wrote, was certainly going to give her an appreciation for her life and her home. She mentioned that none of the women ever got enough sleep. Vietnam was noted for "doing strange things to people." She said, "One day we want out of here so bad and the next we hate the thought of leaving. I think it's partly because of the closeness that we develop here. It was never like this in the States. We're a family here and we all hate to break it up." Linda was getting to be a short-timer—only three more months to go.

Then came February, and life on the base became stricter because of the celebration of the Vietnamese holiday Tet. During Tet of the previous year, 1968, the Vietcong had mounted a deadly offensive. Now the U.S. Army took precautions. Restrictions demanded that everyone remain on base and that the women return to the WAC detachment area by 10:00 P.M. The Vietnamese maids were no longer allowed on the post, so the women did their own laundering of uniforms and shining of boots. And true to form, on 23 February, Linda reported, "all hell broke loose."

She says, "I was blasted out of a sound sleep by incoming rounds. I grabbed my field gear and headed for the door to go to the bunker. Just as I got in the doorway, another round came in and hit the finance building right across the street from my room. I saw the fire flash and shrapnel fly into the air, and I took off for the bunker. I was in my pajamas. We stayed in the bunkers while rounds came in all around until about 4:30 A.M. Then we went out and most of us put our fatigues on. A little while after that, they said a major ground attack was expected so we went back to the bunkers. We stayed about an hour and a half."

A bus came later to take the women to work, and they saw that the enemy had hit the building across the street from headquarters. All day, Cobra gun ships poured rocket fire into the hills on the perimeter below headquarters. Linda watched all of it. There were several casualties. Reports indicated that some Vietcong had infiltrated the post in three places but were still undetected. Linda admitted that the previous night had been the first time she really had a fear of being hit or captured. She said, "I think I'm going to be jumpy for a long time."

The jumpiness continued as the red alerts went on nightly. Linda began to feel that it was almost a hopeless cause to try to go to bed and sleep. The alert sounded, or someone yelled, "Incoming," and the women took off for the bunker. Linda found it impossible to sleep in the bunker. The benches were about eight inches off the ground and narrow. Sometimes the women did not leave the bunker until 7:00 A.M., in time to be taken to work.

The nightly barrage did not depress the morale of the WACs. They learned to take their boots off, but not their uniforms. All of them were getting a bit weary from the constant lack of sleep. The news that two Vietcong were captured on post in a jungle area did not help their serenity, however. They felt a little more confident about their security after the men cleared out the jungle around the WAC barracks and the jets bombed right out on the perimeter of the post. The constant noise of the B-52s dropping their bombs farther away at night also reassured the women.

Sometimes, despite the constant fears of enemy attacks or hits and the noise of the fighting, Linda thought about the Vietcong as people with families.

As her time in Vietnam grew short, she found it difficult to maintain a hatred for the enemy. She had managed to survive traditionally dangerous February; now in March, it would not be long before Linda would fly home. She would leave in May, her yearlong tour over. Her first thought when she heard the noise of incoming fire was, "They can't hit us now; I'm going home soon."

Early in April the Vietcong smashed the post office building of headquarters, destroying it and leaving only an empty shell surrounded by debris. The enemy rocket went in the outside wall, blew out the ceiling all the way across the end of the building, and splintered the doors. Another round that night hit down the street from the WAC barracks. Almost every night the post got hit with something. Linda wailed, "I'm too short for this!"

Linda experienced the normal ambivalence of those soon leaving for home. She said, "I'm getting really excited about going home now and the time is flying. I know I'll have my new Roadrunner, it will be spring in Illinois and everything will be new and clean, and I'll get to be with my family and friends again. I'm beginning to feel like I've been away from home for a year. I'm tired of the dirt, heat, bugs, and all the restrictions. I do like my friends here and I will be sorry to leave them."

Linda spent another night in the bunker, with the incoming fire. She said at the time, "It was very hot and stuffy—worse than usual. It started raining about a half hour before we got out and we waded through red mud and water on the way back to our rooms. That's one thing I certainly won't miss. . . . I really want to go home but the closer it gets the more I wish I were coming back here. I hope my feelings change after I get there."

At a headquarters ceremony, Linda received the Army Commendation Medal for doing an outstanding job during her year in Vietnam. She finished her last paperwork, a request to take a kitten she had adopted, Murphy, home with her. On 14 May she wrote, "I can't believe the end has really come." Two days later she boarded a freedom bird for home.

Linda had a happy homecoming in Danville, Illinois. The new car she had ordered while still in Vietnam, a 1969 Plymouth Roadrunner, awaited her, and she successfully shipped Murphy home. He lived a long and happy life to the age of sixteen.

After a thirty-day leave, Linda reported to Fort Sam Houston, Texas, where she served for two years; from there her duty included many stateside assignments and two tours in Germany. She stayed in the army for twenty-four years, retiring as a first sergeant in January 1989. Her last move stateside was to Chebanse, Illinois, where she is now an administrative assistant at Kankakee Community College.

Linda had forgotten much about her service in Vietnam until she recently reread her letters home and concluded that she grew up in Vietnam. She says, "I went over as a twenty-two-year-old kid and came back as a twenty-three-year-old adult. I still view that year as a good experience, and I have always been glad I was there. Many of the things I looked forward to while I was there did happen, especially being someone special because I was in Vietnam. It may not have been a popular war and the outcome may have been disastrous, but I'm proud to have been an American soldier serving my country."

Anne Philiben in Vung Tau, once a beautiful French resort city; many of its picturesque old buildings were taken over by the U.S. Army.

Carolyn Tanaka inspecting her hits on the rifle range during training. She practiced with a .45 pistol, M-14 and M-16 rifles.

Beth Marie Murphy with the Vietnamese child a GI found in a trash can and brought out to the *Sanctuary* nurses. They cared for—and spoiled—the little girl back to good health.

First Lieutenant Eileen G. Gebhart standing in front of protective sandbags and tents pitched on the sand dunes of Cam Ranh Bay. The tents were erected for both living quarters and the hospital.

Eileen Gebhart plays the piano for the "Choraleers" of Cam Ranh Bay air base. Ed Sullivan sent a TV crew over to tape several of their songs for his Christmas show of December 1966.

Flight nurse Donna Cunningham was in Tan Son Nhut on December 6,1972, when the Vietcong launched several severe rocket attacks against the base. During the last one, Donna stayed in the hospital and delivered a Vietnamese woman's baby.

BUECHLER,DONNA K.   1/LT
354-38-6895PV   4 JAN 70

Flight nurse Donna Buechler was in Cam Ranh when the air base was overrun by the enemy on August 7, 1969. She stayed in the U.S. Air Force twenty years and now professionally counsels combat veterans.

Karen Offutt receives an award for heroically saving many Vietnamese from their burning homes next to the WAC housing in Saigon. She was the only American to risk her life in the fire.

A goodbye handshake. Karen Offutt with Major General Cowles the day in June 1970 she left Vietnam for the United States.

Group picture of some of the civilian women who served in the U.S. Army Special Services. This is a Service Club branch, which provided recreation for the men when free from their fighting duties. The gathering is in Long Binh at U.S. Army Republic of Vietnam (USARV) Headquarters, April 1970.

Ann Campbell, service club director at Bearcat, a recreation center for the 16,000 men on the post. Ann had pulled a ligament, which required a cast for several weeks. Behind Ann is her hooch.

Official photograph of Ann Campbell, civilian attached to the Army Special Services. She served in both Korea and Vietnam.

Marianne Gable Reynolds and two fellow Special Services women at a Saigon meeting shortly after she arrived in Victnam. Marianne helped run the service club in Dong Tam, in the delta, home of the 9th Infantry Division. Leaning over her shoulder is Judy Jenkins Gaudino who later met Marianne at the Vietnam Wall in Washington, D.C. in 1993.

Janice Shomer Kavadas with some of her students at Bui-thi-Xuan girls' high school in the town of Dalat, in the Highlands.

Jennifer Young, Red Cross volunteer, in Vietnam with a favorite puppy.

The Red Cross women in the Central Highlands, assigned to the U.S. Army 4th Infantry Division at Camp Enari. Here they were really a mobile unit, flying daily out to the men in the field.

Dorothy White Patterson (front, second from right) and "the gang" at Cam Ranh Bay in January 1968.

GIs and Vietnam children at a Christmas party in An Khe, 1968. Dorothy White Patterson is in the background.

Martha Royce pouring coffee for the men on the hospital ship USS *Sanctuary.* Christmas, 1970, in Da Nang harbor.

Mary Blanchard Bowe riding in a small helicopter on her way to troops in a forward area. 1968.

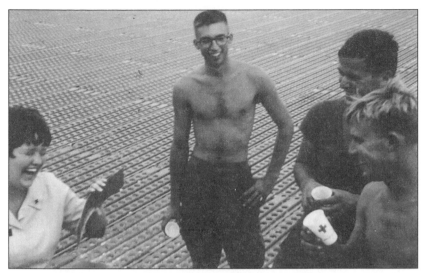

Mary Blanchard Bowe and some of the men sharing a laugh during Red Cross programming June 1969.

Bobbie Keith, stationed in Saigon, became a celebrity as the Weather Girl for the Armed Forces TV, the "Bubbling Bundle of Barometric Brilliance."

Linda Sullivan Schulte (far left) and the group at Tuy Hoa air base take a break from planning entertainment. Tuy Hoa with many amenities was known as the Atlantic City of the South China Sea.

Linda Sullivan and a fellow nurse playing a guessing game with the men outside Phu Bai.

Linda Schulte with the youngsters at the orphanage near Lai Khe. Linda taught them camping skills, songs, and played games with them.

Stationed in Saigon, Barbara Hamilton traveled extensively by hitchhiking from the airport. Here she is photographed sitting in the cockpit of a C-130 transport plane, flying into Cam Ranh Bay in 1969.

Barbara Hamilton at the An Loc Orphanage in Saigon where she volunteered weekends during her two-year tour in Vietnam.

Mary Blanchard Bowe (center) and fellow Red Cross workers meet at the Vietnam Women's Memorial in Washington, D.C., in 1993.

Army Special Services

Ann Campbell

Ann Campbell grew up in New Jersey and graduated from both Seton Hall University and Grace Down's Airline School in New York City. She flew all over the world as a stewardess, then spent twenty-seven months as a civilian with the U.S. Army Special Services at four different service clubs in the demilitarized zone of war-torn Korea before she decided to transfer to Vietnam in the spring of 1969.

Ann Campbell was prepared for anything as the plane landed at Tan Son Nhut Airport, near Saigon. She was eager to get started; she was not frightened or apprehensive. After all, she had spent more than two years in Korea, and before that had flown to all parts of the world, and she had the sensibility and experience of a thirty-four year old. Nevertheless, she was slightly dismayed when she saw the Plantation Service Club complex at Bearcat in the Army III Corps area in the south. Ann was to be director of this club, one of the largest in the country.

Here the post commander was a Thai general with the Panther Division from Thailand. His troops were 70 percent Thai, with some fragmented American aviation units and a small group of Australian navy. There were sixteen thousand men on the post, and two American women—Ann and one other.

When Ann saw the living quarters for the females—the hooch—
she immediately thought of Tobacco Road. The squalid, dilapidated building was an L-shaped wooden tropical structure with fifteen living stalls on the ground level, each with what looked like
cardboard walls. The walls fell short of the ceiling, extending only
to an open space below a rusty tin roof, which covered the entire
building. The roof had barbed wire strung around the beams. It was
a depressing sight. Ann wondered how she would ever make it liv-
able and how she would get rid of all the bugs she saw everywhere.

The largest room was the living room. It had a few chairs, which
she knew had been borrowed from the service club; a small table;
and a television with one fuzzy channel. A wooden counter was the
bar, and behind it was a small refrigerator. Next to the living room
was the kitchen stall, which had a refrigerator, a sink, a hot plate,
and a wooden table. A few dishes, open boxes of cereal, and several
pots were on the table. An ironing board leaned against a wall. The
odor in the kitchen was dreadful.

The bath stall had three toilets, two of which did not work, and
three sinks, two of which did not work. They were all camouflaged
with mounds of dirt and sand. The shower space had a spigot from
which water, deep brown in color, dribbled down. After Ann had
used these facilities for a time, she noticed that her teeth were turning brown, and she began to occasionally brush them with scotch.

The remaining stalls were empty, with the exception of three that
were fitted out as bedrooms, each with an army cot, a metal locker,
and a small wooden dresser.

Outside, nearby and facing the hooch, was the bunker. It was
about fifteen square feet in area and six feet high, and could hold
six army cots. The bottom layer consisted of fifty-gallon drums filled
with dirt. On top of these and down the sides were hundreds of
sandbags, with only a small entrance exposed.

An old fence with broken and missing slats ringed the yard,
hooch, and bunker. A guard was stationed at the fence opening to
give a sense of security to the women. Of course, he did no such
thing.

Two factors were paramount at Bearcat: the filth and the noise.
The hooch in the Thai area was across the road from a huge chop-

per landing strip. There were hundreds of helicopters there, many of which took off day and night. There was a constant swirl of reddish-brown dust in the air, and the puttering of the chopper rotary blades was unrelenting. The noise was so close, it was almost deafening. The flight pattern was directly over the hooch and only inches from the tin roof, which vibrated violently.

The club building was large enough—about fifteen thousand square feet. It had a small library, a writing room, a card room, a tape room, two music rooms, a game room with four pool tables, a large lounge area, two shuffleboard tables, a Ping-Pong table, and many comfortable chairs. It also had a checkout counter with musical instruments, sound equipment, movie projectors, tape recorders, typewriters, games (including chess), and cards. The building included a kitchen, two storage rooms, a latrine, and a large office room. On the surface it seemed to be well equipped, but there were never enough supplies. The stove in the kitchen didn't work, the toilet in the latrine didn't flush, the storerooms had no shelves, and the fire marshal told Ann he would close the club down if she didn't get it wired properly. There were five or six air conditioners working on AC instead of DC current.

Ann immediately set to work to clean and paint, and she went everywhere to beg, borrow, or trade supplies. She was quite successful, and in spite of the shortcomings of the club, it was popular. By demand, it was open every day of the year, anywhere from nine to fourteen hours a day. Ann and one other woman were the official civilian staff. One GI was assigned to work in the club, and two more worked part-time until Ann managed to convert them to full-time.

There were tournaments, bingo, quizzes, and games galore. Usually, prizes were awarded and refreshments were provided, although there was no liquor. Shows came to perform at the club, and the GIs often provided their own entertainment with jazz sessions or impromptu bands.

A few of the Thai officers spoke English, but the majority of the troops did not. However, they were friendly and cheerful, and made themselves clear by body or sign language. In most cases, they did not wear proper uniforms. Many just wore their army pants with no shirts, no shoes, and no socks. Some wore something like a loincloth around their middle and nothing else. But, to a man, they all wore one or many Buddha figures around their necks. The Thais believed that if you wore a Buddha, you could not die. Their government had sent enough Buddhas to adorn the twelve thousand men; some of them wore twenty. They insisted that Ann wear the ones they gave her, saying, "Must wear, Miss Ann, no can die." Ann gladly wore three Buddhas; too often, she heard the sounds of bombing raids nearby.

The Thais posed a few problems. Marijuana was legally issued to them, and the floors in the club were usually coated with a layer of marijuana. And they did not understand the purpose of the tall cylinder-style ashtrays that stood upright on the floor. They removed the tops and used the cylinders as toilets.

The local mama-sans were unreliable. Hired for eight-hour duty to keep the club clean, they usually stopped work after two or three hours and took naps on the floor. Also, their views of cleanliness were not the same as Ann's. On checking one day, Ann found both mud and a dead rat inside the refrigerator.

Ann had the usual practical problems of running a service club; in addition, she had to buck the local beliefs and practices. Several times she found the mama-sans cutting one another with razor blades. They believed that a few cuts on the head in the temple area would get rid of a headache. One day Ann had to get an ambulance to take a mama-san to the medical unit. Her friend had cut her naval trying to get rid of a stomachache.

When Ann could get a Jeep or a truck, she made trips into Saigon and Long Binh for supplies. She was allowed off the post as long as she had a driver and a shotgun rider, but the vehicle was allowed outside the gate only if the minesweeper had cleared the dirt road for safety. At night the Vietcong mined the area, and the next morning the soldiers dug up the mines. Ann was among the few who risked travel by ground vehicle, since there was often sniper fire. Most personnel used only helicopters, which flew straight up before flying forward.

Ann never forgot that the Bearcat base was in the combat area. An evacuation plan for the women in case the Vietcong breached the perimeter was discussed on the post, but after much study the

Americans, who were quartered far from the Thai area, decided that any evacuation of the American women was out of the question. The men could never make it to their area and back out by the planes, which would be the prime targets of attack. The officer making this decision made an offer: if the women wanted cyanide tablets in case of capture, they could be provided. Ann checked with the other woman, but both declined.

The siren for incoming artillery sounded at all hours, sometimes all day and all night. That would be followed by more outgoing. When the siren sounded, everyone on the post was to get into a bunker. This procedure was sorely tested in May, before, during, and after Ho Chi Minh's birthday, when the noise seemed constant. Incoming mortars and rockets hit almost every area of the compound. When the siren went off, it was often hard to hear it in the hooch because of the noise of the helicopters taking off over the tin roof and artillery shells flying overhead. Sometimes the siren sounded after the incoming artillery had landed; other times, a nearby generator sounded exactly like the siren. Often, there seemed to be total confusion.

There were three alerts: green, yellow, and red. Green meant trouble was coming soon; yellow meant an attack was likely soon, so everyone should stay in a bunker or close to one. The service club was to be evacuated and closed down quickly. Red meant an attack was imminent or had already begun somewhere on the compound. Everyone was to go to a bunker and stay there. The red alerts became more and more frequent; some days, the red alert was constant.

Ann had stocked the bunker with essentials, such as a bottle of scotch and small candles with matches. In the bunker, she slept in her army camouflaged fatigue uniform with a flak vest around her chest and her steel helmet with a liner on her head. She kept her jungle boots on, and in her uniform pockets she always had a flashlight, tissues, a nail file, chewing gum, a canteen of water, cigarettes, a lighter, and her noncombatant card. This card was supposedly her ticket to safety in case she was captured. It showed her picture and stated that she was a civilian with an assimilated military rank. Ann thought the card was designed to keep the enemy from shooting her. She always wore her dog tags with a p38, which was a tiny military-style can opener, and a very small screwdriver around her neck, along with the Buddhas.

The bunker was a safety spot, but it was a pretty miserable place. Inside, it was basically mud—very wet mud—with bugs and insects. There were several cots, which had filthy, smelly mattresses, and Ann had wisely installed her folding sun chair to sleep in. The sandbags of the bunker were constantly ripping, having been soaked and weakened from the frequent rains. The air inside was musty and foul.

Many nights when the Vietcong were attacking vigorously, Ann was frightened. She recalls one night when she was terrified. She was in the bunker with several of the staff, including the guard. "Outside there were the violent sounds of war—the incoming rockets, the outgoing mortars, the shrill whistling of shells flying every which way, loud explosions, automatic firing going on, trucks on the road, choppers overhead, red tracers streaming from the choppers as they fired on the enemy. Mortars and rockets were landing all around, even in the yard. The earth mixed with shrapnel was bouncing off the outside of the bunker." Ann prayed that the enemy would be kept outside the compound perimeter.

It was very still in the bunker. No one had said a word for what seemed like hours. All of them could feel the trembling of the ground beneath them. Ann lay quietly in her chair, hoping that she could control her fear.

"I was so tense. My entire body was soaked with my sweat. The flak vest was heavy and so terribly hot. My hair was dripping wet from the steel pot. The air was so stale, it was so hot and humid, I could hardly breathe. Mud was oozing out of the sandbags. I wanted to get up, move around, fire a weapon, do anything but continue to stay in this stinking bunker. What was happening out there? Was the compound being overrun? All I could do was wait and listen. It went on for hours and hours without letting up. The yard was filled with potholes and pieces of shrapnel. Would I see the sun rise tomorrow?"

At about 2:30 A.M., Ann thought she heard a vehicle outside. Before she could consider what she should do if it was the Vietcong, she heard a voice she recognized. It was a colonel from the 222d Aviation Battalion. He wanted to know if everyone in the bunker was OK. Just as Ann was reassuring him that they were all fine, the guard jumped up, cocked his rifle, and headed for the exit, shouting, "What's the password, what's the password?" Ann knew that the colonel would not have the vaguest idea of any password. She tackled the guard, and as they tumbled on the floor together, she said to the surprised soldier that he really didn't want to shoot his battalion commander, did he? The incident broke the tension in the bunker, and everyone began talking at once.

During this same period, the Thai troops outside had been busy. The next issue of *Stars and Stripes* headlined their activity: "Thai Troops Killed 212 VC at Bearcat." It was a great victory, and the compound went wild with celebrations. But the spoils, proudly shown to Ann during the days following the battle, were human ears cut from the dead Vietcong. When she saw them, Ann felt sick.

Another night when the Vietcong attacked, Ann was at the service club. The building and everything in it trembled and fell. Even the ceiling lights crashed to the floor. Ann raced through the building, making sure that the staff went to secure shelter and that the men got down on the floor. When she reached the game room she saw that the Thai troops had completely ignored the siren and were happily playing billiards. They disregarded Ann's order to get down on the floor. They had their Buddhas, which would keep them from harm. In desperation, she tripped one man and pushed him to the floor. The others then voluntarily joined him.

Luckily for Ann, Vietnam was not all fear and work. There were also parties and good times. And going to a party meant just about any sharing of off-duty hours with some of the men down the road. It could be as simple as sitting on sandbags, having a few drinks, and cooking some steaks on an open grill. Ann remembers that just being together constituted a party. "Occasionally someone had a guitar; everyone sang a few songs. There was even a dance now and then. These were precious moments. No formality, no rank, officers and enlisted men were just people needing the companionship of other people. They were good times and good people. . . . These good times were woven in between the anxiety, the apprehension, the uncertainty, and the unknown. I was glad to be alive and so sorry others had to die."

Six months after Ann took charge of the club, its transformation seemed miraculous. The needed repairs had been done, the whole inside had been painted in bright colors, the latrine was flushing, and new wiring had been installed. Club attendance had soared, so that it was the highest of any such club in-country. The good job that Ann had done was recognized by her superiors, who offered her a promotion to assistant area director.

In Long Binh, as assistant area director for the Army III and IV Corps, she supervised the four service clubs in the Mekong Delta—those at Can Tho, Vung Tau, Vinh Long, and Soc Trang. She lived in a room in Can Tho; she was the only special services female in-country who did not live on a military compound. For the next twenty-one months Ann flew in every type of plane available to one club and then another to meet the staff and the post commanders and to help with training and any problems.

When her room was needed by its owners, Ann moved to Long Binh, which she found to be a more civilized area. But she became busier than before; she was in charge of sixty-five women assigned to twenty-two clubs, which varied from a shack to a brand-new building.

The months flew by, and when her year of service was up, she extended for three months—a move she was to repeat many times in the coming period. Her responsibilities kept increasing as clubs and personnel constantly changed. Each time she was to return to the United States, she extended for another three months. And although she got R&R after each extension, she began to tire. She recalls that she could not work enough hours to catch up on the workload. There was just too much work for too few people. "The toll began to be felt. I found myself so tired that my insides began to shake. . . . I was so tired, it was an effort just to keep my body and soul together."

Ann continued the frantic pace of traveling from club to club. In January 1971 she took over as area director for service clubs, stationed now at Nha Trang. By this time she had been in Vietnam for almost two years, and burnout was beginning to take over. She says,

"I had been living out of a suitcase for almost two years. I had more time flying than some of the pilots. My body was constantly in motion, coming and going in perpetual waves. I needed time to think and solitude to rejuvenate my soul. I had no sense of stability, no roots; everything was temporary. It was time to get off the roller coaster." She decided to submit her resignation and ask for a port call of June to return to the United States.

Ann found her decision heart-wrenching. She wanted to stay, but she knew she should leave. Once she had decided, she did not look back, but began to plan for the future. From the PX catalogue she bought a 1971 Chevrolet Vega for $3,000 (only a couple hundred down) and arranged to have it shipped to her in New Jersey. Ann found it hard to say good-bye, but now farewell parties were frequent because many of the personnel were going back to the United States.

At a final farewell ceremony, Ann's staff director presented her with the civilian medal for service in Vietnam. She remembers, "I was so sad and yet I felt ten feet tall. God, I was so proud. . . . I was not just going home, I was ending a period in my life that could never be duplicated, perhaps not even explained, but it could not be erased. My body was twitching with mixed emotions. It was 9:00 A.M. on 18 June 1971, at Tan Son Nhut Airport, Saigon, Vietnam. I boarded the plane for the United States."

Night after night after she returned home, Ann had nightmares. She would wake up in a cold sweat. Her pajamas were wet through; even the sheets were damp. She would sit up in bed, breathing hard, her heart pounding. The nightmares were flashbacks to her Vietnam days; in her dream the women had been left alone on the post with no one to protect them from the Vietcong. These dreams continued for years but became less frequent and less dramatic as time went on. Often during the night she saw the faces of the little children of Soc Trang, Vietnam, who had had their hands and feet cut off because their parents had refused to work for the Vietcong.

Ann began to quietly pick up the pieces of her civilian life. She put Vietnam behind her. She did not speak of her time there because she learned that no one wanted to listen. No one chided her for her service there. In the beginning of 1972 she started working for the Essex County, New Jersey, Department of Parks, Recreation, and Cultural Affairs, and she stayed there for twenty-three years, retiring on 1 April 1995. She never married. In 1974 she purchased her first home, and she stayed there until she moved to Florida in retirement in 1997.

Ann did a great deal in those years after Vietnam. She went back to school and got a master's degree in administration, and then traveled extensively. She took trips that any ardent traveler might envy, to Alaska, Russia, and Scandinavia. She sailed the Caribbean, went down the Mississippi in a steamboat, visited the Grand Canyon, rode in a hot air balloon, went on a safari tour to Kenya, and tracked gorillas in Uganda.

It was not until the first reunion of the special services women of Vietnam in Washington, D.C., in November 1993, that Ann had any contact with the women who had served during the war. In Washington they met, bonded, and marched together in the general parade down Constitution Avenue held in honor of the dedication of the Vietnam Women's Memorial. Ann was exhilarated. The men along the parade route waved at them and cheered for them as they passed by. Ann held her head high and felt a deep sense of pride to have served in Vietnam.

(This material is copyright by Ann G. Campbell, and the author is kindly granted use. See endnotes.)

Marianne Gable Reynolds

Marianne Gable Reynolds was born in Seattle while World War II was full-blown, prompting a nurse to remark that Marianne was just more bomb fodder for the Japanese to kill. Her family moved to California in 1946, and after a few starts and stops, she graduated from Los Angeles State College (now California State University at Los Angeles). In 1966, as vice president of the college recreation club, Marianne was involved with a visit of U.S. Army Special Services leaders from Washington, D.C., who were shunned on campus. Marianne was embarrassed, and thus extended them a warm welcome. She was hooked when the leaders pleaded for help for the troops in Vietnam. She applied to join when she graduated at the end of another semester. Her parents said, "Marianne, you're twenty-three years old. We don't agree with what you're doing, but we'll support you." Marianne left for Vietnam in August 1967.

The plane banked to land at a steep angle at Bien Hoa airport in South Vietnam. Suddenly, it was extremely quiet inside the plane. Perhaps, Marianne Reynolds thought, the men and women were seriously contemplating that their lives were about to change and would never be the same. She certainly was. When they landed, no one was there to meet her. Through a fluke, she had been awaited the previous day at Tan Son Nhut, where she had been scheduled to arrive. Now, as she disembarked, there was nothing to distract her from the memorable smell that enveloped her—the unique smell of Vietnam.

Marianne had her first culture shock as a Jeep drove her through the outskirts of Saigon. She marveled at the hand labor everywhere; work was being done on buildings block by block, with no machinery in sight. The streets overflowed with bicycles, lambrettas, and motor scooters, some with whole families riding on one.

In Saigon, she received a short indoctrination by her advisor, Dorothy Phillips, who was later killed when her Red Cross plane flew into a mountain or was shot down by the enemy.

Marianne proceeded on to Dong Tam in the delta, home to the 9th Infantry Division. There were ten thousand troops and a huge service club called the Ponderosa, with only two women to run it, morning to night. But Marianne considered herself lucky compared to the nurses. She shared dining facilities with them but didn't really get to know them because they were on such chaotic schedules. Marianne lived in the nurses' hooch, but she had her own cubicle in the barracks-type building.

Marianne arrived on base only two weeks after a nurse had died of suffocation when the hospital, which was housed in inflatables, was shelled by the enemy. As the hospital collapsed, the nurse had been caught within. Now there were many alerts, for which all the women went to a bunker. Unfortunately, the bunker closest to Marianne's room was considered unsafe, and when the siren sounded she ran the length of the hall to the good bunker. She always arrived feeling nauseated. She was extremely near-sighted; her contacts had been rendered useless by the contaminated water supply, so she wore heavy dark-rimmed glasses. When the alarm siren sounded, Marianne left the glasses behind and sat in a corner of the dark bunker in a haze of blurry figures, breathing as deeply as she could to keep from throwing up.

Marianne suffered physically as a result of the conditions around her. She got worms from eating pork at a restaurant in Saigon, and she had constant diarrhea and cramps from the malaria pills. Nevertheless, she thoroughly enjoyed her work at the Ponderosa and felt that she significantly contributed to the morale of the troops. The club provided an air-conditioned pool room and library, a Mars station for calls home, and a large open hall where the USO shows were performed. Generally, the men were on their own at the center, with the women not entertaining them but helping to run the facilities. The women did participate in the recreation when they went out to the ships. The women played and ran Bingo on the ships. Only once did they visit the hospital.

The hospital visit was a disaster. Marianne's coworker offered cigarettes to a dying soldier with a tracheotomy tube. The hospital suggested that the women not return. Marianne thought that for her psyche, that was probably a blessing, but she considered the whole episode an unfortunate event.

A more positive move was to visit an orphanage, but here too, the results of the trip were unsatisfactory. Marianne went with the Catholic chaplain. Most of the babies were Amerasian and had been abandoned at the orphanage. When the little ones, about two years old, saw Marianne, with her blond hair, green eyes, and hair on her arms, they were terrified of what they obviously considered a monster, and they cried. After some time, the children became used to Marianne and enjoyed her visits.

Marianne's help was best received at the special services club, but there, too, not everything was perfect. One day Gen. Omar Bradley went to the club. Marianne was working alone and was surprised by the visit, but she greeted him warmly. "Sergeant Bradley, I'm so happy to have you at the Ponderosa Service Club."

General Bradley was not in military uniform, but a civilian white shirt. Marianne reports, "I saw him smile briefly but what I really did notice was his aide-de-camp and our base commander recoil in horror. To my surprise, that evening I was invited to the command bunker to learn army lessons from the base commander's executive officer: 'Now, Miss Gable, when you see one gold oak leaf it's a major; a silver oak leaf is lieutenant colonel, and . . .' The officer went through the whole litany of rank."

At the time Marianne exhibited chagrin, but she became indignant later when she thought, *If they wanted me perfect as a civilian, they should have trained me to all that rank.*

There were positive sides to Marianne's days in Vietnam. She was lucky that her father was the president of a local Lions Club back home and kept her supplied with cookies in coffee cans every week. Needless to say, these were definitely appreciated by the men. Another plus was of a more personal nature: the solar-heated water for the showers was always warm when Marianne went to shower, and the bathroom was always empty, except for an ever-present praying mantis.

The monsoon rains did not leave a lasting impression on Marianne, with the exception of one poignant night. As she was coming home late from the club, she saw the troops sitting on top of their tanks in the driving rain, bent over, with their ponchos as their only protection. The lonely, miserable scene was etched in Marianne's mind.

While Marianne was at Dong Tam, Martha Raye came to visit with a USO show and *Hello Dolly*. That night the base was hit by incoming artillery. Martha had been staying in the post commander's trailer, and she, like all the women, raced for the bunker. Marianne recalls: "We all made it to the bunker and I was again fighting back nausea. In the dim light and my fuzzy vision I could see her, in a shorty nightie with her little legs hanging out, saying, 'Beer, anybody?'"

Martha had scooped the commander's beer out of his refrigerator on her way to the bunker.

Just before Christmas, Marianne was scheduled to be transferred to Can Tho airfield, farther south in the delta. The day she was to leave, an officer at Dong Tam summoned her to his office and forced an unwanted wet kiss on her, and in the process pulled a button off her uniform. Marianne says, "He was so mortified at being caught when that happened, he slunk away to the next room like a caged rat, leaving me there in total shock."

Marianne had been quite successful at avoiding any sexual advances from the men by appearing naïve. She recalls the day she was given a helicopter hop to Saigon for a meeting, and upon landing the crew chief nonchalantly asked her, "Do you ever get hit up for sex here?"

Marianne answered, "Well no, I'm treated better here than at home."

The crew chief was stunned into silence.

Marianne says that her year in Vietnam was the loneliest year of her life. "To do the job right, I was sister and girl next door to all and girlfriend to none. Left a virgin, came home a virgin."

Christmas 1967 in Can Tho was a relatively happy time. Marianne lived off-base in a beautiful French villa. The chaplain asked her to get a choir together for the celebration, which she did, and her parents sent her a piñata of Santa Claus. The women put him on top of their club, called the Tiki Hut. Sadly, they had to take him down when the radar kept picking him up. They also hosted an orphanage Christmas. The troops loved having the kids there. Marianne filled the piñata up with candy, and the children and troops were blindfolded and took turns trying to hit it with a stick. The laughter was wonderful for all to hear.

All this changed at the beginning of the new year, 1968. In January the women were moved onto base to live in trailers. The Vietcong Tet Offensive came in late January. Marianne says she received no warning of it.

"The story of Tet was awakening to explosions and looking out of my trailer to see the skies lit up with flames and the GIs close by, not with their weapons but in their underwear with cameras!"

The story, as Marianne learned it, was that the Vietcong had commandeered a U.S. medical ambulance and had broken through the guard post. They drove down the flight line and put grenades in each plane's wheel wells. They hit the whole flight line that way, with no resistance, and then they jumped back into the ambulance and got through the other gate. It was after the Tet Offensive that Marianne knew deep in her soul that she would not survive her full tour of duty.

Marianne managed to get an in-country R&R to Vung Tau on a landing craft. The men aboard were so happy to see a "round eyes" that they spent a long time showing her their machine-gun practice. Marianne thought these landing crafts were deathtraps for the men because of enemy ambushes, but they all remained unscathed on this trip.

Marianne had a number of unusual experiences. Once she went to visit the army POW camp at the airfield. She saw only one prisoner, who was in a crouched position, with eyes down and hands bound. *And that was the enemy!* she thought. Another time she went by Huey helicopter to Saigon with a body bag in the chopper. She could see the outline of the body, and as the Huey bounced, so did the body—an eerie sight.

On another occasion she rode door gunner on a helicopter. She was attached to the craft only by a seatbelt near the open door. The fright of the situation did not really sink in. Much of what Marianne felt about events in Vietnam, including that trip, was sheer wonder.

One day Marianne took a Chinook helicopter which landed in a Laos special forces camp. No outside troops were allowed there. This visit to Laos was never discussed at the time, because women were not allowed to be in Laos. It was a trust situation to bring Marianne there for half an hour so the men could visit with an American woman. The men let Marianne shoot an automatic gun and a machine gun. A dog with new puppies lent the only touch of home. She remembers the gaunt faces of the men as she left the camp. They were so far in the bush that they would never come close to a service club.

Another time when Marianne was in a Huey heading for Saigon, the craft almost collided with a civilian helicopter in midair. "We dropped elevation like a roller coaster and the pilot was rip-roaring mad, and when we landed he lit out for the civilian pilot."

Late in January Marianne made a momentous decision: she and her husband-to-be, who was serving in Vietnam, would get married. They did so during their R&R in Hawaii, in a traditional wedding. He returned to duty for his remaining month in Vietnam. Marianne sent the special services officials in Saigon a telegram stating that she would not return to the base and flew home to California. She had married an army aviator, and they eventually had two daughters. Marianne's husband suffered severe post-traumatic stress disorder. After ten years they divorced.

Marianne joined the army in 1975 to support her girls, and later remarried and had two more children, both boys. She went back to college on the GI Bill from 1984 to 1989, attending Boston University's overseas program, and earned a master's degree in counseling. Through these studies, Marianne gained a deeper understanding of her divorce and the pain, shame, and guilt from Vietnam.

"In 1993, after twenty-five years of no contact with former workers or talk of Vietnam service, I went to D.C. for the Vietnam Women's Memorial unveiling. That opened Pandora's box. I took from the bottom of my cedar chest three almost-new photo albums to share. At the civilian memorial service the night before the dedication the civilian women from Vietnam met. . . . The emotions flew. Later, walking down Constitution Avenue at the dedication ceremony was the first time I'd seen approval in the eyes of the crowd—what a healing journey!"

When Marianne came home she joined Vietnam Veterans of America, Chapter 95, as a life member and served as its vice president. She also became a volunteer therapist, counseled at the local Vet Center, and eventually hosted a support group for wives and girlfriends of veterans with PTSD.

In June 1996 Marianne retired as a lieutenant colonel after twenty-two years of military service as a public affairs officer in the U.S. Army Reserves. The next year she met her daughter, Sp. Mindy Beall King, in the medical corps stationed at Fort Benning, and together they attended the dedication of the Women's Memorial in Washington, D.C.

Today Marianne says she has empathy for and dedication to Vietnam veterans. Her year in Vietnam was a personally lonely year, but it started a chain of events that has left her feeling happy and blessed.

International Voluntary Services

Janice Shomer Kavadas

Janice Shomer was born and raised in Chicago but moved to Phoenix to attend Arizona State University. She taught school for four years in California and Arizona before she learned, in 1966, of the possibilities of joining the International Voluntary Services (IVS) to teach English as a second language to the people of Vietnam. That Vietnam was a war zone did not deter Janice. She joined IVS, trained in Washington, D.C., and in July flew to Vinh Long in the delta of South Vietnam for Vietnamese language training. She felt sanguine. "Since I wasn't going to be in the military, I didn't feel that I would be in direct physical danger."

In August 1966, Janice Shomer arrived in Dalat, a beautiful former resort city of eighty thousand people in the highlands. Everyone in IVS congratulated her on receiving such a plum assignment. The Vietcong ignored Dalat; it was rumored that they had made a military agreement with South Vietnam to spare the city as a rest and recreation area for all. Dalat, truly a gem set in the mountains, with a lake in the center of the city and two in the surrounding area, boasted a moderate temperature that was never too cold or too hot. Poinsettia flowers bloomed everywhere and roses of all hues grew profusely along the modern paved streets. It took no stretch of the imagination to see Dalat as the popular resort it had been during the French presence.

Janice and her roommate, Kay Haberlach, lived in a modern French-built house with complete amenities, modern plumbing, a hot water heater, and a bathtub. A large fireplace in the living room heated the house, which was owned by the Vietnamese government but made available to IVS.

Kay and Janice shared the use of an American Scout car to go to their various teaching locations in Dalat, but they could not drive outside of the town because the Vietcong were active there and made the roads unsafe for American travel.

Janice found everything in Dalat very different from anything she had encountered previously—the food, the climate, the teaching, and the living conditions. Luckily Kay had been there for several months, teaching at the university, and she helped Janice adjust and feel comfortable in her new surroundings. They hired a Vietnamese woman, Chi Hai, as their cook, housekeeper, and laundress. The American women found her delightful. She was middle-aged, had black-lacquered teeth, chewed betel nut, and took care of them as though they were her own daughters.

Janice taught pronunciation and writing skills to the students at Bui-Thi-Xuan Girls' High School. A Vietnamese counterpart taught grammar and vocabulary to the beginning students on alternating days. The classes were large—usually about seventy twelve-year-old girls.

The older girls were, Janice says, delightful students. "They were serious about their studies and curious to learn as much as they could from the only American they had ever met." Thirty years later, Janice still corresponds with one of those students, who is currently head of the English department at Dalat University.

In the 1960s, English teachers were in great demand in Vietnam. The IVS teachers were especially popular because they were not allowed to accept payment for extra teaching. None of the teachers minded that restriction, since they received a regular salary of $80 a month, which was deposited in their bank accounts in the United States, as well as $5 in military money to spend at the PX and a living allowance in Vietnamese money, equivalent to about $70. This was guaranteed for their two-year stay. It was not a princely sum— about $960 a year—but with a roommate to share expenses, it was adequate.

Janice taught not only at the girls' high school but also at a Catholic seminary, a boys' technical school, and the Vietnamese Psychological Warfare College. She also taught adult classes at night and gave private lessons to some of her colleagues at Bui-Thi-Xuan.

Janice had a special relationship with two Catholic nuns at the orphanage in Dalat. She taught them practical, everyday conversation, and also introduced them to the small American military detachment there. The mother superior wanted the help of the American soldiers in providing a merry Christmas for the orphans, and the soldiers were eager to participate. They got into the swing of their duties easily; they decorated a Jeep like a sleigh, secured a Santa and dressed him in a traditional red suit, and brought great quantities of food and gifts. It turned out to be a wonderful celebration. It was debatable who had the most fun, the children or the soldiers.

Once exposed to the orphans and the mother superior, the men fell into a pattern of helping out when needed. They made repairs to the buildings on request. On their time off, they found spare materials and tools and went to the orphanage to do what they could to patch up the buildings. The nuns couldn't pay the men money, but they always had cold beer for them, as well as offering a pleasant change from the nightmare of the war.

Although Dalat did not suffer from Vietcong attacks, the threat was always there. Most of the residents had relatives who were in combat, and many of these people had already been killed. The basic food supply for daily living was unaffected by the war because the townspeople raised chickens, ducks, and pigs, and the farmers provided fruits and vegetables of many kinds.

The war cast a sober atmosphere over Dalat. The students maintained perfect attendance and applied themselves well to learning, and a great number of their parents actively participated in parent-teacher meetings and other school functions.

Janice felt welcome everywhere. The Vietnamese constantly expressed their gratitude for the Americans' concern and caring. Though Janice expressed no sentiment for or against the American military presence in Vietnam, she felt that being there was necessary. Many Vietnamese teachers told her that they wanted the Americans in Vietnam because they knew the country would be taken over by the communists if the Americans left. Janice reported that the educated people did not want a communist government. However, she never publicly voiced any political opinions. "I went to Vietnam to teach English, not to promote any political ideology," she says.

Dalat was peaceful until the Tet Offensive of 1968, when the Vietcong attacked many major cities to show their strength. At that time, Janice was on a trip to Japan, so she knew nothing about the attacks on Dalat until she returned to Saigon and was not allowed to go back to Dalat. The authorities felt that conditions there were not secure for civilians.

The offensive did not do much damage to Dalat. Janice was told that a small band of Vietcong had entered Dalat and occupied the large shopping center in the middle of town. They had managed to raise the Vietcong flag for a short period of time, but destruction and casualties were limited. When Janice returned, she saw that bullets had hit the empty home, but had only slightly chipped its stone front.

While in Saigon, Janice and other civilians who could not return to their posts stayed at the IVS house. The house, however, was not in a safe location, since it was in the line of enemy mortar attacks on the airport. Janice felt it was nerve-wracking just to wait, so she volunteered to help the Red Cross workers at the American military hospital in Saigon. She did not have any nursing skills, but she passed out magazines, newspapers, and chocolate chip cookies, which had been air-mailed daily from the United States. She wrote, "I talked to the wounded, wrote letters for them, played cards—anything to pass the time until they recovered or were sent back to the States. The wounded seemed comforted just seeing someone from home."

As Janice's two-year stint in Vietnam was coming to an end, she was faced with a decision about the future. Should she take a teaching job in Laos, which IVS offered her, or should she go to graduate school at Southern Illinois, where she had applied? She told herself that she would finish her master's degree if she could get a teaching assistantship. She was granted the assistantship, so that solved the problem. She planned to return to the United States. Janice flew home in April

All was not smooth sailing at Southern Illinois University, which had a Center for Vietnamese Studies. The students on campus protested the program and also the bombing of Cambodia. Student riots forced Southern Illinois to close temporarily, along with a number of other universities across the United States, in April 1970. It was, as Janice said, a time of turmoil for the whole country.

Janice finally finished her graduate degree, and then married Dennis Kavadas, whom she met at Southern Illinois University. She taught at the Center for English as a Second Language on the university campus, and taught at O'Fallon High School in Illinois and in Athens, Greece.

When her husband finished his degree in mathematics, they were both looking for teaching jobs. They heard about opportunities to teach on the Navajo Indian Reservation in Shiprock, New Mexico. They visited the area and felt it was just right, and they both began teaching there in 1978. Janice again taught teenagers of a different culture.

Janice and her husband spent twenty years among the Indians, and then retired in 1998 to his hometown on the Greek island of Lefkas in the Ionian Sea. They spend their days sailing, gardening, swimming, and fishing. Janice feels it is fitting that she is again in a new culture for her retirement years.

Janice remembers Vietnam fondly. "I was always treated with respect and gratitude by the community, my colleagues, and my students. They knew I was not part of the military, and I was there because I wanted to be. After I left Vietnam, one of my students from Bui-Thi-Xuan wrote me a note. She glued a dried flower to the paper and below it printed neatly, 'Forget me not.' I never will forget."

United Service Organizations

Mara Hodgkins

Mara Hodgkins was born and educated in New York State. She joined the Women's Air Force and married while in the service, but divorced ten years later. She did not elect to stay in the reserves, but rather took a job as a head bank teller. It was not a very remunerative or rewarding job, so when the Vietnam War accelerated, she was ready to do something to help in the conflict. She had had experience as a special services officer in the air force, so it seemed only logical that she would apply to the USO. She applied, was accepted, and shipped out for her job as program assistant in Saigon in December 1967.

The incongruity of the Vietnam situation was apparent to Mara from the beginning. The flight over was on a packed commercial airline, which provided a smooth, comfortable trip. Looking down, Mara could see that Vietnam was a beautiful country. The water and beaches were attractive, as were the waving rice paddies that seemed to flow like river water in the slight breeze, and spreading banana plantations abounded. It was only when the plane landed that Mara could feel and see that war was all around them. There were Vietnamese military manned bunkers, which were surrounded by all kinds of weapons, strategically placed around the airport.

Saigon was a hot, bustling, crowded city, and the USO club there was the largest in South Vietnam, on a busy divided street. Mara's first night in Vietnam was spent at a big Red Infantry party at the nearby Di-An base. The army men picked her up in a Jeep and gave her one of their helmets, cautioning that there was always sniper fire on the road by the rubber trees. It was true. As they rode in the dark through the rice paddies and plantations, tracer bullets whizzed past.

The party lasted all night.

Life in Saigon was pleasant, even luxurious, for Mara. The living quarters were spacious, and the women all had maids—who had little concept of property rights. If they wanted the women to share items such as their lingerie, they would just take what they needed. ("I wash each time. You have. I no have. So I take home.") The great restaurants in the city offered all kinds of meals for a song compared to the United States. The wine flowed, and there was good food and rooftop dancing while the enemy bombing lit up the skies over Cholon five miles away.

The USO club was always busy, and in spite of the war and knowing the conditions that the GIs endured out in the boonies and fire bases, Mara felt no fear. She was supposed to project an image compatible with her job, and she did. She was calm; her feeling was, "Whatever happens, happens."

The women previewed shows for the GIs from the Philippines and Australia, and only once did they have to cut off a rather risqué presentation that was being given continuously at the fire bases. The club offered all kinds of parties—for birthdays, for coloring, and for foods. They had free shower-shave service and table games and puzzles. The women provided anything they could think of that was suitable to amuse the troops. One month was hot dog month; another was pineapple sundae month. Sunday mornings there were free pancakes. There was bingo, Ping-Pong, and checkers. For a time, there were Vietnamese classes. The door count kept climbing. One quarter the count was 94,710.

In January 1968 Mara was assigned to be an associate director of the club in Vung Tau, a beach city south of Saigon, which was the Vietnamese resort area. There, she says, the club acted just like a stateside tourist agency. The USO staff took the soldiers in from the boonies on all kinds of trips: to see the local Buddha shrine, to a beached Greek freighter, and to a spot called VC Hill. The war was all around them, but the staffers tried to keep up the home-away-from-home atmosphere. They offered patio barbecues, movies, contests, and recreation such as pool and cards.

After three months, Mara was assigned to be an associate director of a club just north of Saigon, the Di-An Club. Here an old theater was used to continually show first-run movies. Mara estimates that she saw *The Sound of Music* about twelve times. However, the club often had to be closed because of enemy activity in the area. It was not safe for Mara to live there, so she drove out each day from Saigon. Sometimes on the road she came across American troops spraying tear gas on huts to flush out the enemy, and she heard the sporadic firing of weapons while going to and from the club, but she never felt personally menaced.

By the time of the Tet Offensive in February 1969, Mara was the director of the USO club at Qui Nhon, farther north, on the coast of Vietnam. The club was housed in a converted two-story military barracks adjacent to the airfield, so it was convenient for the GIs who flew in from the fire bases for in-country R&R. The beach was nearby, and although it was crowded with refugees who had fled from inland, it was an attractive area. Here too, however, the club was often closed because of enemy activity. During the Tet Offensive, the South Vietnamese USO gate tender proved to be a turncoat and killed all those he had worked with. It was a wild night, with tracer bullets spinning by the club, which had to close and be left to the rat and roach inhabitants.

Daily activities included shows, for which a parachute-covered outdoor patio was built to accommodate the many soldiers who wanted to attend. There were food programs, and gifts sent from the United States to be contest prizes. There were photo boards where staffers hung Polaroid snapshots they had taken of the GIs. The shower-and-shave kits were popular too, but often they were of no avail, because the town was frequently declared off-limits as a result of the fighting.

As director, Mara was always busy and was sometimes confronted with special problems. There is one day she remembers well. A young GI came to her office door, which was always open. In his hand he had a wad of military currency plus some American bills. He told Mara he was only in for the day and never had a woman. He said he needed "companionship," and he was willing to pay for it. Mara suggested that he have some free coffee and talk to her Vietnamese counter girls, who spoke good English because they attended English classes. Then, she said, he should go to the music room and bang on the drums for a while, then take a cold shower.

After a time the young GI came back with the same handful of money and told Mara, "It didn't work." Mara felt sorry for him, as she had felt sorry for all the GIs who had to go right back to the war at their fire bases after their day in town.

The USO staff tried to help the men in every way they could think of, including supplying them with goods to purchase as souvenirs from Vietnam. The Montagnard people were clever craftspeople, and many GIs bought their products, including mousetraps made from bamboo, palm, and woven reed, and palm baskets and hampers, all made under the auspices of the Christian Service Association in Pleiku.

The club also sold unframed oil paintings that were painted on canvas, wood, or velvet by the local artists. Mara found that she couldn't get enough of them to keep up with the demand. There was never time to put them up on the walls before the supply was exhausted. The most popular were the tigers on black velvet.

For the most part, the local Vietnamese were open and honest. When the staff noticed that their lingerie sets were disappearing, they knew the maids had taken them with the rationale that they did not have any of their own. However, the authorities took a sterner view. They checked the Vietnamese every night at the gate for any pilfered articles. The only way to avoid confiscation was to secure a gate pass release, which was given for the trash items being removed. These were often just empty containers, coated cardboard, or flattened soda cans, which they used in their living quarters. Especially coveted were the nontarnish frozen strawberry pails, which the Vietnamese used for hauling water on the ends of a wooden bar carried across their shoulders.

They even wanted the leftover hamburgers, hot dogs, and french fries that the GIs left. These were denied them as unsuitable for recycling for human consumption. But the USO contacted a nearby orphanage that had a pig farm and was eager to have the leftovers. Mara was sure that the pigs didn't get all of the food.

Even though she was the director, Mara made certain that each morning and afternoon she spent at least fifteen minutes socializing with the GIs. She found most of them stoic. They sat quietly and usually answered questions with just, "Yes, ma'am," or "No, ma'am." Mara found that they needed a great deal of coaxing to enter into any type of silly or fun activity. For some of them, Mara learned, one day at the club was not enough to loosen up. Some still weren't relaxed after three days. After all, it was a sobering time.

Mara recalls one trip to a fire base to visit the men that was quickly shortened. The pilot of the helicopter stated matter-of-factly that they had to leave—now! Mara rushed over to the helicopter, which had the doors off to allow for the weapons, and climbed in. She buckled her seatbelt just in time to see the river below from a tilted helicopter vantage. Her seatbelt held her in. The guns of the helicopter were blazing. The pilot looked over his shoulder and said calmly, with a straight face, "Just practicing, ma'am," which Mara knew was not a true statement at all. The base was actually being overrun.

Another time Mara was helping to unload wounded men who had been in a big skirmish from the helicopters into the holding building, where the medical staff would assess their wounds. One young soldier who she was helping had his shattered arm in an air-pillow type of plastic bag that covered his entire arm. The bag had gotten punctured, and it was leaking. All the young GI kept saying was, "I'm sorry for the bleeding on the floor, ma'am." Mara knew he was in pain. As she said later, it was a sad time for everyone.

Mara went home after eighteen months. She felt that she had been a dove when she volunteered to go to Vietnam. Doves, she had reasoned, are considered peaceful, gentle, loving creatures. They symbolize the spiritual tone of life, and she felt that peaceably trying to work things out was best. After she was in Vietnam, she decided that this policy did not work there. She says, "All those boys dying while politicians sat around tables discussing what was to be done. . . . Too long and drawn out. Wasteful . . . of lives!"

She went to Vietnam with the idea of providing "a relaxing spot away from all the hurt and unfamiliarity that was there." She came back a hawk. "I then felt that a war should be just that. Like the hawk, go after what you want and get it. War is hell, and it should be over and done with as quickly as possible, in my view. Don't stretch it out when lives are at stake. I don't like bombing, but the South Vietnamese were peaceful-type peasants who didn't for the most part care where the road went. The North Vietnamese wished to gain the South's rice paddies, et cetera, and they were the aggressors. How to stop them? Not sure. But if bombs were required, so be it. I wished to help. And I wish McNamara never had written his book to clear his conscience."

When Mara was back in the United States, she did not feel rejected or ostracized because she had served in Vietnam, but she did feel unneeded in her new posts. She worked in two different USO clubs as a member of the YMCA. One was in San Antonio, Texas, and the other was in Charlestown, Massachusetts. Mara found both clubs to be top-notch, but felt they were not needed. The military had many city choices; they could go bowling, to the drugstore, or to libraries—they were welcome almost anywhere. In addition, Mara found the rules and restrictions of the clubs extremely petty. For instance, there were rules about the length of volunteers' hemlines, and dancing close was forbidden; dancing partners were required to be an arm's length apart. To Mara, there was just too much "little stuff" that seemed unimportant after the war.

Mara went back for a second tour of duty in Vietnam within eight months, in August 1970. She served in Cam Ranh Bay and in Da Nang. Her second eleven-month tour was similar to her first, with the exception that Cam Ranh Bay had "miles and miles" of supplies, which were eventually abandoned. Mara had wondered many times whether the Vietnamese would ever be able to figure out what to do with them when they were available. She had found that the Vietnamese "just used things until they quit."

The situation in Vietnam had changed. The war was de-escalating, and the military had many forms of entertainment in their own compounds. They had pizza parlors, snow cone machines, and musical instruments, and Mara again felt that her service was unneeded. She returned to the United States, leaving the USO. Her job had been done. Mara says, "Lots of us lost loved ones over there. I met a GI in the club who said he'd come back to take us both home. It was never to be."

Mara was fearless during the Vietnam War because she personally experienced little that could cause her adrenaline to run high. She was fortunate that she saw little of the physical damage done to the fighting men. There are no terrifying recollections. Today there is, however, a bit of wistful sadness as Mara speaks of her photos. "There's no one who really looks at them anymore except me. And I have lots of memories."

Mara has thoroughly enjoyed her retirement years; they have been exciting years, because she has traveled extensively. She currently takes a trip each month, traveling with such organizations as the Sierra Club, Saga, Elderhostel, and Earthwatch. In the beginning of her travels she decided on destinations alphabetically. The A's included Alaska (five trips), Africa, Antarctica, Australia, and Argentina. Then Mara began skipping around: Costa Rica, the Galapagos, Russia, and other parts of Europe.

She also finds the time to do volunteer work in her community and to take care of her beloved puppy, Taffy. Mara's retirement is happy, active, and rewarding.

American Red Cross

Jennifer Young

Jennifer Young grew up in Webster Groves, a suburb of St. Louis, Missouri. She spent three years at Purdue University in West Lafayette, Indiana, followed by her senior year as an exchange student at the University of Madrid, Spain, before her graduation in 1968. She joined the Red Cross to volunteer in Vietnam for the simple reason that she wanted to help; she wanted to "support our fighting men." After a summer tour of Europe, she returned to the United States, and in the fall she entered the Red Cross orientation program in Washington, D.C., before setting off for Vietnam.

Jennifer Young felt like the new kid on the block when she arrived from Saigon for duty in Dong Ba Thin, headquarters of the 18th Engineer Brigade and the 92d Assault Helicopter Company, just north of Cam Ranh Bay. It was the week before Thanksgiving, 1968. Her four Red Cross coworkers glowed with truck driver tans, and their soft, worn, faded blue uniforms contrasted starkly with Jenny's pale skin and bright uniform with its still-stiff insignia. A twenty-one-year-old, tall, slim, blond neophyte, she had just arrived to spend a year helping to raise the morale of her country's troops.

Red Cross bemoaned the unofficial name given to its volunteers,"donut dollies," a hangover from World War II when the young women actually passed out doughnuts and coffee. Now the women were in Vietnam to keep the men's spirits high by entertaining them. Technically, the program for which the women volunteered was titled Supplemental Recreational Activities Overseas.

After her arrival, Jenny first settled into her closet-sized quarters in the house trailer on base, then began to learn the routine. The five women of the group shared the duty. They worked in pairs, with two pairs out in the field and the odd woman dispensing coffee and Kool-Aid and supervising the activities at the base recreation center.

Jenny's first assignment was to the next overnight run down the coast to Phan Thiet, where units of the 101st Airborne and the 7/17 Cavalry were based. That run was one of the two regularly scheduled runs; the other was a two-nighter to Tuy Hoa, an air base on the coast to the north of Dong Ba Thin. Jenny and Jodie, her partner for the day, left the base at 6:00 A.M. on what was Jenny's first helicopter ride. The Chinook, a large double-rotor helicopter, gave off so much prop wash that Jenny was forced to take out her contact lenses and store them for her entire year in Vietnam. Luckily, she could manage without them.

She thought the flight was wonderful. The pilots invited both women to stand up front behind their seats as they flew low and buzzed the destroyer USS *New Jersey* and a sampan—the large and the small. They found another case of the large and the small when the helicopter landed at Phan Thiet. On the landing strip, a burly blond MP in full uniform, more than six feet tall and at least 220 pounds, guarded a Vietnamese person who was blindfolded, shoeless, and barebacked, and who seemed to Jenny to be about fourteen years old.

Out in the field, the Red Cross women planned all kinds of amusements for the men in the units in more forward areas. Most of the time the women planned games for the men to play, and most were patterned after the current TV game shows popular in the United States. The men played the Red Cross versions of *Concentration, Jeopardy, The Price Is Right, Name That Tune,* and similar shows. The women made their own materials, artwork, and questions. The men sometimes seemed reluctant to participate in this kind of entertainment; many told the women that they only came "to please you girls." Jenny noted that in the next breath they quizzed her on what games were going to be played the following week. Sometimes they radioed the game answers to their buddies at the next fire base to help them win.

By the afternoon of the first day, Jenny was suffering jetlag from the trip to Vietnam. Her arms felt like seventy-five-pound sandbags. When the program was over, Jodie wanted to watch some of the men play basketball and also to try their buckin' bronco, made from a blanketed oil drum suspended from four ropes over a sandpit. Jenny just wanted to sleep. She took a key to the hooch that the sergeant major of Phan Thiet lent the Red Cross women every Monday night.

Jenny fell asleep almost immediately. Not much later, a tremendous banging on the door woke her with a start. A soldier shouted that he wanted to see the sergeant major right away. Jenny explained that he wasn't there, and that the Red Cross was occupying the hooch for the night. The soldier insisted that she was lying— that the sergeant major *was* inside. After much argument and door banging, the soldier left.

This incident was just one of the many insinuations of bad character that haunted the Red Cross women during their days of service in Vietnam. Many of the men, particularly among the enlisted, claimed that no woman in her right mind would volunteer to be in Vietnam. Their purpose in being there, they said, was to make money—lots of money—and to make that money, they reasoned, the women must be there to serve as call girls, imported for the officers. Jenny was shocked by that attitude, which was so contrary to the men's open chivalry and their appreciation of the women.

On Jenny's second morning the women endured a wild Jeep ride before spending the day with the troops. The Jeep driver skirted in and out of the South China Sea waters, and a swerve drenched Jenny in salt water. When they returned to the road, mists of tar flecked Jenny's skin and clothes as the driver took a shortcut through a petroleum dump. No matter what, the shows went on.

Jenny was given a day's reprieve from the runs. The next day she took the recreation center duty. The servicemen were courteous, fun, and good companions.

The women of the team thought Jenny should have the experience of the two-night Tuy Hoa trip, so she and Cathy caught a C-130 from Cam Ranh Bay early the next morning. This plane's crew had the women stand up front and report the port calls to the ground controllers, who were startled to hear feminine voices from above. Jenny thoroughly enjoyed the new experience.

The job at Tuy Hoa was twofold: to see the air force units on the base and to go to the army units of the 173d Airborne around Phu Hiep. They arrived at Tuy Hoa in the early evening, and after settling into their designated quarters in a dormitory, immediately went out to visit some troops. They loaded a large coffee urn onto a Jeep and drove around the perimeter, stopping at every guard tower. At each tower it was the same: "Halt, who goes there?" The women answered and then climbed up to the top with the coffee. They stayed for a time at each tower, talking to the two men on duty.

Long before curfew Jenny felt extremely tired, and she and Cathy went back to the dorm, which, they had discovered, they were sharing with a troop of Korean entertainers—strippers who were performing at the enlisted men's and noncommissioned officers clubs. A separate small room, designated by a sign that read "Red Cross Girls Only," held a bunk for Jenny and Cathy. They had no trouble falling asleep. But there was trouble after the strippers returned to the dormitory at 3:00 A.M.

They shouted and scuffled so noisily that Jenny and Cathy woke up. Two of the inebriated girls were fighting, shrieking, and howling. Cathy called the air police, who quickly came, broke up the fight, and took one of the Korean strippers off to the base infirmary. The group's manager had climbed in the window to seek solace with one woman, which had enraged another, who began the physical attack.

Cathy accompanied the air police and gave a statement about the incident. When she returned, she told Jenny that they would not stay in that dormitory another night. The air force would have to find a different place for them.

The question of housing became moot. Jenny and Cathy spent the next day with the army, visiting the men at the field hospital in Phu Hiep. By the time they returned to Tuy Hoa, the base had been alerted of an imminent typhoon. Cathy knew from experience that they had to scurry to leave or they might be socked in by the weather for days. She managed to get them aboard the last C-130 out of Tuy Hoa before flying became impossible.

For the Red Cross women in the field, the expected proved to be the unexpected. Weather forced the women to make many unscheduled overnights.

Jenny's first weather-related incident occurred at Bao Loc, in the interior toward the highlands. A fog socked the two women in the night before Thanksgiving. Their chopper tried to make it out, but turned back. The men at Bao Loc were expecting their return, and so had prepared a place for the women for the night.

The Hilton Hotel couldn't have provided more thoughtful amenities. Two aviation officers vacated their wooden-floored tent, and someone carefully laid out two washbasins, two towels, two washcloths, two bars of soap, two toothbrushes, and two tubes of toothpaste. Another donated a flight jacket for Jenny to wear in the chill air. She did wear it, and later wore it to bed over her uniform.

Another soldier escorted them with a flashlight through the dark to the mess hall, where all the electrical generators were in use for the cooks to prepare the next day's Thanksgiving meal. The women chatted with the men as they cooked. Just as a tray of raw biscuits was placed in a gas oven, Jenny's eyes started watering, and everyone began to run out of the hall. Someone grabbed Jenny and propelled her toward the door. "Go outside," he said, "and face the wind, and let the tears flow." Jenny did. Later she learned that they had all experienced something that happened on occasion—they had been "CSed." Jenny never found out what that meant, although she was told that it stood for "concentrated stuff." It seemed to her as though they had all been exposed to tear gas.

The next day while the men at Bao Loc were eating their Thanksgiving dinner, Jenny and Linda, her partner on that trip, were flying back to Dong Ba Thin, where they later dined on leftovers.

Every run proved to be unique. Ba Ngai was a mobile run in a Jeep or a three-quarter-ton truck, and once in a huge semi-tractor-trailer. On one visit the women could tell something was amiss. That morning someone had attempted a fragging—an assassination of an officer by one of his men, who had rolled a grenade under the sleeping officer's bunk. Luckily it did not explode. A member of the Criminal Investigations Division was on his way. The women knew that this was not the time for their participation games, so they were relieved when the commanding officer suggested that they just circulate among the men and talk to them. Perhaps with them, the men would relax and the tension would be eased. Jenny, however, inwardly objected to the commanding officer's additional request. If they heard anything about the fragging, they were to report it to him. The men might reveal something to the Red Cross women.

Jenny and her partner circulated and did not hear a word about the fragging, and they did not ask. The morale problem had solved itself. She could not bear the thought of having to incriminate one of the men.

A completely different atmosphere existed when Jenny returned on a run to Ba Ngai about a month later, at Christmastime. When the brightly decorated semi-tractor-trailer arrived, a happy spirit filled the air. The trailer had tinsel, garlands, a tree, and even a plump GI dressed as Santa Claus. The women had packed hundreds of gift ditty bags, filled with combs, mirrors, decks of cards, ballpoints, packs of Kool-Aid, socks, and other small knick-knacks. People back in the United States had made the bags and sent them to the Red Cross. The women gave each GI a ditty bag and a personal Christmas greeting as they passed by the open trailer door.

Recreation center duty exposed the women to many emotional situations, which ranged from joy to sorrow. At the center they sang with the men; played pinochle and Ping-Pong with them; and shared word games, string tricks, and ESP tricks with them. Jenny explains, "Anything for a moment's entertainment; anything to get a soldier to smile." They tried out their newest weekly mobile program with the men as the team participants. Jenny says the Red Cross women invented Trivial Pursuit fifteen years before its time. They staged goofy fashion shows, held Jell-O-eating contests, and judged talent shows. They considered their nickname, the donut dollies, to be an expression of affection. They saw the men laugh and they saw them distraught. And sometimes they had surprising experiences.

One day when Jenny was on duty at the center, a GI shyly came up and asked to speak with Jenny privately. When they were alone, he asked Jenny to teach him some bust exercises. "My goodness, why?" she asked. The GI was reluctant to explain, saying that Jenny was too nice a girl to hear the reason. The discussion went around in circles until they made a bargain. Jenny would teach him two she knew if he would explain why he wanted them. It turned out just as Jenny had suspected: "He was a pimp, with a stable of Vietnamese prostitutes who thought bigger chests would mean more money. I remember thinking how shocked Washington Red Cross would be at one of my first center recreation activities."

Many of the men were regulars at the center, and the Red Cross women knew them well. They often comforted them in some personal unhappiness. Some of the men received Dear John letters and poured out their sorrow to the women, wanting to share the pain of their ended romances. Jenny knew the Red Cross women filled a role here. "From us, I think they sought sympathy. We could lament and give them our female reaction. Maybe through us they got a small, much needed, female reaffirmation of their self-image. They also could express the sadness of a lost love."

Jenny recalls "the deep anger and frustration of one of our center regulars." She says, "He told me he'd really taken to heart the army training films about wild strains of VD. He was avoiding all possibilities. Then he came back from R&R and got a diagnosis. He'd caught VD while on R&R in Hawaii—from his wife. I'd never seen such a jumble of emotion—sadness, anger, helplessness, bitterness, resignation, and on top of everything, a noble attempt to understand his wife. He seemed so lost."

The women's reactions to the casualties of the war varied person by person, but often it was numb acceptance. On Christmas Eve, Jenny and the others learned of a helicopter going down; the entire crew was killed. One of the door gunners had been a center regular—according to Jenny, a sweet young kid. There was no dramatic scene around Dong Ba Thin when the word came, just numb acceptance.

"We felt the loss," Jenny says, "but no one showed it beyond a sad shake of the head. The pervasive feeling was, 'When your number comes up, there's nothing you can do about it.' I suppose that philosophy was what got a lot of people through their tour. It certainly influenced me; I developed no fear of our daily helicopter jaunts or mortar attacks, or of visits to small fire bases." Jenny learned not to inquire about missing faces in the participation games out in the field.

There was, however, a universal sense of unfairness if someone who was scheduled to go home in a few days was killed. A superstitious feeling existed about having only a few days left to spend fighting in-country. Sometimes one of the other men took over a mission so that a man who was "short" would not go out and increase his risk of death; sometimes the man purposely defied fate by actually seeking out risk, as if to flout destiny.

In January, the Red Cross headquarters in Saigon decided to close the unit at Dong Ba Thin and move it to Tuy Hoa. Two of the women were reassigned elsewhere, one who was short went home, and Linda and Jenny went to Tuy Hoa, where two others from different units joined them.

The Tuy Hoa base, which housed several F-100 fighter squadrons, proved to be a social one with many amenities. The newest would be the Red Cross recreation center, and they would be the only women on the base. From the time they arrived and were whisked off to a fancy party at the officers club, Jenny, Linda, Candi, and Dorset attended one social function after another. Almost every day, they received invitations to picnics, barbecues, and parties of all kinds given by the various units on base. One evening the brass invited them over for a steak dinner at their quarters. They arrived promptly at the appointed time of 6:00 P.M. and found a general fussing over the baked potatoes and a full colonel ironing the tablecloth.

This sociable pattern lasted just four weeks for Jenny. She was promoted to program director at Cam Ranh Air Base. This air base proved to be even more social than Tuy Hoa. There were many nurses there. The squadrons gave parties with live bands, the officers club showed all kinds of movies, and the men and women played beach volleyball and swam off a lovely white sand beach. The nearby naval air facility even had a swimming pool. Washington headquarters had warned the Red Cross women that the more civilized and sophisticated rear areas might present a greater challenge to them than the remoter sites. Jenny discovered that they were right; the more stateside the base, the lower the morale. The men faced boredom.

At Cam Ranh the seven Red Cross members worked hard and long. They ran two recreation centers on opposite sides of the base, seven days a week, fourteen hours a day. A curfew kept them from burning the candle at both ends, but nevertheless, Jenny and the others found that they were exhausted, and they were frustrated that they could not be out in the field.

Luckily there were several exceptions to constant center duty. Cam Ranh Air Base had inherited the Bao Loc run from Jenny's old Dong Ba Thin unit, and she took that duty whenever she could. Also, once a week, on the invitation of the hospital, the women walked the wards. These men couldn't take part in any type of participation game, but the women brought activity books, and they found that the men were delighted just to have them there to talk to. In this duty, Jenny was lucky; she realized that this was a medical ward, because she saw no casualties from the fighting.

There was only one disturbing encounter. On the mental ward, one of the men was strapped to either side of his bed by leather wrist cuffs. He kept calling Jenny to come to his side, and finally she did. He pulled at his cuffs and pleaded with Jenny, "Get me out of here, get me out of here. Please help me!" Jenny felt inadequate. "All I could find to say was, 'Oh, but you need to stay here where they can help you. Everything will be okay.' Everything will be okay? Who was I trying to kid? I briefly looked at him again and couldn't come up with anything else to say. I glanced away and moved on."

Jenny found that Cam Ranh Air Base was too stateside for her taste, so she was elated by her promotion to unit director, assigned to the 4th Infantry Division of the U.S. Army in the central highlands. This was a real field assignment. The Red Cross unit there was completely mobile, since the recreation center of the division headquarters was run by the army's special services women. The Red Cross women flew out from headquarters at Camp Enari to the fire bases and the landing zones of the "Famous Fighting Fourth," where the men often lived in underground bunkers.

The women were housed in a long Quonset hut. At the front was a small dayroom area; individual cubbyholes for the women lined a long hallway. Each contained a bed, a table, and a footlocker. For privacy, long strips of plastic hung in the entryways. Outside, a dilapidated sandbag bunker stood next to the hut, and an MP was posted nearby. The showers and the nonflushing toilets were located down the sidewalk. The army special services women lived in a Quonset hut nearby. A seven-foot gray wood fence surrounded the entire area. The men called this female compound Fort Apache.

Jenny's spirits soared with each day's flight; she found the helicopter trips exciting. She and the other Red Cross women soon became good friends with the Huey and light observation helicopter pilots. They cajoled the pilots to fly them to as many of the fire bases and landing zones as possible. The pilots cheerfully transported them, and the women always hoped that the men would remember where they left them so they could return to pick them up. Jenny claims that the light observation helicopters were like flying eggshells with no doors; one could affect the line of flight by putting an arm out. One day when they were airborne, a Huey made a steep turn and a stack of C rations dropped away. Jenny made sure that she was securely fastened at all times.

The men had given names to all the 4th Division fire bases, landing zones, and brigade headquarters, such as Tiger, Gypsy, St. George, Meredith, Dot, Bison, Oasis, and Mary Lou. One day Jenny unexpectedly landed on Landing Zone Ann, an unscheduled stop at the very top peak of a mountain, really just a narrow ridge about one-fourth the length of a football field.

"It was really narrow. They popped green smoke for our chopper's landing. I swear, on that ridge it seemed that the tail rotor was out over one side and the nose over the other. It was a very small LZ, all bunkers. The latrine was a square crate with lye sprinkled at the bottom and no sides."

The women used their program bags to carry candles, cards, books, combs, pens, pocket mirrors, and so forth, which they gave to the men they visited. On this trip, by the time they reached Ann, they had given away all the items except for some hard candy. Jenny felt truly sorry that they had nothing more to give these men on their desolate mountaintop.

Hazards existed out in the field, some of them completely unexpected. One day Jenny and her partner June were visiting a landing zone where the men had lined up, a dozen at a time, to get one of June's famous haircuts. To amuse herself while waiting, Jenny visited the landing zone mascot, a monkey who was hopping around on a soldier's shoulder. Urged to shake hands with it, Jenny stuck out her finger, and the monkey promptly bit it. Jenny had painful visions of injecting needles in her stomach, but she was assured that the animal had had its necessary shots. She felt indebted to the veterinary corps in Vietnam.

Sometimes the women rode in the same helicopter that transported hot food to the men. Then they helped by serving it, often out in the open by the pup tents, since no mess tent had been erected. Sometimes the men who had been out on patrol straggled in, apologizing for their dirty, tired appearance.

The women always wore their light blue uniforms so they would be visible and the men would know that there were women on the base. Jenny heard the rumor that their blue uniforms made them great targets for Vietcong snipers, who supposedly would receive a reward for hitting one of them, thus damaging the men's morale. Jenny did not seriously worry about this possibility, although there was always danger out in the field.

Danger did strike one of the Red Cross's favorite fire bases. The women had regularly visited St. George, so they were quite shocked one morning to hear that it had been nearly overrun the night before. An army official asked the women to visit the St. George men who were no longer at St. George, but in the 71st Evacuation Hospital in Pleiku.

"We rushed over there with a vengeance—after all, these were *our* guys. Not only that, but these were the ones who always wanted to know about next week's program as we packed up each time. We couldn't believe it. But we got to the hospital and believed it. Here were the guys—previously laughing, joking game players—hurt, and hurt badly.

"We had to put on our smiles and not let them know we were

fighting back tears. We had to let them talk about what happened if that's what they wanted to do, or talk about anything *but* what happened. One guy wanted to talk, but to do so he had to press on a plastic device at the base of his throat. I held my breath and dug my fingernails into my palms as I conversed. The whole day was an emotional drain."

Jenny got to know the men when they came in from the bush to a fire base for what was known as a stand-down. During the stand-down the men would rest, bathe, and get hot food. They usually had time on their hands and thus were great program participants. One day, however, there was no time for games. The men were busy being reeducated. They had been fighting the North Vietnamese Army; now they would be fighting the Vietcong in a different kind of war, for which they needed knowledge of jungle tactics, booby traps, and punji sticks.

Jenny and the other Red Cross women often became friends with some of the Vietnamese. The mama-sans came every day to clean their rooms and do the laundry. Gaio, Jenny's mama-san, was young, sweet, pretty, and very pregnant with her third child. Her husband was in the Army of the Republic of Vietnam and was not at home, but her parents were when Jenny visited her in a village just outside Pleiku. Jenny noted the primitive conditions there: poverty, dust, and mud houses for homes.

Besides the Vietnamese in the central highlands, where the 4th Division was stationed, the Montagnards, a singular people, lived. They did not look Vietnamese or even Asian. They lived in their own villages in a tribal society. The men wore loincloths and the women went about bare-breasted. They hunted with crossbows and ground meal with stones. The 4th had civilian affairs teams assigned to these villagers to help with civil defense. They seemed loyal to the Americans and sympathetic to the South Vietnamese cause. They could, the army believed, be counted upon to stand and fight.

Jenny and June flew to one of the Montagnard villages to visit the men of the 4th. The locals extended hospitality to the women, who, Jenny was sure, were the first American women they had ever seen. They treated them to rice wine, which the women drank out of a straw from a large pottery urn. Jenny says the urn looked as though it was filled with hay, and the liquid tasted like bacon rinds.

When the women were back at the recreation center at Camp Enari, they were busy preparing their programs; they needed to decide on the shows, make the props, and figure out any dialogue and procedures. They also designed birthday cards, with a different card for each month. They found out who had birthdays during that period and where the mimeographed greetings could be sent. They addressed hundreds of cards.

Daily living always held surprises. One evening Jenny and some of the other women went to a movie projected onto a bed sheet at the officers mess hall, and when they returned to Fort Apache they found a note with some of their daintier underwear. Jenny read the note: "Donut dollies. This is to inform you of my deep remorse and regret due to a flagrant violation of moral principles. In a rare moment of unbridled passion I found myself compelled to abscound with these delicate articles of apparell. I was not responsible for my actions because of the flames of desire that welled within my burning breast. With most profound regrets, The Wayward Spider." Underneath the writing was a drawing of a spider on its web. And below that: "P.S. I hope you will find it in your heart to forgive this indisgression."

Finding out the identity of The Wayward Spider kept the women amused for a few days. They were determined to find out who he was. He had unobtrusively entered the hallway of their Quonset hut—an area off-limits to the men—and pilfered the garments from the interior clothesline that the women had strung down the hallway. They hadn't even noticed that any articles were missing, and here they were returned!

Days went by without a clue, but then someone let something slip, and the women discovered that their Wayward Spider was a Cobra pilot of 1/10 Cavalry Delta troop. They called him Spider from then on. Jenny reluctantly kept a tight rein on her heart to resist his charm and his antics. One night, his buddy said, he overindulged and decided to crawl along the beams over the band that was playing at their club that night, and he fell off and into the drums.

The days and nights were unpredictable. Jenny used the bunker only twice, but she thought the sessions there were miserable. The women could hear the artillery, but Jenny couldn't tell outgoing from incoming. Helicopters and fighters scrambled, and flares went up around the perimeter. The women sat in a rat-infested, mildewed bunker. Jenny says, "There was nothing to do but sit in the dark, listening to the sounds, hoping no one was getting hurt."

Jenny's time to leave Vietnam came as no surprise. She had been short for quite some time, and there were too many parties not to realize that there was a leaving time for everyone. Jenny explains her feelings then. "Partings were hard. . . . The 'world' was a very desirable destination, but it was also something that would engulf each of us. . . . Gone would be the camaraderie so unique to this experience. I remembered someone leaving Vietnam, when I was so new in-country. He had said, 'You know, as great as it is to be leaving, it's really sort of a bummer.' I now knew what he meant. . . . It was hard to let go, and it's still hard to let go."

On the plane crossing the Pacific headed for home, Jenny had plenty of time to think. She felt lucky that she had not experienced any real danger or trauma. During her year's tour she had seen "low morale, waste, stupidity, corruption, filth, and the clashing of two cultures." She had also seen sweetness and courage. "Paradox," she wrote later.

Back in the United States Jenny's family greeted her lovingly, but she worried about her younger brother facing the draft. Now twenty-three years old, she felt a letdown.

"I had experienced two unusual years back to back, where I witnessed headlines firsthand. Of those two years, my year in Vietnam would influence me for the rest of my life.

"Six weeks later I was in Chicago enduring a long, cold Midwest winter. I was in an all-female environment; for lack of anything better to do I was attending a business skills school to learn shorthand and polish up my typing. I went to classes in the morning, worked as a typist in a local bank in the afternoon, and worked back at the school office at night. I lived in a women's club. It was a miserable time.

"When I heard the announcement about Nixon moving troops into Cambodia, I cried and cried, pacing up and down in my little dormitory room. I cried because I wasn't still there. I cried for the guys who would still have to go to Vietnam, since it appeared we just couldn't end things over there. These guys just might include my two younger brothers. I cried for humankind, wondering why we keep repeating history—war after senseless war. I cried for the people of the United States, because I knew we'd been in Cambodia all along and therefore our government was capable of deception and distortion in what it told its people. I cried for myself, because I realized how much Vietnam was a part of me, and I was around no one who could understand."

Jenny was restless. She wanted a warmer climate, so she moved to Dallas. After a year there she met the man she would marry. He was a two-tour Vietnam veteran and an undercover narcotics agent. He and Jenny spoke of Vietnam only once or twice in the seven years before they divorced in 1979.

Jenny stayed on in Texas, working in human resources, first for a large oil company and then for the largest Texas bank. She did volunteer work for the Red Cross at the Veterans Administration Hospital and joined the Dallas Ski Club. Jenny stayed in Dallas for eighteen years until she accepted a position with a large bank in Boise, Idaho, where she continued to do volunteer work. She never remarried; her subsequent relationships were with men who had not gone to Vietnam. They only expressed passing interest, if any, in her background.

However, in Boise Jenny found that she was geographically close to Julie, one of her Red Cross cohorts at Cam Ranh Bay. They went on an organized trip to Vietnam together in November 1995. The memories came flooding back as they visited the places where they had served. Some of the mountain roads were at such high elevations that looking down at the terraced farming below, Jenny felt as though she were in a helicopter again.

Jenny was reminded of Vietnam again when she took a job in Santa Barbara the following year with an oil company exploring for oil in Venezuela, among a number of other locations. Jenny visited Venezuela five times in one year.

One recent Christmastime, Jenny went to an open house and met someone who mentioned Vietnam. He had been a marine. Jenny told him she had been there twice, in 1969 and 1995, but she wasn't a nurse. He looked at her and then asked, "Were you a donut dolly?"

Jenny recalls her reaction: "It was sort of nice to hear that question asked after all these years. We talked about the Vietnam Memorial wall and my experiences there. In describing the statue, how the artist had achieved the look, and how the three men symbolized the last patrol coming in, tears started running down my face, something that hadn't happened to me in years. Later, as he left the party, he sought me out and asked for a hug. We didn't have to say anything. That's the bond that's always out there."

Dorothy White Patterson

Dorothy White grew up and was educated in Illinois. After she graduated from Illinois State University in 1964, she taught for a year before volunteering for the Supplemental Recreational Activities Overseas (SRAO) Red Cross program in Vietnam. She took a year's leave of absence and joined the program. She trained for several weeks in Washington, D.C., in July 1967 before she flew off on a Braniff plane headed for Vietnam.

On the approach to Vietnam, the pilot announced that he would make a rapid descent to the airstrip at Bien Hoa, since enemy gunfire made it dangerous to descend gradually, and that the stewardesses would tell the passengers good-bye from inside the plane, avoiding any risks. The pilot's message made Dorothy wonder if she really knew what she had gotten herself into. She felt relieved when all the passengers exited the plane without incident. After customs checked their luggage at Tan Son Nhut Airport in Saigon, the Red Cross women boarded a bus for the Meyerkord Hotel downtown. They stayed in Saigon for five days for further orientation, at the end of which they received their duty assignments.

Dorothy considered her assignment a plum: the luxury army base at Cam Ranh, thirty minutes from the air force base. Here the

Red Cross operated two recreation centers: one at the headquarters of the field depot and the other at the 22d Replacement Center several miles to the north. The women lived in what they claimed were the nicest quarters in the country; three of them shared a three-bedroom, air-conditioned trailer.

At the recreation centers, Dorothy helped dispense coffee and Kool-Aid to the men, joined in many of the card games, and spent a great deal of time just visiting. Her favorite center was at the 22d Replacement Center, which, after the Tet Offensive of that year, quickly became filled with young GIs, most of whom were scared and wanted a sympathetic ear. Since they hadn't received their permanent assignments yet, they were fairly steady customers at the Red Cross center.

Dorothy found it hard to believe that she lived in a war zone, because she dealt mainly with behind-the-scenes people, not men fighting out in the field.

Technically, the Red Cross women here were called club mobile units, but they made few trips out of Cam Ranh. Dorothy found that the daily routine began to assume a boring sameness. She and the other women enjoyed many beautiful beaches, since Cam Ranh was a peninsula of sand, but they really delighted in the trips to several signal corps units by helicopter. The men participated enthusiastically in the Red Cross games, mainly because the games gave them a chance to spend time with the only American women around their center.

Dorothy stayed at Cam Ranh for six months. Memorable events there included battening down for a typhoon that never appeared and visits to the local orphanage—especially the Christmas party when toys sent by the women's families were distributed to surprised children.

Dorothy and some of the other women made occasional visits to Binh Ba Island, just off the coast, where U.S. Navy advisors trained the South Vietnamese Navy in the techniques of warfare. Dorothy was appalled at the primitive conditions there, and seeking to improve the sanitation in the area, she and some of the other Red Cross women brought bars of soap to give to young mothers so they could give their children good scrubbings. The women received a shock when they saw the mothers using the soap to scrub the pigs, which were kept on raised wooden platforms so they did not stand in the mud and dirt. Pigs made money for the local families, and the children could get cleaned when it rained or by swimming in the bay.

A few times Dorothy also visited Dalat, an R&R center in the central highlands. Dalat was nestled high in the mountains. The Americans taught the Vietnamese how to garden successfully; the produce prospered, and the women who visited Dalat always came back to base with copious supplies of lettuce and other fresh foodstuffs.

Dorothy transferred the next year to An Khe, also in the central highlands, a spot that was completely the opposite of Cam Ranh. While sand surrounded Cam Ranh, high-altitude trees and mountains clustered around An Khe. During Tet of 1968 the Victcong blew up the airstrip at An Khe, so Dorothy's move was not made until some time after it was scheduled. At An Khe the women lived in private hooches like those occupied by the GIs. Mosquito netting covered the beds. There might be hot water on a sunny day; otherwise, cold showers became a part of the daily routine. The women also caught the rainwater that ran off the roof so they would have a supply if the water tanks were not filled.

At An Khe all the men were infantrymen of the 1st Air Cavalry and the 173d Airborne. They headed out to the field to fight and only came back to base for a short recuperation or rest time; then they headed back into the battle.

The men, usually tired and scared, needed to talk to the Red Cross women to vent their feelings and frustrations. Dorothy found that she really had to fight to keep up her morale and not become depressed. She and one of her coworkers, Jan, became especially attached to the men of the 173d Long Range Reconnaissance Patrol. The men went out in groups of seven or eight and scouted the area for enemy troops. The danger proved great, with high casualties.

The women spent a lot of time in helicopters and Jeeps visiting troops at fire support bases around the countryside. They visited landing zones with names such as English, Schuler, Ollie, Mustang, Uplift, and Pony. Usually, two women worked at the recreation center each day and the rest flew out in teams of two in different directions. Sometimes they accompanied the mail runs and only had brief visits at the various bases that received mail. On other days, they went on hot meal runs and helped serve the food to troops who had been existing on C rations for several days.

Though security remained tight for the base that housed the women, sometimes the women evaded the rules. One day Dorothy and a few of the other women talked some GIs into taking them to a local village just outside the base, looking for a Vietnamese rice separator they hoped to buy. They walked up and down the streets of the village without success and finally returned to base. They were chagrined when they discovered that they had acted foolishly: the local village was a stronghold of the Vietcong.

The twenty-four women who had left for Vietnam on the same day met again on 23 July 1968 for the return trip to the United States. As a group of Red Cross women in their new, clean uniforms deplaned from the bright blue Braniff aircraft, Dorothy and the other women who had finished their tours boarded in their faded, slightly soiled old uniforms. Dorothy envied the new women for the experiences they would have, yet eagerly awaited picking up the threads of stateside living.

Dorothy returned to her teaching job, from which she had taken a year's leave of absence. She received a warm and interested welcome. She spent most of her first year back giving slide shows and talks about her experiences in Vietnam. She met her husband-to-be the summer he returned from his tour in Vietnam, and they were married in July 1974. They have a daughter who is now twenty-one years old and a senior at the University of Illinois.

Dorothy is still teaching first grade and is still communicating with other Red Cross workers who were in Vietnam when she was.

Martha L. Royse

Martha L. Royse was born in Missouri, attended school there, and then went to college at Illinois State Normal University with a major in health, physical education, and recreation. While she was working at her first job, teaching in Illinois, World War II broke out and she was recruited for the USO. She served with the USO in club work in Texas, Utah, and Hawaii until the war ended. A stint with the YMCA followed, and then Martha was recruited by the American Red Cross as a hospital recreation worker. She was at Elmendorf Air Force Base in Alaska while Vietnam patients came through for three years, and then went to a mainland naval hospital before being assigned to the USS Sanctuary off the coast of Vietnam.

Martha Royse flew into the Saigon airport on 6 December 1970, and stayed in the city for a few days while the Red Cross supervisors gave her a quick orientation to the area and the work facing her. Then she boarded a small plane and flew to Da Nang. The Red Cross staff met her there and arranged for her to board a small craft which took her out to a hospital ship, the USS *Sanctuary*.

The USS *Sanctuary* was a floating hospital that rode the waters off the coast of Vietnam between the 15th Parallel and the demilitarized zone. It had 750 beds—bunks—and four operating rooms. Half of the ship's six hundred personnel worked in the hospital, with the staff normally including two dozen navy doctors, three dentists, twenty-nine nurses, and two Red Cross workers.

The hospital's facilities included a heart-lung machine, a kidney machine, a blood bank, an optical shop, and a dental clinic. Although it had been commissioned in 1945, the *Sanctuary* was recommissioned in 1966 to support the Vietnam conflict.

Martha was impressed. The only disturbing factor was when she felt a touch of apprehension as she began climbing the accommodation ladder to the upper deck of the ship. It was a bit scary, but later on the repeated process became, she says, "no sweat."

Martha's Red Cross roommate had arrived a few days before and now took over the job of acquainting Martha with their cabin and the rest of the ship. Martha took an instant liking to her roommate; she was young and friendly, and seemed talented. The cabin had an upper and lower bunk, one closet, a pull-down desk apiece, a bath basin, two big drawers under their bunks, and a hallway to the showers and toilets. Several decks below was their office, about twelve feet square, with two desks and storage room for games, guitars, tapes and tape players, and other recreation items, as well as a stock of ditty bags filled with toothbrushes, combs, mirrors, and other personal items to be distributed to the men who were brought to the ship.

Two groups of professionals ran the ship: the crew, who took care of the ship, and the hospital staff, who took care of the patients. Martha liked them all. Large helicopters flew the patients to the hospital ship from aid stations, or sometimes directly from the field, the men still covered with mud. The medics were alerted when patients were arriving, so when the helicopters landed on the aft deck, they were there with stretchers to carry the wounded down to the triage ward nearby, where the doctors immediately examined them and designated where each patient was to be taken.

The surgery suites were located several decks below the top deck because that area was more stable, suffering less from the movement of the ship. Treatment was given as quickly as possible, and as soon as a patient stabilized, he was prepared for air evacuation to Japan or the United States. Or, if he was patched up quite well, he was returned to duty.

Instead of beds in the wards there were suspended bunks, two and sometimes three high. The first comments the patients most often offered were, "Oh boy, white sheets and a mattress," and then, "Whee, pretty young nurses in their beautiful white uniforms."

The Red Cross women provided nonmedical services for the patients which helped alleviate stress and worry. They sent and received messages using the ship's radio facility. Either the families sent reports about their health and welfare or the patients sent such messages back to their families. If the families requested, the doctors sent their patients' reports back through the Red Cross chapters in the United States.

One of the less serious duties Martha and her roommate performed was to deliver new baby announcements to the crew from their wives back home. Recreation activities for all those who were physically able to participate included games, cards, listening to tapes, playing guitars, and making small voice recordings to be mailed home. Martha was often called upon to write letters for the men who were unable to do so, and to carry out other requests they might make.

It was only a matter of days after Martha arrived on shipboard that plans were made for the Christmas celebration. Everyone pitched in to decorate the wards in as cheerful a holiday fashion as possible. Luckily, groups and individuals back in the United States had made quantities of delicious cookies which the Red Cross sent to the ship, so there were plenty of supplies for the coffee and cookie calls that were held for everyone in the aft lobby. On Christmas Eve Bob Hope and some of his troops, notably Les Brown and Lola Felani, went out to the ship and put on a show on the top deck for the ambulatory and wheelchair patients. After the show, Hope toured the wards to greet those who were unable to make it to the aft deck. Then several Santas distributed Christmas presents to everyone—presents that had been donated by groups such as the Colonial Dames of America.

Daily shipboard living and working were fairly routine. The exciting times occurred when the ship took on fuel, supplies, movies, or people. The last were carted aboard in a sling chair that moved parallel to the supplying ship. The total process of loading up took several hours. Perhaps a more pleasurable event, although a less frequent one, was when Martha, off duty, took a small craft ashore to shop at the PX or go to the Red Cross club.

The USS *Sanctuary* was scheduled to leave the area. The Department of Defense had announced earlier that year that the ship would be retired as part of a phased reduction to achieve a smaller, more modern navy. The ship had treated more than twenty-three thousand U.S. and Allied troops and civilians since 1967. In May 1970, it sailed for the United States.

Martha went with the ship to Hong Kong, then flew back to Vietnam to finish her yearlong tour. She was assigned to the U.S. Army Hospital in Saigon for the next seven months. The hospital had formerly been a school and was spread out over several blocks. The job for the Red Cross women was basically the same as before: to handle the social work problems and communications for the bed patients, and to work with various volunteers who shopped, wrote letters, and did other personal chores for the patients. Some of Martha's patients recovered sufficiently to be returned to duty, while others were medevaced to the United States. Life in the big city of Saigon was far different from that of the shipboard days.

The time at the hospital was busy and went by quickly. Soon Martha's tour was at an end. She flew back to the United States in December 1971.

Unlike many women who returned from duty in Vietnam and Southeast Asia, Martha found that her family and friends were interested in hearing about her service, both on the ship and in the Saigon hospital. She encountered no one who was hostile because she had helped out in the Vietnam War. Before she began a retelling of her life in Vietnam, she always prefaced her remarks by stating that if any circumstances were such that she, as an individual, could help in any way, she was ready to do so, no matter what it meant.

Martha recalls that when she joined the American Red Cross as a professional worker one of the major questions she was asked was, "Can you be mobile?" Little did she know then that mobility would mean twenty-four moves for her, both stateside and overseas, in Alaska, Libya, the Philippines, Germany, Korea (in a MASH), and Vietnam, over a period of thirty-one years.

Since retirement, Martha has been involved in volunteer jobs such as Meals on Wheels, Tele Care, and Friends of the Library. She is doing some traveling and enjoying her friends and her cat.

Mary Blanchard Bowe

As an army dependent, Mary Blanchard Bowe moved with her family often as she was growing up. Mary lived in New York, Greece, Washington D.C., Italy, Taiwan, New Mexico, Georgia, and Texas before attending and graduating from St. Louis University in St. Louis, Missouri. When she was a senior at the university, one of her roommates decided she wanted to join the Red Cross. That idea sounded good to Mary, and her reaction was, "I'll go try it too." After graduation she volunteered for Red Cross duty in Vietnam and was accepted. Her protester sisters were opposed, but her parents felt she was old enough to decide her future for herself. Thus, in July 1968 Mary flew off to Vietnam.

Mary Bowe's plane took off from Travis Air Force Base near Sacramento, California. About a half-hour into the flight, the captain came on and told the passengers that he would be turning back because part of the wing had fallen off. The military men roared and cheered, because now they had an extra day before going to Vietnam. The next morning when the plane took off again, the men seemed subdued; this trip would surely take them back to the war.

After a long flight Mary arrived in Vietnam, and as her first assignment, she joined the Red Cross women at Dong Ba Thin, the base for the Army Corps of Engineers. The day proved to be an unfortunate introduction to the life of a troop morale builder in Vietnam. Five of the men from the base had been killed; the funeral was the day Mary landed. Mary was shaken. She sensed the sad atmosphere and later recalled that "all of sudden the reality of war hit me real hard. I didn't even know these guys, but I just felt a tremendous loss. I suddenly realized, *This is it; this is Vietnam.*"

Mary spent her time on two basic projects at Dong Ba Thin. One centered on helping the five other women with the creation and preparation of the materials for their programs, whether for the troops at the recreation center or for those out in the boonies. Mary became friends with a quiet, capable GI who came into the center often to talk. She discovered that whenever she told him about a program or game she planned to develop, he quickly and easily sketched it out for her. Mary found his work just what she needed, and she began calling him Art, short for artist. Art was a gunner in a helicopter. He and Mary spent many hours talking together, becoming good friends and enjoying each other's company. Then the unexpected happened.

"One day I was riding in a helicopter up to visit a unit and the gunner said to me, 'Did you know Art died?' I was so shocked because I had just seen him the night before. I think the thing that stands out most in my mind was that he risked his life. He saved all of the other people in the helicopter when it crashed and started burning up. He went back to save them and he got burned himself and just died. I think that was one of the saddest moments that I had over there."

Mary and the other Red Cross women rotated their jobs of running the center and going out into the field to carry out their programs with the troops. She and the others visited Cam Ranh, Tuy Hoa, Phan Thiet, and the radio research center.

Mary's second occupation at Dong Ba Thin consisted of writing to all the radio stations she could to secure music to play on a tape recorder. She and one of the other women wrote and wrote and wrote, and finally they got two tapes back. They played them over and over in the recreation center, and the men thought the records, including the commercials, were wonderful.

Soon Mary was transferred to Pleiku, where the army's 4th Division was stationed at Camp Enari. Here she flew in helicopters almost every day; the women were in a mobile unit and flew to all the fire bases they could reach, using whatever helicopter team was in the area. Among the helicopters was a little chopper Mary called "the bubble," which had no doors and only enough room for three people. A passenger sat on either side of the pilot. Mary had never before flown in any craft that small, and she was truly frightened, but after fifteen minutes of pilot loops and ups and downs she found that it was a wonderful and exhilarating experience. From that time on she loved to fly. She found flying over the tops of trees a magnificent way of clearly seeing the beautiful country below.

One day a week Mary worked at the recreation center on base. Various attitudes toward possible personal danger surfaced there when they experienced incoming enemy fire.

"One time I was just so tired that I decided to sleep. Suddenly there was incoming and the siren went off. We all were supposed to go to the bunkers. I said, 'Well, if I'm going to die, I'm going to die asleep, because I'm so tired.' So I just stayed there in bed. Our director came, and she was so angry with me. 'Don't you know you could have been killed?'

"Yeah,' I said, 'but I was so tired.' What good would it have been if a shell had hit, or a mortar had hit? What good would it have been for me to be in the bunker?

"Some people had elaborate ways of going to the bunkers. There were people who would take whatever kind of liquor they could find and just sit in there and drink. They figured if they were going to die, they might as well die happy—partying. There were other people who took books and stuff like that. The bunker was kind of a place where a lot of things happened."

At Camp Enari Mary learned to be a disc jockey and to cue records. She had become friends with one of the women of the Army Special Services, Candy, who shared the compound with the Red Cross women. When she was called back to the United States because of the death of her mother, Candy asked for volunteers to take over her radio show for the American Forces Vietnam Radio and Television. Mary eagerly volunteered, and from that point on she received a modicum of fame as "Mary, the record librarian."

"What I wanted to do", she said of her evening radio show, "was to take requests from the guys that were on fire bases and in the field. They thought that was a great idea. So I was called 'Mary the record librarian' and they always played the song 'Along Comes Mary' before I came on the air."

The Red Cross women visited the fire bases, did their programs, and then asked for requests for the show. The reaction was great. Some men said they really liked Mary, the record librarian. Others, who didn't know Mary was a doughnut dolly, said that the record librarian was "so down to earth, and so funny, and that she didn't know what she was doing." In later years Mary realized she was young and "so crazy . . . acting so silly and everything. Here these guys were going out on patrols and in long-range action units. They must have thought, 'Wow, this girl is really dingy.' But at the time I was naïve, and I was just spreading sunshine, so to speak."

Mary knew that she never achieved a proficiency that would qualify her for a disc jockey position in the United States, but in Vietnam, she said she "got good enough so I did the programs by myself. If I fouled up, it wasn't that big of a deal. The show was great. It felt like I was holding people in the palm of my hand, from that one little tiny room. I had a lot of help from the AFVN [Armed Forces Vietnam Network] team stationed at Pleiku; they kept me on my toes."

The requests came in from different units, and Mary tried to make sure that she got them all in every night, dedicated to the men so that they would know somebody cared. "It made me feel good. Of course, I really enjoyed it when I went on forward runs. They never knew who I was."

The women planned to go out and visit the troops on the fire bases at Christmastime, but there were no helicopters available. At a dinner at a general's compound, Mary managed to tell the general about the thwarted trip. He immediately and generously offered his helicopter and his aides to take the women to as many fire bases as time permitted. In her enthusiasm for the outing, Mary insisted on playing Santa Claus in the outfit the Red Cross women had received from the United States. She stuffed her stomach area, plastered on a cotton beard and mustache, and topped the outfit with a Santa hat. Mary knew she looked hilarious, but that was what she wanted to do.

They left at 6:00 A.M. on Christmas Eve and flew to ten different fire bases, where they saw nearly nine hundred men. Mary sat in the front of the helicopter, and on arriving at each base, she leaned out and shouted, "Ho ho ho, merry Christmas." She had a hard time moving around in her stuffed suit, and it was very hot, but the men took turns sitting on Santa's knee. They took many snapshots and everyone sang carols. Mary was thrilled. "It just made me feel so good to see all that smiling and laughter and fun. I guess I made an impact on some people's lives, and I know the visits made an impact on mine."

Mary continued her Santa work that evening when the women went around the perimeter of the base camp, caroling for three hours. When the compound was secure it was difficult to allow travel around the perimeter, especially for women, but the army chaplain got permission for Santa—Mary—and her elves—the other Red Cross women—to go with him as he said mass and passed out communion. Mary said later, "I felt touched by the experience of singing carols with war all around us, and celebrating at mass made a definite difference in my outlook on life and the true meaning of Christmas." As Santa, she shook hands with all the men.

On Christmas Day Mary was Santa again, first along the bunker line at Camp Enari, and then at the Dak To and Oasis fire bases. The men in these remote areas were enthusiastically appreciative of the chance to sit on Santa's knee or to pinch Santa in the stomach. Mary enjoyed it all.

Mary had been keeping a journal; now the entries became concerned not so much with activities, but with thoughts and feelings. As the war went on and the days went by, reports of more and more casualties came in. A high school friend, who Mary describes as "nice and gung ho," was killed. Mary found it difficult to cope. She wrote: "I guess I just reached the 'too many' stage at that point. This war . . . I came here with enough strength to cope, but I'm afraid I don't have enough strength to understand the whys. . . . I can't begin to express how awful I think this war is. Taking from us so many wonderful people; where does it all stop?"

Mary began to wonder about her role.

"Does a smile and a game really take away the tragedy of fighting a war? I wonder. I will continue to smile for my guys here . . . but I need the strength and the reason behind it all. The reason behind the senseless killing, to be able to *really* smile and *really* feel. I feel like some kind of a traitor sometimes, because I honestly want us to get out. I can't take any more deaths. I truly want us to reach out and take hands and have peace."

For a time Mary turned to her religion, which she called the one stable part of her life. On one run back from the camps at fire base Mary Lou, Mary's helicopter ran into a severe storm and the pilot had to land by instruments. When she was up in the chopper and couldn't see a thing, Mary became really afraid for herself and wondered what death would be like.

She wrote: "So I prayed. Yet these guys face this feeling every day out in the boonies. They must have to grow up fast. . . . Why should anyone really be sacrificed? I can't help agreeing with the thought that this has been eight years of a senseless war. But then again, I have a twinge of patriotism about the feeling of freedom which I have enjoyed my twenty-two years. Then it comes down to the same idea of what is really necessary to perpetuate our safeguard for freedom. Who is to say?"

Mary spent a great deal of time thinking about life and death. She could not help it. As part of their Red Cross duty, the women went on hospital runs to visit the wounded men and try to bring cheer into their lives, if only for a few minutes. One day they went to the 71st Evacuation Hospital. Mary was always sent, because it was known that she agreed to go whenever she was asked. It was hard for her because of the injuries she encountered, and the trips made her sad, but she always ended up going on the runs.

One day she visited a unit that had been caught in a Vietcong ambush, from which only twenty-five people had escaped. When Mary saw the men, she felt "useless in offering any type of help. I saw so many familiar faces, with arms off and shot up. I just felt completely down and out."

Mary wrote after this visit: "I just want to escape from everything and everyone. Today I want to go home, to do crazy things; to walk on the beach and look out and see a happy world where people laugh and look into each other's eyes and see good, not bad. To laugh long and hard and feel fun and happy. . . . I want to just run home and forget that I ever saw such suffering. When I returned from the hospital, I spent some time thinking how lucky I was to be me."

Luck did play a part in Mary's life in Vietnam. One day they visited a fire base and were waiting for a helicopter to return to base. One came along, but Mary could not get on because it was full; she was told to wait for the next one. The helicopter took off. It was almost immediately hit by enemy fire, and went down. Mary watched it with an amazed feeling; she could have been on that chopper.

Enemy fire slammed Camp Enari often, usually by mortars at night. But one day just before Mary transferred out, she heard incoming rounds at about 8:30 A.M. She was in bed and had no energy to move. She knew she should go to the bunker. She recalls, "I just rolled over and said, 'Well, maybe they're going to hit me, but if they're going to, they're going to hit me in my sleep.' Because I was so used to getting up early, that extra hour of sleep when you worked at base camp was really cherished." As it turned out, a bunker was hit and a mess hall was demolished. Thirteen were wounded.

Mary spent her last two months in-country in humid Qui Nhon on the coast. Life at this base varied greatly. Sometimes the enemy fire on the TV mountain and on the tank farms in the area was flagrantly fierce. On other occasions both the troops and the women shared enjoyable events. On July 4th the recreation center sponsored a scavenger hunt, and for the first time in a long time, Mary found herself laughing.

Mary mentally prepared to go home. She wondered how she would find the American way of life.

She wrote, "I cringe when I hear the news from home. It wouldn't be so bad if the guys here knew that they had a little support from the home front. But all they hear in the news media is about the youth and the harassing groups and everywhere they turn there is dissension. They have that constant question I always hear, 'What am

I doing here? Why? Why doesn't anyone like me? Why don't the people support us? Why are they against us? What did I do to them?' I have no answer. I just smile and have a program to take to them."

Mary was now "short," the name for someone ending a tour of duty and leaving Vietnam. Again, all kinds of thoughts assailed her. She sensed the bond she would always have with the Vietnam veterans. She was bitter about the friends who had died. She was glad to be a short-timer, but also felt that when she left her whole life would end. "As happy as I am to see my family and take a bath, I'm scared and I feel lonely. I admit I am tired of smiling and the age-old question of 'Why are you here?' and yet I'm not tired of the attention and the love that I have felt here."

Mary knew she would miss all the people she was leaving behind. So it was with a bit of sadness, combined with joy about returning home and a fear of what she would find in American society, that Mary boarded the freedom bird for the long trip back to the United States in August 1969.

After Mary got off the plane late at night, as she was waiting for a friend to pick her up, she saw two women in the airport shoving and pushing on a machine. They got very upset because the coffee did not come out of the machine properly. One remarked, "Dumb machines," and the other chimed in, "They never work."

Mary first thought, *A machine, an actual machine!* Then her reaction changed. "I thought about what I'd been through and how these people were getting upset about something so stupid as that. I was home."

Mary was met at that late-night arrival by a friend who brought champagne to celebrate. Mary kissed the ground, she was so glad to be back. She spent the night at a motel and enjoyed the luxuries of a bathtub and a toilet. The next morning she could hardly wait to get dressed and go shopping.

"While I was in one store and was paying I struck up a conversation and it led to me being in Vietnam. The lady got enraged, threw the change in my face, spat at me, and called me a warmonger. I got out of there fast, tears rolling down my face. As I stepped outside and started walking a car backfired. I hit the dirt immediately.

When I realized what had happened I got up, embarrassed. It was strange; I felt out of place.

"I flew into San Antonio after visiting my brother's family in San Diego, and I arrived with huge hives on my face—a reaction to food or to the incident, I never knew. Again I soaked in a tub in the comfort of my parents' home, feeling safe and realizing that I should keep my mouth shut.

"On return I had my tonsils out and then took off in my VW bug to see the U.S.A. I went to San Francisco to search for a job and an apartment. I worked at United California Bank. I had many moments of depression and crying jags. I later learned it was post-traumatic something."

In general, Mary encountered a half-hostile, half-apathetic attitude toward Vietnam veterans. She learned not to talk about her experiences, and no one asked or wanted to hear about her days in Vietnam. Except for her family, she was received only lukewarmly by the people she later encountered.

Mary worked at the bank in San Francisco for two years and then graduated with a teaching certificate from Trinity University in San Antonio, Texas, in 1972. She embarked on a bilingual and English teaching career, and to date has completed twenty-seven successful years.

Mary remembers many events of Vietnam clearly after thirty years. Being in Vietnam changed her from an innocent, naïve, wild, fraternity party college girl into a sensitive, thoughtful, responsible adult, aware of the fears and horrors of war.

June Smith

June Smith grew up in a tiny West Texas town sixty-seven miles from Lubbock. She graduated from college, and after a few months of teaching thirty-two second graders, she decided she must do something other than teach. A friend told her about the Red Cross program in Vietnam, and she applied and was accepted. She trained in Washington, D.C., and flew off on a Braniff aircraft in July 1969.

June Smith and the other Red Cross recruits from her training class, along with assorted military males, landed at the Tan Son Nhut airfield in Saigon. When the door of the plane opened, the air that rushed in smelled and felt to June like an old wet wool blanket. After they went through Vietnamese customs, the women made a stop at the Red Cross offices; then they were taken to a downtown Saigon hotel. They lived there for a week, assimilating more instructions: how to make and present recreation programs for the men, how to take two types of malaria pills, and how to maintain liaison with the command at military bases. They also learned a smattering of local customs and of the Vietnamese language.

The Red Cross assigned the women to their living complex, known as Fort Apache, at Camp Enari. This was the home base of the 4th Infantry Division, in the highlands near Pleiku. Immediately, June got sick with dysentery. She recovered slowly. When the women began their programming, June was kept on runs around the base camp, where the latrine was handy, while the other women went out in the field to the fire support bases.

Housing for the women was in two Quonset huts. It was hard to do much to personalize their quarters, but June found some brightly colored Christmas wrapping paper. She taped it to the plastic window, hoping it would lend her sleeping cubicle some cheer.

The monsoon season came with the fall. It rained with torrential force and for a time did not let up day or night. The dirt roads became impassable and the drainage ditches on base turned into rushing rivers. The sucking mud created by the downpours often took the boots right off of a person's feet. One time June and her partner Linda were caught at Camp Holloway in a bad rain and couldn't get back to Camp Enari. They went to bed in a hooch borrowed from a captain. No sooner had they retired than Holloway began receiving incoming fire. The women reached the nearest bunker, a little dugout underground. They crawled on their stomachs to get into it; they could not stand up, but by necessity walked around hunched over on their knees. When a rat ran into her hair as she lay trying to sleep, June crawled out of that bunker. She finally stayed in the command bunker for the night.

During the monsoon season June and her partner of the day ran their programs at a fire support base. When the chopper came to fetch them, June could not find her raincoat, so she left without it. The rain slashed down as the chopper pilot made his way back to Camp Enari at high altitude, and June got thoroughly chilled. The next day the doctors diagnosed her with pneumonia. June ended up at the 21st Field Hospital at Pleiku. She was the only woman in the hospital, so she was placed in a cubbyhole from which a desk and chair had been removed. The staff tacked up a sheet around the space; in essence, June had a private room. After a ten-day hospital stay, she recovered and was again able to participate in the visits to the men in the boonies.

The women created three new programs each week. They brainstormed on Saturday mornings, and then they divided the tasks of making the props, game boards, cue cards, or whatever was needed among the women in the unit. June admits that these programs "might seem trivial and silly," but, she says, they diverted the men's attention away from the war for at least a few moments.

Not long after June recovered from pneumonia she transferred to Cam Ranh Bay. She found the amenities there relatively luxurious. The eight Red Cross women lived in two trailer houses within an area of other trailer houses for army special services women, USO women, and other civilians.

Cam Ranh was a replacement depot for personnel coming into the country at that time, so there were always new faces. The women rotated between center duty and programming in the forward areas. Morale at the Cam Ranh base camps was low, mainly because the men didn't want to be there; they wanted to be out in the field. One day June and her day partner, Carol, had a miserable time. They went to three stops, and there were only two or three people at each. So they cancelled the rest of their runs for the day and went over to the noncommissioned officers club and ate hamburgers. That was the first and only time June failed to perform her duties. She found that the poor morale of the men severely dampened her enthusiasm.

On Christmas Day, the Red Cross women helped the engineers host a highly successful party for a group of Vietnamese orphans. Soon after that, June transferred again. She hitched a helicopter ride to her new post, Nha Trang, where she helped to close out the camp center because the Red Cross thought that the war was winding down. (It was then 1970.) She did some programming at the base camps and at some of the fire support bases before she moved on to An Khe.

To her surprise, the men of the 4th Infantry Division, whom she had met when they all were at Camp Enari, were stationed there.

June and the other Red Cross workers went on fire base runs and also visited the hospital as part of their routine. At the hospital June saw all kinds of patients, and the visits depressed her. An Khe received incoming fire from time to time, and one night June ran down to the bunker for the hospital patients but found it full. She went down the road, sat on the front steps of the chapel, and looked out over the open field where the helicopters were parked. To her astonishment the helicopters were being blown up by the Vietcong, who had somehow gotten onto the base.

Although the Red Cross women were known as donut dollies, they did not pass out doughnuts. However, June's group at An Khe decided to be the exception. The cook made a giant batch of doughnuts, and the women flew out into the field and distributed them to the grateful men.

Toward the end of her tour of duty, June saw or heard about a number of events that greatly distressed her. She heard that the men on perimeter guard saw the Vietcong come through the wire and requested permission to fire, and that permission was denied. When June heard this she felt depressed. She wondered: were the Americans in Vietnam to win the war, or just to go through the motions, wasting U.S. servicemen's lives? At the helipad, she often saw the choppers bring in body bags. That sight and her visits to the hospital severely upset her, as did the conditions she saw out in the boonies.

"It seemed like the guys became younger and younger and more ragged as the months went by. On several of the fire support bases the boys had been out three months with no stand-down. Their uniforms were in shreds and their behinds were showing through. Their combat boots were rotting on their feet. I kept thinking, 'Is this the way the United States government takes care of its own?' I took pictures of these young troops in their ragged uniforms. Some nights I would come back home to my room and cry thinking about what I had seen and the conditions that these young men had to live with out in the field. But they never complained."

On one of her last forward runs, June returned to Camp Enari, her first unit. She and her partner visited the perimeter guards, who were still securing what was left of it since the 4th had moved to An Khe.

June wrote of her visit: "It was a strange feeling flying into what had once been such a thriving, alive base camp. The buildings were deserted; a lot of them were torn down. I had a chance to go back to our old hooch, in Fort Apache. It was like visiting a graveyard. The Quonset hut was still there but the bath fixtures had been ripped out. The floor tile for the front room had been pried up.

The furniture was all gone. It was pretty well ransacked. I walked through the quiet mess and went into my old room. The Christmas paper that I had put over the window as decoration was still there. I peeled it off. There was my cardboard name tag, which I had been given in D.C.—I had accidentally left it on the sill and it had been hidden by the Christmas paper. I picked it up and took it. It was time for me to go."

June Smith left Vietnam on a commercial plane bound for Japan, took a week and a half delay on the way home, and arrived in California in mid-July 1970. She had minireunions there with friends from Vietnam and then flew on to Lubbock, Texas, where her parents and sisters greeted her with big "Welcome Home" banners.

Not long after arriving home, June became restless and began to seek a job. She hoped for one that would involve travel. She applied to five different airlines, but they all told her she was too tall to be considered for the position of hostess. She was too underweight and undereducated to be hired by the FBI as an agent. She was unmarried, so ARAMCO in Saudi Arabia did not want her.

She finally found a job as a programming assistant at a Lubbock radio station. From there she took a job as a secretary at a Dallas television station; then she switched occupations and became a Dallas police officer, and later a special agent for the U.S. Drug Enforcement Administration. This job ended when she broke her back and arm in an off-duty accident. When she recovered, June returned to Dallas, where she worked in banking until the bank was merged out of existence.

The idea of teaching attracted June again. She volunteered as a mentor for a South Dallas high school, and finally, she moved back to her small hometown in West Texas and began to teach elementary school again.

June remarks, "I have now come full circle. . . . I am right back where I started from some thirty-five years ago."

Linda Sullivan Schulte

Linda Sullivan was born in Richmond, Virginia, grew up in Baltimore, and graduated from Western Maryland College. She was active on campus and vocal about protesting the Vietnam War. When Army Commanding Gen. Lewis Walt returned from Vietnam and lectured at the college, he challenged Linda to go to Vietnam to see the truth about the war for herself. She accepted his challenge, and three weeks after her graduation in May 1968, she left on a bright blue airplane for Saigon and a year's commitment to the American Red Cross.

When the blue plane filled with servicemen and -women lifted its wheels from the runway at Travis Air Force Base in California, headed for Vietnam, everyone cheered—an act that was unusual for those taking off for the warfront.

The plane had started in that direction the previous day but had turned back, dumped fuel, and returned to the base when the crew became aware that something was drastically wrong with the right engine. The plane vibrated severely, and when it touched down, part of the engine fell off and skipped along the runway. Thus, the cheers on the following day were for safety, not for the destination.

Like most newcomers, after Linda landed she was briefed at the Military Assistance Command Vietnam headquarters in Saigon and received her orders for her first unit assignment, in Lai Khe, just north of Saigon. She was to work with the 1st Infantry Division, known popularly as the Big Red One. Linda climbed aboard a helicopter and the pilot made the trip at treetop level, hoping to spook the new Red Cross woman. Linda wasn't fazed; she loved flying of any kind.

Lai Khe, an old rubber tree plantation, charmed Linda, as did the infantrymen stationed there. Their leaders, Commanding Gen. Keith Ware and the 3d Brigade's Col. William Patch, and the three other Red Cross women welcomed her warmly.

Linda's first assignment in the field was full of mistakes. Linda and another new worker, Suzi, gave the helicopter pilot the code word for their destination, a special place near Loch Ninh, which was an old airstrip controlled variously by the "good guys" and the "bad guys." They landed, got out, and waved good-bye to the pilot, who protested leaving them on the strip. Linda and Suzi expected the GIs to appear, but they did not; all they saw were women in pointed hats and black clothes working in the high grass alongside the landing strip. Soon another helicopter landed and Gen. Orwin Talbott, assistant commander for the Big Red One, came striding over to them.

"What in the hell are you doing out here?"

General Talbott had been flying reconnaissance, and when he looked earthward, he had seen the two blue dots on the runway. He directed his pilot to swoop down and fetch them. The code word was obviously wrong; this area was unsafe. So the general rescued the women, plucked them out of the red clay, and escorted them back to the base.

From that time on, Generals Ware and Talbott became good friends with the Red Cross women. They often invited them to the officers mess for what the women called marvelous meals. And the women took General Ware's German shepherd, King, to their hearts.

Then came Friday, 13 September 1968. General Ware and his crew were watching a ground fight from his helicopter that day.

Linda says, "Something happened and the command chopper crashed, killing all onboard. I cried myself to sleep that night and had barely gotten myself together by the time of the memorial service the next day. As I entered the chapel, I noticed the eight pairs of boots and helmets lined up in a row at the front. Next to the helmet with the general's stars was a leash. I couldn't stop sobbing. If there was a defining moment for me this was it. I realized that there was more to peace than merely wanting it."

Linda and the three other Red Cross women in Lai Khe continued to plan entertainment for the men. Two of the women stayed at the recreation center on base while two went by truck, tank, or helicopter to where the troops were stationed. They presented their program for the men in the field; some days they hit as many as ten posts.

Linda found that morale was low. She worked long hours every day, either in remote areas with the men or on the base, where the women played requests over the radio for the men in the bunkers or sat and talked with the soldiers—or, more often, listened. Linda found that everyone needed a friend. Some men felt guilty because they had survived; a few had received Dear John letters from home. Others told of their frustrations and defeats. They all seemed to be starving for support, and Linda, who by now had wavered in her antiwar stance, was delighted to help provide that support by bringing cheer and evoking a smile.

She was no longer convinced that the communists were merely defending what they thought was theirs, especially when she saw what the war did. The Vietcong blew up hospitals and sent children wired to explode among the civilians, and mama-sans into the compounds with satchel charges to blow up the enemy Americans.

There was death and danger all around. Once the Red Cross women's helicopter crashed, sucked down by the jet wash of a friendly jet that was doing a flyby over one of the American bases. The helicopter never flew again, but the women did—six more times that week. Linda was exposed to rockets flying into camp. She saw dead bodies littering certain roads, and snipers fired at the women. Their Red Cross hooch at Lai Khe was shaken by a satchel charge that went off several hooches away. Life was precious and easily snuffed out. The women visited camps with their homemade games, which in a way were silly, but which caused the men to relax and enjoy themselves. Once, they heard that a base they had just visited had been overrun, and many of the men they had just seen had been killed.

The hospital visits were bittersweet. Linda was happy to lift the spirits of the men, as the appearance of "round eyes" always did, but the visits also brought pain.

"One patient was a young man with his head completely swathed in bandages. Only his upper cheek and mouth were exposed. His hands were covered in bandages. He wasn't able to speak. His prognosis wasn't good. I couldn't think of anything clever or meaningful to say. So I simply said, 'Hi,' and put my hand on his wrist. I felt compelled to sit with him for a while. When I got up to leave, I said only, 'Take care. I'll be thinking of you.' A solitary tear appeared on his exposed cheek."

On another hospital run, Linda found herself talking to an eighteen-year-old who had shot himself in the foot. He had severe damage to the foot, and the doctors were uncertain as to whether he would ever walk again. Linda asked him why he did it, though secretly she knew. It was, as she suspected, to get out of Vietnam. But, the soldier told Linda, he had not known that it would hurt so much.

Linda asked him, "What on earth did you think it would do to you?"

The answer: "When John Wayne gets shot, he just keeps going. It seemed so easy."

Linda found the men sensitive, caring, and afraid, but always grateful for the presence of the Red Cross women. The men of the 3d Battalion helped Linda when she volunteered at the orphanage next to Lai Khe. They organized a Girl Scout troop and practiced camping skills, sang songs, and played games.

Two things of significance happened in October 1968. Linda had a birthday, and in celebration she received a certificate of honorary membership in the Big Red One; and she was reassigned to Dong Ba Thin, a small outlet across the water from the huge base at Cam Ranh Bay.

Programming was a challenge; the men to be entertained included American special forces and Republic of Korea forces. But

Linda's stint here was brief—just long enough to spend New Year's Eve watching the Americans send off mortars from the air base across the way at Cam Ranh Bay.

In January 1969 she was transferred again, to Tuy Hoa Air Base, which was considered the Atlantic City of the South China Sea. The Red Cross women had extremely comfortable accommodations: four of them lived in two air-conditioned trailers on the base. Because there were so many amenities on base, Linda found that the men, used to comforts like those they enjoyed at home, presented a greater creative challenge than they had met in less luxurious areas. Linda and the other women worked hard to think up, plan, and produce programs to entertain the men. They held marathon races, performed theater, and ran scores of trivia contests. The men were not bored; they seemed to enjoy the amusements.

One of the benefits of being a dounut dolly with the Red Cross was the granting of several R&R trips during a commitment. A tired dounut dolly was considered a liability. Linda took one R&R in Australia and another in Cambodia. The latter was a feat, since Cambodia did not accept or recognize America or its citizens. Linda went to Hong Kong, got an Australian visa, and caught the next flight out to Phnom Penh, Cambodia. She traveled north to Siam Reap to explore the temples and artifacts of Angkor Wat, a special pleasure for Linda since she had been an art and religion major in college. She had difficulties with monetary irregularities (illegally changing money in Hong Kong before arriving in Cambodia), but she managed not to be detained for that offense, and she caught the last plane out before the Siam Reap airport was closed for the week.

Again Linda's assignment changed. Her last three months in Vietnam were spent at Phu Bai in I Corps. This was the northernmost area closest to the demilitarized zone, and headquarters of the 101st Airborne Division, popularly known as the Screaming Eagles. Here her job was the same: to help plan and carry out the programs for the men, to alleviate the stress of the war, and to relieve any boredom. Two women worked at the center on the base and two took off in helicopters to the remote fire support bases, where the men were truly isolated. The soldiers ate two C ration meals and one out of cans every day. They did not have movies.

The dounut dollies tried to visit as many fire bases as they could each week, always hoping to bring levity and smiles with their program—a set of games they devised and changed every two weeks, which the men often initially found silly but eventually enjoyed, becoming boisterous, loud, and hysterical. They were dirty and tired, and they were happy to be away from the war for a short time. Linda found that easing tensions and bringing smiles to the faces of these men, who constantly faced death, was all the reward she needed.

Linda extended her tour of duty for several months and did not return to the United States until August 1968.

Linda returned to her family and friends and found that she had grown apart from many of her protest-oriented college friends, but had grown closer to her family. She had plans to travel around the country to visit the men and women she had met overseas, but on the third day back, when she stopped by the Red Cross chapter in Baltimore, she was offered a public relations job and she took it. That night she put her diary of phone numbers and addresses in her footlocker along with all of her other pieces of Vietnam memorabilia. They stayed there for ten years before she took anything out to look at it again. "It was almost too painful and I was afraid I'd get lost living that past experience."

Yet Linda realizes that her Vietnam experience defined her in many ways, and its imprint was to help her in times of need in the future. "Seeing the life and death and the realities of an experience like serving in Vietnam sorts out the important things from the inconsequential. Real values were etched in my feeble brain at an early age. The Vietnam experience also taught me that risk is good for the soul. People thought back then that I was crazy to go to Southeast Asia. It brought me wonderful experiences, terrific opportunities for travel, and countless other personal benefits. It gave me great self-confidence and a feeling that I could accomplish anything if I put my mind to it. Successfully surviving the Vietnam experience certainly was responsible for this."

From her Vietnam days until the present, a great deal has happened to Linda Sullivan Schulte. Her first job was the start of thirty years in the public relations and corporate communications field. Linda ran her own firm for a number of years, with an old friend as a partner. With other friends as partners, she opened a restaurant and bar. She owned a racehorse and several dogs. She took flying lessons. Whatever she did, she did with confidence.

When she was in her late twenties Linda was struck with multiple sclerosis, with a total loss of eyesight in one eye. In 1985 the disease put her in a wheelchair, where she remained for, she says, nine years, four months, and sixteen days.

Through determination and extensive physical therapy (she became an outstanding wheelchair tennis player), with a dedicated neurologist and great luck, she walked again. Today she is an executive with a nonprofit organization that provides employment opportunities for people with severe disabilities. She is a writer and photographer, and has used her photography skills to publish a book of photographs of people with disabilities. She served on the city council of Laurel, Maryland, for two terms before she ran for mayor and lost by a mere one hundred votes.

Linda gives her Vietnam experience much of the credit for her success in the postwar years. And indeed, courage, determination, and strength of character have much to do with her overcoming multiple sclerosis to engender her triumphs in the business world.

U.S. Agency for International Development

Barbara Hamilton

Barbara Hamilton lived and went to school in a middle-class neighborhood in Concord, California. She attended the University of Puget Sound, Diablo Valley College, and a secretarial school in Berkeley, California. She had a number of jobs, including working for a Head Start project, but she yearned for an occupation that involved travel. Finally she found it through the U.S. Agency for International Development (USAID). Her assignment was in Vietnam, but first she was sent to Washington, D.C., for a one-month training course.

After exotic tastes of Tokyo and Hong Kong en route, Barbara arrived at Tan Son Nhut Airport in Saigon, Vietnam, on 10 December 1967.

"I had just turned twenty-three years old. Military was all around the airport—tanks, airplanes, guns, missiles, sandbags, bunkers, weapons. All the American soldiers were wearing weapons; many were carrying M16s. Soldiers never went anywhere without their weapons. I was taken to the Excelsior Hotel on Nguyen Hue Street ("the street of flowers") in downtown Saigon, where I lived for six months until my apartment was ready. This was just before Christmas, and I recall buying a palm tree with Christmas decorations on it, which I had set up in my hotel room. Our hotel, which was filled with American civilians who worked for USAID, the embassy, and various other U.S. government agencies, was located near To Do Street and the famous Continental Hotel as well as the Mekong Delta River. It was a wonderful location.

"From the first night I arrived in Vietnam I would hear rockets in the distance. Going up to the roof of the hotel, I watched the helicopter gun ships firing across the Mekong River—a steady stream of red-orange flames being fired in the distance from helicopter gun ships into the land below. I tried not to think about what destruction and death the flames were bringing, but I was unable to stop the pictures in my mind."

A USAID bus picked Barbara up at her hotel each morning and got her to work by 8:00 A.M. The workers went back to the hotel at noon and returned to work at 2:00 P.M. to work until 6:00 P.M. When she first arrived, there was an 11:00 P.M. curfew in Saigon.

Barbara worked as a secretary in the USAID Department of Education, a job she held for her first eighteen months in-country. Her office was responsible for building and setting up schools and educational systems and providing teacher training for the Vietnamese. Later she moved to the contracts office, which was charged with assigning contracts for building schools, roads, and other facilities in Vietnam.

Barbara had been in-country for seven weeks when the 1968 Tet Offensive by the Vietcong occurred. She had gone to dinner at the home of a friend who was a professor at Saigon University. After a fabulous dinner, she recalls hearing firecrackers all night.

"Bombs were going off in the distance, but I really didn't notice that much because that was the norm at night in Saigon in 1967. I was told that there were always firecrackers the night of Tet. The bombs and rockets and mortars were a bit more frequent and louder that night, but I thought it was because it was the Tet New Year celebration.

"Early the next morning there was a knock on my hotel door. A man from USAID, who also lived in my hotel, said Saigon was under attack by the North Vietnamese. We were not to leave our hotel. We were confined to the hotel for seven days with a twenty-four-hour curfew. There was a BOQ [bachelor officers' quarters] across the street from my hotel. Armed marine guards and military police would come to the hotel and take us across the street in armed vehicles for our meals there. The soldiers were armed with weapons and machine guns. It was an eerie feeling being in a big, busy city and seeing no cars, bikes, motorcycles, or people on the streets, which were totally deserted and quiet. The sounds heard in the city were the firing of weapons and bombs, rockets, mortars, helicopters, and planes.

"During this time, we would go up on the roof of the hotel and watch the helicopter gun ships flying over the city. We could see the top of the American embassy from the roof of our hotel and could see the helicopters trying to take the embassy back from the Vietcong, who had taken it over for a short time during this offensive. At night the rockets and mortars were constantly going off.

"We were told to throw our mattresses over us when we heard the mortars coming into the city, which was often. The explosions from the rockets and mortars going off all around the hotel were really terrifying. When I heard the swishing and whistling of the incoming before they hit their target, I could feel my adrenaline pumping, my heart beating faster, and shaking. We learned very quickly to tell if the sounds of the rockets and mortars were incoming.

"Buildings and cars would be hit all around our hotel and explode and then catch fire. In the morning, we would look around and see how close the rockets and mortars came to our hotel. Often they hit just across the street, where the buildings would still be on fire. They hit all around our hotel, always missing it. This, to say the least, was not at all what I had expected or been prepared for.

"One day during our seven-day confinement in the hotel, Red Cross representatives came to our hotel and said blood donations were desperately needed for the wounded at a local hospital. I volunteered, and that afternoon the MPs came to escort us to the hospital. There were five Jeeps that arrived. We were in the middle Jeep with two Jeeps to the left front of us and two Jeeps to the right front of us with soldiers armed with M16 rifles, grenades, and the full military gear.

"The MPs drove up to the parking lot of the hospital, and in the lot were piles of lifeless nude Vietnamese bodies. Several Vietnamese men were making wooden plywood coffins and placing these bodies in the coffins. I remember not saying a thing, just kind of staring at the bodies. I think I was in shock. It seems like slow motion when I think about it. I had never seen a dead body before and here there were hundreds of bodies piled high. The scene of the bodies piled high was real and ugly. I can still picture it clearly in my mind after thirty years."

When the South Vietnamese and the United States finally regained control of Saigon, the USAID personnel were allowed to go back to work, but this time curfew was from 7:00 P.M. until 6:00 A.M. It hardly gave the women time to rush home from work and eat out, but they made it. After Tet there were many parties in the hotel. Having worked ten hours a day, six days a week, the women were eager for entertainment in the evenings.

In 1969 Americans were permitted to visit Cambodia, and since Phnom Penh was just a short flight from Saigon, Barbara and two friends caught the first flight out and visited the ancient ruins of Angkor Wat for three days. They were lucky; Cambodia was only open for three weeks before the communists took it over again.

In Saigon one of Barbara's greatest pleasures was to volunteer at the An Loc orphanage on the weekends. There were hundreds of babies lying on mats on the floor, and each day more were brought in from the entrance gate. There were also older children who had lost their parents in the war or who had been abandoned. Many of the children had missing limbs, blown off by mines. Barbara had a favorite baby, and she asked the doctor what was wrong with him. The answer was simple: "lack of human contact." One week Barbara came to the orphanage and found that he was not on his mat; the helpers told her he had died. She was devastated but continued to come to help out at the orphanage.

After Barbara had been in-country for six months, she moved into an apartment. Her routine continued in the same way. A bus picked the women up each morning to take them to work, and if they went somewhere at night, or if they went shopping downtown, they called the motor pool and a car and driver were sent for them. Barbara had a maid to clean her apartment, cook, and shop for fresh fruit, vegetables, and flowers for her.

Life for the American women of Saigon was very social. There was a party almost every night, and on the weekend many of the women were invited out to the U.S. military camps in the field for parties with the GIs. The camps would send a helicopter gunship for the women at the Saigon airport, and it would be escorted by four helicopters on each side. It was always an exquisite trip; the land below was full of lush forests, green rice paddies, mountains, and beautiful white sand beaches.

Barbara traveled extensively: to Cam Ranh Bay, where the air force and navy had many F-4 Phantom fighters and ships; to Da Nang; and to Nha Trang. She also visited a special forces camp on China Beach. Many places were forbidden, but Barbara always managed to get where she wanted to by flying around on C-130 transport planes, hitching from the Saigon airport. She managed to visit the ancient capital of Hue that way and then spent the night on a sampan on the Perfume River there. American women were not officially allowed in the boats on the river because it was dangerous, since there were Vietcong and North Vietnamese Army troops all over the area. But, Barbara says, "Our bodyguard was on a sampan right next to ours with his M16 at all times. It was an exciting adventure that I remember clearly."

In 1969 Barbara attended the Bob Hope Christmas Show at Long Binh, where there was a "sea of thousands of green uniforms sitting in front of a stage watching."

Because she enjoyed the first two years so much, Barbara extended her stay for another year in Vietnam. She was saving money and getting in a lot of travel—her original dream.

But after that stint, it was time to go. On 13 June 1970, Barbara left Vietnam to return to the United States.

Barbara resigned from the U.S. Agency for International Development and took the long way home. For seven weeks she traveled through India, Lebanon, Iran, Turkey, and Greece, and then she met her mother in Italy. They traveled through Europe together and had a wonderful time. They even managed to get to Denmark to visit her mother's relatives.

When Barbara and her mother landed on U.S. soil, Barbara felt that the attitude that greeted her was a real culture shock: "My brother was not interested in hearing about Vietnam, as he had filed conscientious objector and was still concerned over his status. My friends in Berkeley, the few who would even talk with me, were not interested either. Several of them said that if everyone refused to go to Vietnam, there would be no war."

Barbara says, "I got a job as a secretary in San Mateo, California. I was lonely and unhappy. I missed my friends in Vietnam and the excitement of living and traveling overseas."

In March 1970 Barbara married the special forces officer she had been dating in Vietnam, and they were sent to Okinawa, Japan, for his duty. He was gone for much of the next two and a half years, in and out of Vietnam, Cambodia, and Korea, while Barbara got a job in Okinawa as a secretary for military intelligence and took Chinese cooking and flower arranging classes. She also made a trip to Vietnam to visit her many friends who were there.

In 1973 Barbara and her husband, who retired from special forces, returned to San Francisco, where Barbara gave birth to a daughter, Kirsten, in 1975. She and the infant joined her husband in London and they all proceeded to Saudi Arabia, where he was posted. Barbara got jobs and stayed for a year and a half, but then returned to the United States with Kirsten in 1977 and filed for divorce the next year. She secured a job with the navy in the San Francisco Bay Area.

Barbara and her daughter moved to Florida in February 1981. She married her second husband and was employed by the U.S. Attorney's Office, and the next year worked on the 1982 President's Drug Task Force. Her son Mark was born that year, and in 1984 the whole family trekked to Thailand, where Barbara worked for the Drug Enforcement Administration in Bangkok.

Three years later they were back in the San Francisco Bay Area. Barbara continued her government job, and at the same time attended John F. Kennedy University to get a college degree at the age of forty-nine, and later a master's in clinical psychology. Now Barbara is serving an internship as a counselor. She will not only work as a marriage, family, and child counselor, but will also counsel Vietnam veterans. Barbara believes that her own experience serving in Vietnam has given her a special understanding of others who also served, among whom there may be some who have been adversely affected by their individual experiences. She is looking forward to practicing her new career as a therapist full time.

Bobbie Keith

Bobbie Keith grew up and was educated in many countries, since her father was a colonel in army intelligence. Her early schooling was in Massachusetts and South Carolina; high school was at an air force base in Japan; and college was at Sophia University in Tokyo for two years. At other times she lived in Italy, Germany, Texas, California, and New York. Bobbie was living in Virginia when two of her friends convinced her to volunteer for USAID in Vietnam. She trained extensively in Washington, D.C., and in Rosslyn, Virginia, before she took off for Saigon.

Bobbie Keith arrived in Vietnam in April 1967. The first thing she noticed after she got off the plane was "the hot, sticky climate punctuated by the smells—rotten fish mixed with a spray of jasmine scent, an array of fragrances affronting the nostrils." Before she had a chance to absorb the new ambience, a sponsor met her and escorted her to her hotel, the Astor on Nguyen Hue Street, "the street of flowers." The traffic in the city astonished Bobbie: "an ever bustling array of mopeds, cyclos, small cars, citrons, bikes, and the women in their native dresses."

The Astor was primitive. There was no hot water, and Bobbie had a small room with a small cot and a separate bath with a shower gadget over the commode area so she could sit and take a shower. The women had to eat all their meals out; across the street was an American mess facility where they usually went for breakfast, cafeteria style. Fresh eggs were served only on occasion. Usually, the eggs were dehydrated, but bacon was available—and extra-strong GI coffee.

Bobbie was surprised by Saigon. She found it much more modern than she had expected. Passing through the streets to the hotel, she saw glamorous-looking beauty parlors, indoor shopping malls, night clubs, many restaurants (predominantly French), and seamstress establishments where one could have clothes made. The Vietnamese women on the streets appeared to be quite fashionable. They wore the latest outfits, had well-coiffured hair, and were well made up. Bobbie noted that aside from seeing an occasional American in uniform, one would never know a war was going on. The coming days and nights would soon change her mind.

The Astor Hotel housed mostly USAID employees, as well as members of the International Control Commission—Poles, Indians, and Canadians. The USAID employees received instructions not to fraternize with the Polish members, since they were from a Soviet Bloc country and contact with them could lead to a breach of security. After work hours they socialized mostly among themselves, but they never talked about the war. "Perhaps," Bobbie says, "we thought if we didn't mention it, we were not giving it any credence, and it would go away. Yet from the rooftops at night, you could watch the fire flares light up the sky and helicopters circle around the outskirts of the city, presumably in search of the Vietcong."

Her work environment pleased Bobbie. She worked at one of the USAID annex buildings, the Mondial Hotel, located near Cholon. The building was next door to a bachelor enlisted quarters, where the employees could have coffee, lunch, and dinner.

"I worked with a great group of dedicated people. We had Vietnamese on the staff, as well as third-country nationals like Bella, from the Philippines, who worked as an accountant in the budget office. USAID employed many women in various capacities; for example, we had 180 nurses in-country when I was there.

"My workload fluctuated from heavy, bordering on overwhelming, to often boring. I had my own office and a secure vault to take care of the classified material. Non-Americans, or those who did not have top-secret security clearances, were not permitted in my office area.

"We were driven to and from work in buses with bars on the windows for security, presumably to keep the Vietcong from throwing things in the windows. Sometimes we had armed guards onboard with us. We were picked up from our hotels or residences and delivered."

The work hours constantly varied. The pickups and returns were changed constantly, in terms of both times and routes, so that the Vietcong could not learn their pattern and then attack.

The austere buildings looked like barricades behind concrete barrels, barbwire, and security guards. Inside, the marine security guards checked all ID cards and did sweeps of the premises to make sure that no one left any classified data out and that all was secure. There were forbidding bars on all the windows of the building.

The employees had all signed an agreement that they were in Vietnam to meet the needs of the government service—which meant they worked long hours, sometimes on weekends and holidays, and no one broke that agreement unless they wanted to be shipped home. Everyone Bobbie knew worked many hours of overtime.

Although lunch hour was a liberal two hours, in line with local custom, the employees could go out for longer breaks or take naps.

Bobbie worked in the commodity import program, an economic assistance program that was designed to keep the economy from falling apart.

She noted that even rice was brought to the country, because the local harvesting and distribution had been interrupted. Rice was used as a weapon by both the Vietcong and the Americans.

Bobbie found that her secretarial job was neither interesting nor demanding. She did not have many responsibilities other than keeping the office running effectively and keeping up with all the typing and filing. However, she says, "I worked with a great crew of people; all believed they were there to make a difference. The esprit de corps was terrific among everyone."

For their evening meals the USAID members went to either the Rex or Brinks bachelor officers' quarters near the hotel, where movies were shown and popcorn was available. Sometimes they went to the International House American Club for sing-alongs in the cocktail lounge (which sported a piano player) or to the numerous bars, which were crowded with soldiers and bar girls. They usually gathered on the roof of the Astor to socialize, sing songs, and tire themselves out for sleep.

In May 1967 Bobbie ventured out of Saigon to visit some of the men and women who had been in training with her in the United States. They were now posted as provincial representatives to Can Tho in the delta, which Bobbie says was a "quaint hamlet with obvious French influence in the architecture of its buildings." She added, "I felt as if I had gone to a French Foreign Legion post." On the way there Bobbie got a good glimpse of the scenic countryside of Vietnam: "Rice paddies full of bouncing hats with mountains in the background, lots of tropical flowers, varied colors. But when flying in a helicopter, I could see the bomb craters that dotted the landscape and smoldering vegetation. The devastation to the land was something you could not miss."

The next month Bobbie was reassigned to the Excelsior Hotel, which was a step up in living accommodations. Here she had a bathtub, a balcony, a small refrigerator, a table and chair, and a real bed, not a cot.

"I could barbecue on my balcony and wash the dishes in the bathtub—what a treat it was. I had a little hotplate and usually boiled corn and barbecued chicken on the grill. One evening a rocket exploded in front of the USO, directly across from the hotel. The casualty was a young child, seemingly not yet seven years old. I stood frozen on my balcony in disbelief as I watched his mother pick up his bleeding body and jump into a cyclo taxi. Whether or not he survived, there was no way to find out. I gathered he was just another nameless victim of the many rockets the Vietcong lobbed into the cities throughout Vietnam. The human devastation of it all became very real to me. The reality that it could have been me was even more terrifying.

"My friends and I sipped another gin and tonic and never talked about it. I, among others, concealed disbelief and fear. That's how we managed to survive the insanity of it all—by ignoring it."

One Sunday Bobbie was having brunch at the International Club when Colonel Nash came up to her and said she looked like a weather girl. He urged Bobbie to go to the TV station and audition for the part. When a friend teased Bobbie unmercifully, she decided to go for the audition, and she became the weather girl, the "bubbling bundle of barometric brilliance." She received instant fame in Vietnam. She was a pretty, vivacious young woman with long blond hair; it was inevitable that she would become the weather girl of AFVN-TV. It was a volunteer job for which she received no compensation. She performed that job along with her regular USAID work. But, Bobbie said, it meant more to her than any money could pay. She was to take many trips out into the field to visit the men, in addition to announcing the weather within the TV studio.

At first they started promotions on TV, advertising the airing of the weather show for 8 July. Along with these promotional spots, Bobbie was escorted around Vietnam to make personal appearances and announcements on TV and radio.

"The first shows were awkward, as I had to sit on a stool which restricted any movement. This didn't work well, so they later decided I could stand up with a wand and point. I had little to no flexibility until a new director took over and made the show more fun, as we started copying ideas from the TV show *Laugh-In*. I would get doused with buckets of water when announcing rain. It happened so often, the first weather set had to be redone, as it had become faded with water stains.

"Sometimes we did really silly things like arrive on set via a motorcycle, and fly around the set on a broom for Halloween. With all the tragedy happening in Vietnam, we wanted to make the show fun, not serious. The men who put the show together were great; I was treated as if I were their kid sister. They'd play pranks on me to get me to laugh and lighten up. I generally never knew what was going to happen toward the end of the show."

Bobbie became a celebrity. It was flattering to receive so much admiration, but she also received a great deal of teasing when she was recognized. Her face often flushed when the GIs applauded en masse as she stood up in a public place to walk to the toilet facilities. Wherever she went, the men recognized her and whistled and applauded.

Bobbie taped a number of shows in advance before she visited the troops. She spent a day filming, changing clothes and temperatures. Those shows were believable because the weather remained fairly constant—hot, humid, and rainy.

Bobbie made her first trip out to the boonies in August to September 1967 to see the 199th Light Infantry Brigade. Their task was to protect the perimeter of Saigon by flushing out the Vietcong so they could not get into the city. Their information officer, Andy, picked Bobbie up in Saigon and drove her out into the field where the headquarters was located. From there she flew on a loach—a small, open-sided helicopter—to other areas where the men were located. They stopped off and saw about six to ten men at a time, then got back on the helicopter for another area of six to ten men. During the visits, Bobbie shared Cokes with the men, chatted, and asked how they were faring.

Bobbie always came back from these visits with the names of men to mention on the show. They loved that. She also mentioned the men who wrote to her, and there were hundreds and hundreds over the months. Bobbie mentioned the men and their hometowns, as well as sending out special salutes to them. Bobbie closed each broadcast with words such as, "This evening, I'd like to send a special salute to little Richie on the LST *Garrett County,* serving down in the Delta," and, "This is Bobbie wishing you all out there a pleasant evening weatherwise, and you know my wishes go with you for otherwise."

Bobbie felt that the weather girl slot opened a whole new world for her. Invitations poured in to the studio for Bobbie to visit the troops all over Vietnam. So she flew around to different camps on many handshake morale tours; on these she learned more about the fighting than she ever had from her USAID office.

Bobbie found that the men were often shy and reserved, and many were so surprised to see a "round eyes" out in the field that they did not know how to react. Bobbie says, "Some scratched their heads in disbelief; others stared at the ground and could not make eye contact, perhaps due to shyness. I never ever once had a problem with anyone making off-color remarks—or what we call sexual harassment these days. The men were usually curious about why I was in Vietnam, and where did I come from. Some said I made them homesick and smelled like their girlfriends (with White Shoulders, the perfume I always wore when going on a trip). I had to wear boots—white ones—because of all the mud and muck. The men were always willing to share their rations or a sip of Coke or a candy bar, even chewing gum. I never heard them complain at all."

A navy pilot, Commander Corie, organized the second trip out to see the men in September to October. Bobbie flew on his helicopter to the LST boats in the delta to visit the navy crewmen. They picked the men up and returned to Tan Son Nhut Air Base outside Saigon. They boarded a C-141 troop cargo plane and flew to an offshore island, Con Son, for a one-day R&R.

"The island was beautiful—lush tropical vegetation, with monkeys, parrots, and a sandy white beach where we would cook out and have a food bash along with some beers. Then swim and roam around the beach area until it was time to board the plane and return to the war."

Commander Corie organized these trips quite often, and other women were always invited, some of them from the USAID office. It was always sad, though, to head back to the mainland—and, for the men, the battle zones. If an expedition to the island wasn't feasible, sometimes Bobbie just accompanied Commander Corie down to the LST boats to deliver the mail, and they would spend the day flying from one boat to another.

Bobbie received so many invitations at the studio, she spent almost every weekend out in the field in different locations. In addition, she and her friend Pat Zanella (another USAID worker) volunteered as candy stripers for the Red Cross at the 17th Field Hospital in Saigon, making Kool-Aid and snacks for the wounded patients, as well as helping the disabled men write letters home.

In November Bobbie made a trip to Nha Trang, home to the Green Berets, 5th Special Forces. Before she left she taped a number of weather shows so that she could have three days away. At Nha Trang she was quartered in her own room in a Quonset hut on the beach. From the headquarters they flew by helicopter to visit small base camps. By evening she was always back in Nha Trang, wined and dined at both the officers and enlisted clubs. She was the only woman, and she really had to be on her toes to be fair and dance with everyone she could.

Both Bobbie and Pat accompanied Commander Corie once again at Christmastime 1967. They flew down to the delta and brought mail and packages to the men on the LST boats. Santa Claus was along on this trip, and on Christmas Day they flew to three different boats and sang carols. At the end of the day Commander Corie took a detour and brought them to a remote spot in the boonies where thousands of men had gathered to watch the Bob Hope show. Bobbie says the show was great, and included a dance and song by Raquel Welch in a short red knit mini. She brought the house down. Bobbie noticed that the men plummeted from high spirits to quiet exits as they headed back.

Bobbie never watched any TV while she was in Vietnam, so she never saw her own weather show. "Perhaps if I had," she says, "I may have had too much fear or embarrassment to continue doing it."

She was a great morale booster for the men. The letters increased in number. They ranged from polite greetings and questions about where she was from to writing about themselves and saying that she reminded them of their girls back home. There were invitations to visit them in the field, and some men asked if they could buy Bobbie a drink or coffee in Saigon if they ever got there. There were literally thousands of letters, plus many gifts. Bobbie received a number of stuffed koala bears from the Australians. Sometimes the men sent photos of themselves with their families, or of themselves out in the field. Bobbie says she was modest enough to know that she was the weather girl by a fluke, and that she and all the other "round eyes" were popular and in demand because there were so few of them.

Bobbie continued to visit the men. She revisited units where she had been before, and she visited the 4th Infantry in Pleiku, the long-range reconnaissance patrols (LRRPs), and the 25th Infantry.

She visited the 1st Cavalry, who dubbed her a "miniskirted heat wave who raised troops' temperatures." The 1st Cavalry made Bobbie an honorary member of the 1st Cavalry Division Association of the United States and presented her with a fatigue jacket, which is now covered with patches from all the units she visited.

Bobbie was still living at the Excelsior when the Tet Offensive of the Vietcong hit in 1968. The residents were not allowed to leave the hotel, so they could not go to work for a week or two because of the fighting going on in the area. They had to wait for all of the Vietcong to be flushed out of their hiding places. Bobbie and Pat volunteered to help serve food in the mess across the street, since many of the Chinese mess helpers could not get into downtown Saigon because of the ongoing battles.

During the May offensive, the Vietcong habitually rocketed the city each morning before the sun was up. Bobbie grabbed her mattress and slept in the bathtub, thinking that even if the building was hit, the bathtub would survive.

When refugees flooded the streets of Saigon to escape from the surrounding battles, many lived in front of Bobbie's hotel.

Intending to be kind, Bobbie gathered up some crates of C rations someone had given her to dispense among the Vietnamese. She decided to share them with a refugee family in front of the hotel. She says, "I put a box down in front of an older lady who was squatting on a bench. She looked at me with such hatred and spat in my face." *Perhaps,* Bobbie thought, *it had been the Americans who had destroyed her house or caused her pain and grief, not the Vietcong.* Either way, the woman was another nameless victim.

That summer some marines marched into the TV studio with the complaint that Bobbie had not visited as far north as Quang Tri, where they were stationed. This was prejudice against the marines, they claimed. As a result, a trip was arranged for Bobbie. She was escorted up to the area, which was beautiful, mountainous terrain with white sand beaches and a cooler climate than in Saigon.

Just after Bobbie and her escort officer, Dan, had finished dinner at a mess facility, the sun suddenly disappeared, and it was very dark. A blast went off in the distance, and sirens sounded. Dan rushed Bobbie into the nearest bunker. It was underground and was very modern inside, with light bulbs on the ceiling. There were a dozen or so men in the same bunker; they quickly hung up an army blanket to give Bobbie her own space. Bobbie curled up in her own little corner behind the blanket and tried to sleep. She was relaxed enough that she could do so, and the next thing she recalls is Dan standing beside her, saying that they could now leave the bunker. It was then that Bobbie learned that the Vietcong had penetrated the perimeter of the camp.

The visits continued, first to Phuoc Vinh and Camp Gorad, where she also visited some medical wards. Then it was on to three brigades located at Tay Ninh, Lai Khe, and Bien Hoa. At Tay Ninh, Bobbie played cards and talked with the men of A Company, 2d Battalion, 8th Cavalry. They were having a few days break at the VIP center after eighty-seven days in the field. At Lai Khe, Bobbie toured the enlisted men's club, and at the next stop, the VIP Center at Bien Hoa, she mingled with B Company, 5th Battalion, 7th Cavalry.

During the week, it was always back to work at the USAID offices. Bobbie remembers odd bits from her time in Vietnam. She recalls watching a little black fuzzy puppy, tethered to a flower market stall on Nguyen Hue Street, grow up day by day, only to later see it being roasted on a stick. They called these dogs "chow hounds." Bobbie had fed the puppy table scraps regularly. Now she felt sick when she saw what had happened to it. She acquired a Siamese cat and eventually shipped him home to her parents, who called him Mau Mau, their Vietnamese refugee.

Bobbie's last official trip in Vietnam as Bobbie the weather girl took place when she was catapulted onboard the USS *Enterprise* in June 1969. Captain Harnish lent her his posh quarters, and guards escorted her almost constantly. Bobbie visited the men in the mess facilities and took part in a radio show onboard as well as a closed-circuit TV interview.

By June 1969 Bobbie was no longer permitted to sign off each show with, "This is Bobbie saying goodnight. I wish you all a pleasant evening weatherwise, and you know my wishes go with you for otherwise." The format of the show changed so that after the weather, Bobbie signed over to the anchor, who then closed the evening news broadcast. Objections had been raised that Bobbie's goodnight was too suggestive. Also, she was no longer permitted to dance at the end of the show or to use any gimmicks or stunts.

She says, "The show, in reality, was no longer for me—I was totally getting burned out from just about everything by July 1969. So I had put in my paperwork to resign from U.S. government service and was waiting for the approval to leave Saigon." Bobbie says that had she not had the naivete of youth, she would not have survived Vietnam.

"Nothing seemed real; nothing appeared permanent. I thought what we were doing was right, but by the time Tet hit, I began to question the wisdom of our leaders who placed our military forces in such a quagmire. I left, not just brokenhearted over the things I witnessed—the destruction caused by the war, the deaths of so many—but also very skeptical. The landscape of Vietnam was pockmarked with bomb craters everywhere.

"When I departed from Vietnam I was totally burned out by it all, a little disillusioned, and sick of government propaganda, as it just seemed to make less and less sense. Once my resignation papers were approved, I headed for Katmandu, Nepal."

Bobbie Keith traveled to India, Turkey, Israel, Greece, Senegal, and Germany, and then returned to Virginia, where her parents lived. By 1975 she worked for the Department of State, she served in Germany, Jordan, France, Turkey, Colombia, and Morocco. She returned to Washington, D.C., in 1988 to work at Main State.

Main State was only two blocks from the Vietnam Veterans Memorial, and one day during her lunch break, Bobbie walked down to the wall. She found that what she had tried so hard to block out of her mind and erase overcame her. She felt confused and angry.

"I would not have believed it could happen, but having talked with others, who said it was a normal reaction, I did not fear being near the wall. About a year later, after meeting Morris, a park ranger on site at the wall, I started volunteering, one among 150 yellow hat volunteers who devote their time to assist visitors who make their pilgrimages to the wall. They say the wall has a healing impact on people, and I can tell you from firsthand knowledge that it is indeed true."

In 1994 Bobbie took the government buyout because both of her parents were ill. She packed her bags and moved to Florida to take care of them. Her father died and was buried in Arlington Cemetery, since he was a combat-wounded veteran from World War II who also served in Korea and Vietnam. Bobbie now takes classes at the local community college, goes kayaking in the waterways, and attends the county meetings of the Vietnam Veterans.

Bobbie Keith is proud of her service with USAID in Vietnam, and perhaps even prouder that she made a contribution to troop morale as Bobbie the weather girl.

Epilogue: The Others

Perhaps the account that follows expresses the feelings of many of the women whose stories I could not include in this book. Many women were so adversely affected by the horrors of the Vietnam War and the sights, sounds, smells, and feel of death that they could not share their stories with me. They still see the torn and broken limbs; they still hear the moans of the dying. To some, it was all so very useless. These were the stories I could not tell.

Connie Rosendale of the Army Nurse Corps was one of these others. Unable to write on her own, she dictated some impressions and thoughts about her service in Vietnam to a friend, a fellow nurse, who recorded them on her laptop computer and sent them to me. Here is Connie's story in her own words.

"I served in Long Binh, 1968 to 1969 (eleven months). Prior to this, I was at North Camp Drake, Japan, in the 24th Evacuation Hospital. I was in the neurosurgical unit, in the operating room. Because of that experience I was sent to the neurosurgical unit in Vietnam in 1968.

"Why is it difficult for me to talk about it? It's OK to talk about happy things in service, but in Vietnam there was so much suffering among the Americans, Vietnamese, everybody. There was no joy at all there. We were overwhelmed by sadness.

"I had just come from Japan, where we treated the injured from Vietnam. I don't have trouble discussing Japan because there were breaks. We worked five days a week; it was clean; there was no starvation and there were outside things to do for recreation and relaxation. We could go to Tokyo and forget about the war for a while.

"In Vietnam, you couldn't get away. We worked seven days a week, for twelve-hour shifts. One week we worked 7:00 A.M. to 7:00 P.M.; the next week 7:00 P.M. to 7:00 A.M.

"If it had not been for the helicopters, at least 50 percent of the GIs would have died in the field. Vietnam was uncultured. The only cultured people were the educated ones; these included the doctors we worked with. They believed they would not be able to practice if the communists took over. The educated people were in favor of democracy, not communism.

"The war had been going on for many years. The French deserted Vietnam. Then the U.S. got involved as army advisors. From there, the army increased the U.S. involvement.

"At times when there were so many casualties, we had to triage the wounded. The worst cases were held in the back ward for twenty-four hours. If they were still alive we operated. We first operated on the cases that would take a short time in the OR. Then we took the more difficult cases. Any that could be held until a quiet time were postponed until there was a lull in the fighting.

"We also operated on the enemy, and that got me very angry because we knew these were the men who were shooting at our soldiers. Most of us felt this way, but there were some doctors who just loved to operate, and they were glad to operate on the Vietcong just to practice surgery. It was good experience for them. And they didn't need consent forms for any patients like we do in the United States, so they could just proceed as best they could.

"Most bothersome and depressing to me were the spinal injuries who could not do anything because they were paralyzed from the head down. They couldn't even take a pill or put a gun to their heads to end their lives. Who would want to lie like that for their entire future of fifty to seventy years? They could never live a normal life.

"Persons who had sustained head injuries were generally not aware of their condition because they no longer had the capacity to realize the shape they were in.

"My husband was at the 3d Ordinance (called the McNamara group), where the recruits were of low IQ. One said, 'I'm Ho Chi Minh.' The other boy shot his brains out. In the neurosurgical unit we got the boy with the head injury, but he was already dead.

"Another boy, a twenty-six-year-old lieutenant, had been injured twice and each time had been sent back to the front. He asked me, 'Please Connie, talk to the doctors. I'm sure if I go back, next time I'll be killed.' I tried, but the doctors felt he was needed and that this boy just didn't want to go back. He was sent back, and about one week later he was blown up while in a Jeep, along with his driver.

"There was just so much useless killing. What was the sense? We lost the war anyway. While there, we first thought we were winning the war.

"When we returned, even my parents said, 'Don't talk about it.' The war had become even more unpopular by then than when we went there. Even McNamara's recent book acknowledges we should not have been there.

"It brought me into contact with what life was really all about. From an above-middle-class family, I had had everything I could want. In Vietnam I came into contact with poverty, which I had really not seen much of, because in the United States I worked in the OR and didn't have patient contact except with the sedated or anesthetized patients. Now I was talking to the injured and getting to know them as individuals.

"The sick kept asking, 'What is the purpose of all this?' We were supposed to keep the North Vietcong out, but we were not succeeding. They were everywhere. One was the barber, and he killed one of our soldiers in the barber chair.

"One case was taken to the OR immediately upon arrival. I started to loosen his boots so his legs could be amputated, but when I took off his boots, his feet were in them. They had been blown off. I was new; it was my second day. I was ready to go home after that. This image has stayed and will stay with me always. It was a young guy, maybe nineteen.

"Funny how I got to Vietnam. My husband-to-be had given me a diamond engagement ring shortly before he was scheduled to be sent out from Vietnam. A couple of days later I got orders to Vietnam. To be together, he got his stay in Vietnam extended. We took a short break, five days, to get married in Hawaii.

"We were allowed two R&Rs. The second was in Hong Kong. Those were the only pleasant memories, but even there, we knew we had to go back to that dirty country where everybody had dysentery. Malaria, too, but I was lucky not to get it even though I did not take the pills that made me sick.

"Some of the Vietnamese patients had diseases we had never seen before, contracted from working in rice paddies and dirty water. We worked in rubber shower thongs for six months during the rainy season. The groundwater was up to our ankles.

"The OR was a Quonset hut divided into three sections, with low wooden partitions. The doctors, to be funny, would throw sponges and dirty cotton over the partition, so of course we could never accurately count the sponges. When you are in that depressing environment, you have to do something to let out your frustrations, and this was just one of them.

"Most of the GIs could get marijuana, heroin—anything. Most were under the influence of drugs while fighting. Even in the OR, the soldiers working there were taking drugs. We had a lot of nurses just out of school, and they were still gullible, not really mature enough to cope, so they too used drugs to help them cope. There was so much frustration. I at least had my boyfriend, who was later my husband.

"I wonder how many soldiers who were in Vietnam are still in VA hospitals. Probably the boys I took care of have died by now. Paralyzed, discouraged people don't live long. They usually gave up hope. Not like Christopher Reeves, who has probably had counseling to help him cope with his injuries. These boys had psychologically given up hope of ever having a normal life. Who wants to think, at age nineteen, that you'd never be able to move by yourself again or have a normal life?

"Nobody in the United States wanted to talk about it. The only opportunity was when we were with other military people. Civilians didn't want to hear our stories. When we came back, I was not expecting a parade, but neither did I expect to be shunned. We were even advised not to wear our uniform while traveling by plane.

Those who were in uniform were looked down upon. People thought we were coming home with diseases. They probably thought we were druggies or hippies, as it was the '60s, and stories about drugs in Vietnam were broadly known.

"I can't say I'm sorry I had the army experience, because it taught me many things about life. For example, how life can be short for some and long for others. It taught me, after having lived a sheltered life, about a broad range of lifestyles and how the other side of the world lives. I learned that not everyone needs to conform to what my lifestyle had been. In fact, I learned to dance while in the army. My family and church background did not include dancing or drinking.

"Inside myself, Vietnam is something I have put in the recesses of my mind. One day the 24th Evacuation Unit was featured on TV and my niece called me to watch, but I couldn't watch it. I just couldn't think again about all those boys killed and maimed. I was in the TV news program. My niece saw me. I just didn't want to be reminded of the war. When people talked about Vietnam during a social occasion, I would just leave the room.

"It changed my attitude about life. I became more tolerant. When someone makes a judgment, I feel they have the right to be different than I am.

"People didn't feel they wanted to show gratefulness to the returning soldiers, but now I don't care anymore. After all, what did we do for the United States? We were trying to help the Vietnamese, but most of them didn't really care if the country was communist or democratic as long as they could get their rice and fish. The United States had no business there."

Endnotes

Army Nurse Corps

Anne Philiben wrote up a long account of her tour as an army nurse in Vietnam in 1996. We had a good exchange of letters clarifying a number of items, including the bee-hive round.

Connie Connolly wrote up her account for me. In addition, she sent along the Spring Quarter 1996 edition of the *Vietnam Veterans of America, Florida State Council,* which printed her speech and picture (as Connie Shephard), and the 14 November 1987 *Florida Nursing News.*

Mary Dickinson responded to my notice for women to write me, which the Vietnam Veterans of America Chapter 228 published in its newsletter in New Jersey. She also included a chapter of a story in *Good Housekeeping* (May 1988) chronicling her belated bout with post-traumatic stress disorder as a result of her Vietnam experience.

Carolyn Tanaka provided me with a voluminous amount of material. In answer to my plea for additional details, she sent along a twenty-two-page history and a large portion of her memoirs, which were taken from her diary and the letters she wrote home from Vietnam.

Diane Corcoran wrote up her account for me in response to a notice that the Retired Army Nurse Corps Association kindly published.

Navy Nurse Corps

Beth Marie Murphy wrote to me about her experiences in Vietnam and her post-traumatic stress disorder problems as a result of a notice on the Internet, which another Vietnam veteran, Karen Offutt, was instrumental in arranging.

Kay Bauer wrote an extremely detailed, lengthy account for me during the very beginning period of research for this book.

Air Force Nurse Corps

Monna Mumper wrote many times, amplifying her original account, which perhaps was in response to my "In Search Of" item on the Women in Military Service in America Web site, which that organization kindly ran.

Eileen Gebhart wrote me in response to a request placed with the Society of Retired Air Force Nurses. An exchange of letters followed, each answer containing even greater detail about her Vietnam experience than the previous one.

Donna Cunningham read my request for Vietnam accounts in one of the air force publications, *Mail Call.* She wrote a very lengthy, extremely detailed account of her service flying air evacuations out of Yokota, Japan, and then continued her story through her Saigon duty, where she was the last air force nurse to leave Vietnam in March 1973. This chapter was based on that material.

Donna Buechler was suggested as a good subject for this book by Elise Hines of the Army Nurse Corps, who had told me her own story for my previous book, *They Also Served: American Women in World War II.* I wrote to Donna, and she sent me a full chronological account of her tremendous difficulties with post-traumatic stress disorder, later filling me in with other needed details. All of this material was the source for this chapter.

Women's Army Corps

Karen Offutt and I got together through the Internet. She was also instrumental in placing my request for women to write me on the Internet. She has had a difficult time with post-traumatic stress disorder since her Vietnam experience. The material used for this chapter is copyright 21 July 1998 by Karen Offutt, and I was granted use of it for this book.

Claire Starnes contacted me though the Internet and sent a very detailed account of her Vietnam experiences. She put that material under copyright in her name and granted me one-time use for this book.

Linda Earls also contacted me through the Internet. She worked up her account for me by going through all of her letters home during the year she served in Vietnam. It was a long process, but well worth it.

Army Special Services

Ann Campbell was one of the first to contact me in the beginning of my research for this book. She sent me more than sixty pages of raw material for her chapter, and we agreed that all of the material she sent would be under copyright to her. Ann granted me permission to use her material for this book.

Marianne Reynolds telephoned me. By this time a notice for women Vietnam veterans to contact the author had appeared in many veterans' publications, so it would be hard to pin down all sources of contact. After Marianne called, she wrote up and sent to me a long account of her Vietnam service, which provided the basis for this chapter.

International Voluntary Services

Janice Shomer Kavadas carried on a correspondence with me, augmenting her original account of her service. Like the rest of the women, she was most cooperative in filling in requested details. All of this material was the basis for the chapter.

United Services Organization

Mara Hodgkins was one of many Americans who served in the USO centers during the Vietnam War. It is impossible to recall how we first got together, but we were in touch periodically after the initial account of Mara's service, filling in additional details for use in her chapter.

American Red Cross

Jennifer Young saw my notice in the Red Cross *Oversea'r* and wrote. About thirteen years ago she had started her own book, an oral history of donut dollies, getting tapes to transcribe from several of her friends and acquaintances. Jenny offered me her material and then graciously contacted the other women who had submitted accounts to her long before to see if they would give their permission for their material to be sent to me. They did, and Jenny sent it on.

Dorothy Patterson contacted me by e-mail as a result of the Internet notice. This chapter is based on the material that she sent me through the U.S. mail.

Martha L. Royse telephoned me, and I sent guidelines. She sent her account and then a more detailed description of her duty aboard the USS *Sanctuary.* Her chapter was based on the firsthand material she supplied.

Mary Blanchard Bowe gave Jennifer Young permission to send her previous material to me. It consisted of not only an account of service, but a great number of journal entries written at that time in Vietnam. All this material formed the basis for this chapter.

June Smith also gave permission to Jennifer Young to send her material to me. However, she also wrote up additional information to augment that report of long ago, both of which formed the basis for her chapter.

Linda Sullivan Schulte wrote up a special account for me, in addition to sending along the notes she had made at the time of her Red Cross service in Vietnam, which she had previously sent to Jennifer Young. She also enclosed many clips about the multiple sclerosis that had put her in a wheelchair for more than nine years. Her determination to walk again triumphed after a nationally famous period as a top wheelchair tennis player.

U.S. Agency for International Development

Barbara Hamilton was in touch with me some years ago, when she started but did not finish an account for me. More recently, she wrote a full account, which I used as the foundation for her chapter. Barbara and five other USAID workers had a reunion in Montana in the summer of 1998, the first time that they were all together in thirty years.

Bobbie Keith, the weather girl of Vietnam, and I were great patrons of e-mail for this chapter. Bobbie wrote often with her impressions of duty and Vietnam activities. We had quite a running correspondence. Her chapter came out of all this communication.

Epilogue: The Others

Connie Rosendale and I met in my home in Delhi through a mutual friend, Betty Bowers of Delancey, New York. Connie and Betty are both nurses, and although Connie could not write about her

Vietnam experience, she dictated it to Betty, who typed it on her laptop computer and got it to me. I used this account verbatim because I felt that it was representative of the great number of women who were so affected by the Vietnam War that they could not participate in writing their accounts of their service.

Selected Bibliography

Pamphlets and Booklets

Neel, Spurgeon. *Vietnam Studies Medical Support 1965–1970.* Washington, D.C.: Department of the Army, 1991.

Springfield, Illinois, Vet Center. *Helping the Healing.* Springfield, Ill.: Department of Veterans Affairs, 1993.

Technical Assistance Information Clearing House. American Council of Voluntary Agencies for Foreign Service. *Development Assistance Programs of U.S. Non-Profit Organizations in Vietnam. January 1975.* New York: Technical Assistance Information Clearing House, 1975.

USO 1993 Annual Report. Washington, DC: USO World Headquarters, 1993.

Vietnam Women's Memorial Project. *Celebration of Patriotism and Courage.* Washington, D.C.: Vietnam Women's Memorial Project, November 10–12, 1993.

Books

There are many books out about Vietnam, but perhaps two of the most important recent ones are:

McNamara, Robert S., with Brian VanDeMark. *In Retrospect. The Tragedy and Lessons of Vietnam.* New York: Random House, 1995.

Hendrickson, Paul. *The Living and the Dead.* New York: Knopf, 1996.

Index